Marx's Method in *Capital*

Marx's Method in *Capital*

A Reexamination

Edited by
Fred Moseley

HUMANITIES PRESS
New Jersey

First published in 1993 by
Humanities Press International, Inc.,
Atlantic Highlands, New Jersey 07716

Library of Congress Cataloging-in-Publication Data

Marx's method in Capital : a reexamination / edited by Fred Moseley.
p. cm.
Includes bibliographical references and index.
ISBN 0-391-03785-4
1. Marx, Karl, 1818–1883. Kapital—Congresses. 2. Marxian economics—Congresses. I. Moseley, Fred.
HB501.M37M393 1993
335.4'1—dc20 92-22220
CIP

A catalog record for this book is available from the British Library

There are some differences from one article to another in the hyphenation of technical and semi-technical terms. The various contributors have used different editions of Marx's *Capital* when drawing their references, and these sources are themselves inconsistent. No attempt has been made to standardize this usage from article to article.

Printed in the United States of America

Contents

Introduction

That the method of analysis employed in Capital *has been little understood is shown by the various mutually contradictory conceptions that have been formed of it.*

—Karl Marx

Marx's statement above (in the Postface to the second German edition of *Capital*) unfortunately remains largely true today. The vast literature on Marx's economic theory has generally not paid sufficient attention to the methodological principles upon which Marx's theory is based. The most important unresolved and largely unexamined methodological issues relevant to Marx's economic theory are the precise meaning and significance of dialectical logic; the relation between essence and appearance; the role of unobservable variables; the relation between subjects and objects; the order of determination between aggregate economic magnitudes and individual magnitudes; the relation between Marx's logical method and that of Hegel; and, finally, the implications of all the above for the overall logical structure of the three volumes of *Capital*.

In the Marxian literature, there are three main prevailing interpretations of Marx's logical method in *Capital*: (1) the "logical-historical" interpretation suggested first by Engels (1906) and later developed by Meek (1976); (2) the "successive approximations" method introduced by Grossman (1929) and adopted by Sweezy (1968); and (3) the Sraffian interpretation, based on linear production theory and represented by Morishima (1973) and Steedman (1977), which has been widely adopted in recent decades.

According to the logical-historial interpretation, Marx's logical categories in *Capital* correspond to an idealized periodization of the actual process of history. The clearest and most influential aspect of this interpretation is its assumption that the subject of Part 1 of Volume 1 is not capitalism but rather a precapitalist "simple commodity production," in which producers own their own means of production and there is no wage labor. In this respect, Marx's method is regarded as essentially the same as that of Smith and Ricardo. According to Meek, Marx's primary concern was to contrast the basic characteristics of simple commodity production with those of capitalism (Meek 1976, 154–56).

According to the successive approximations interpretation, Volume 1 begins with a number of simplifying assumptions in order to focus the analysis initially on the most essential characteristic of capitalism, the origin of profit. In Volume 3, these simplifying assumptions are dropped in order to provide a more realistic explanation of the prices of commodities and other phenomena of capitalism. The two most important simplifying assumptions of Volume 1 are, according to this interpretation, that the prices of individual commodities are equal (or proportional) to their values, and that the composition of capital is equal in all industries. Even though these assumptions obviously contradict reality, they are made in Volume 1 to show that the profit of capitalists is produced by the labor of workers.

Finally, according to the Sraffian interpretation, Marx's method is assumed to be essentially the same as Sraffa's method of linear production theory, in which the fundamental givens are the technical conditions of production and the real wage. These fundamental physical quantities provide a system of simultaneous equations that determine the exchange ratios of commodities and the rate of surplus value or the rate of profit. According to this interpretation, Volume 1 of *Capital* is concerned with the "value system" in which the labor values of individual commodities and the rate of surplus value are derived from the given technical conditions and real wage. Volume 3, on the other hand, is concerned with the "price system," in which the labor values of individual commodities are transformed into their corresponding money prices and determined along with the rate of profit, again with the technical conditions and the real wage taken as givens.

All the authors of the essays in this volume agree that these three prevailing interpretations of Marx's economic theory are fundamentally erroneous.[1] The reasons given for rejecting these interpretations and the alternative interpretations proposed differ somewhat from author to author, but they all agree that these three interpretations are not only inadequate but also lead to mistaken conclusions concerning the nature and the adequacy of Marx's economic theory.[2] Therefore, the authors argue that a thorough reexamination of the methodological foundations of Marx's economic theory should be undertaken, first of all to better understand Marx's theory in terms of its own logical method, and secondly to be able to more properly evaluate the logical coherence of Marx's theory.[3]

The essays in this volume attempt to explore these important and usually neglected methodological issues and to stimulate further research along these lines. The authors originally presented their papers at a small working conference on Marx's method in *Capital* held at Mount Holyoke College, 2–7 June 1991. The papers have been revised for this volume. The eight authors are evenly divided between economists and philosophers, reflecting the interdisciplinary nature of the subject of the logical method of Marx's economic theory.

It should be emphasized that the contributors to this volume by no means constitute a new monolithic group whose members all share the same interpretation of *Capital*. As will become apparent from the summaries of the essays below and from the essays themselves, there is at least some disagreement on all the important methodological issues listed above. There are also varying degrees of disagreement on the interpretation of important parts of *Capital*, such as the derivation of abstract labor as the substance of value and the derivation of money in Chapter 1 of Volume 1 as well as the determination of prices of production in Part 2 of Volume 3.

The first four chapters of this volume all argue that Hegel's dialectical logic had a decisive influence on Marx's intellectual development and ultimately on the logic of *Capital*. Tony Smith argues that, contrary to the prevailing view within the Marxian tradition, Marx used in *Capital* a systematic dialectical method that is similar to that found in Hegel. Smith first responds to various traditional Marxist arguments against Hegel's dialectical logic and argues that all these objections are based on a misunderstanding of Hegel's systematic logic, which is best understood as a reconstruction in thought of the social world, a reconstruction that begins with the empirical appropriation of that world. The categories employed in this reconstruction are immanent to the social realm and are not imposed externally. Smith argues further that the underlying logic of *Capital* is such a systematic dialectical ordering of economic categories. He presents a summary of Volume 1 of *Capital* based on this interpretation. (Smith 1990c presents a more complete elaboration of this interpretation for all three volumes of *Capital*.) Smith acknowledges that there are several theoretical projects in Marxism and that different logical methods may be appropriate for these different projects, but he argues that when it comes to an analysis of capitalism, a method of presentation based on systematic dialectical logic has both theoretical and practical advantages. Smith concludes with a brief sketch of how his interpretation of Marx's systematic dialectical logic can be applied to two specific problems within contemporary capitalism: the dynamics of technological change and the strategic objectives of working-class politics.

Patrick Murray also argues for the influence of Hegel's logic, and especially his logic of essence. Contrary to Joan Robinson's criticism that smatterings of "Hegelian stuff and nonsense" weaken *Capital*, Murray argues that it is precisely the lessons learned from Hegel that are responsible for the unique achievements of *Capital.* Murray first traces Marx's critical engagement with Hegel's logic in Marx's early philosophical works and argues that one of the main lessons learned from this engagement was that essence and appearance are not logically unrelated ontological realms. There is instead a necessary logical relation between essence and appearance: "essence must appear as something other than itself." The task of theory is then to explain why essence must necessarily appear in a particular form. Murray argues that this necessary relation between essence and appearance is the key to Marx's theory of money and to Marx's critique of Ricardo's failure to provide a theory of money. Based on a nondialectical model of essence and appearance, Ricardo's theory was concerned only with the essence of value, the determination of exchange values by labor times. Marx, on the other hand, raised a question that Ricardo never addressed: Why does value necessarily appear in the form of money? Marx's analysis of this question enabled him to derive money as the necessary form of appearance of the abstract labor contained in commodities. This analysis also provided the foundation for Marx's critique of the "time-chit" proposals of the Proudhonists and for the further analysis of prices in the three volumes of *Capital.* (Murray 1988b presents a more complete elaboration of these arguments; Banaji 1979 and Zeleny 1980 present similar interpretations of Marx's theory of money.)

The next chapter, by Christopher Arthur, also argues that Hegel's logic, in spite of its avowed idealism, is indeed relevant to Marx's analysis of capitalism. Arthur argues that the exchange of heterogeneous commodities constitutes in practice a form of abstraction that is analogous with the way Hegel sets up logical categories in thought. The development of the forms of value into money and capital creates a peculiar kind of "inverted reality" in which the universal dominates the particular—just as in Hegel's ontology. Thus an analysis of the forms of value can draw on the parallel found in Hegel's logic. After a summary of the relevant points of the Hegelian method of systematic exposition, Arthur presents an analysis of the forms of value from commodities to money and then from money to capital. This presentation is based on concepts borrowed from Hegel's logic (quality, quantity, measure, essence, appearance, actuality, and so on), thus demonstrating the relevance of these concepts. In the presentation of these forms of value, Arthur initially leaves aside any concept of labor as the "substance" or "essence" of value, intentionally departing from Marx. However, Arthur concludes by providing a novel proof that Marx is indeed right in giving central importance to labor as the common element of value: If the form of capital is to have actuality in Hegel's sense—namely, to be self-subsistent—the process of self-valorization must ground itself in the production of the commodities by wage labor.

Geert Reuten also examines the relation between Hegel's systematic dialectical logic and the logic of *Capital* and, of all the contributors, is the most critical of Marx's logic. Reuten argues that although there are various ways in which *Capital* can be interpreted as using systematic dialectical logic (for example, the interpretations of Smith and Murray), Marx is not systematic enough in his conceptual development. First, Reuten argues that the commodity is not an abstract all-embracing concept. Second, Marx's abstractions are not dialectical, but analytical or reductive. Third, Marx's logical development is not dialectical—it does not proceed internally from contradictions and their transcendences—but is instead based on conceptual analysis.[4] Reuten then examines the following three different approaches to value theory: concrete-labor embodied, abstract-labor embodied, and abstract-labor value-form. The first two are different interpretations of Marx's value theory and differ only in whether a distinction is made between concrete and abstract labor. Both of these interpretations follow Marx in assuming that labor is a "substance" of value that exists prior to exchange and in some way determines prices. The third approach breaks with Marx's "substance" of value and moves in the direction of a market concept of value, emphasizing the real abstraction of labor in the market. Reuten concludes that Marx's value theory is in need of reconstruction along the lines of a systematic, dialectic value-form approach (elaborated more fully in Reuten and Williams 1989).

Paul Mattick presents the main dissent within this volume to the view that Hegel's logic is important to an understanding of Marx's logic in *Capital*. Mattick argues that Hegel attempted to derive his system of concepts by means of dialectical logic that he then applied universally to all forms of society. Marx's logic, on the other hand, is based on the opposite principle: that there is no general theory that can be applied to all forms of society and that the concepts in a theory of capitalism should be derived not from a priori logical deductions but rather from the historically specific features of capitalist social relations. Mattick argues further that the order of concepts in *Capital* is determined in part by Marx's purpose of providing a thorough critique of classical political economy. Thus *Capital* begins with the commodity because that was the starting point of classical political economy, but Marx ultimately shows that this starting point is inadequate and that a superior starting point of a theory of capitalism is the class relation between capitalists and wage laborers. Mattick then reexamines Marx's derivation of money in section 3 of Chapter 1 of *Capital* and argues that, in spite of the Hegelian language employed, the logic of this section is not Hegelian. The necessity of money is derived not from a purely logical argument of contradiction and resolution but from the practical requirements of social practice (the need to represent and coordinate individual labor as social labor). Finally, Mattick argues that Marx used Hegelian language in the first chapter and elsewhere in *Capital* because it suited his purpose of critique of classical economics. Hegel's illusion that his concepts generated their own movement mirrors the illusion in capitalism (which was represented and systematized by classical political economy) that the products of labor generate their own movement and are independent of the specific social relations of capitalism.

Martha Campbell explores Marx's critique of the naturalism or universalism of bourgeois economic theory, including both classical theory as represented by Mill and neoclassical theory as represented by Wagner. Campbell emphasizes that Marx's concept of economic relations is completely different from either of these theories. For Marx, economic relations are property relations, meaning, in the case of modern society, not only property in its legal form as private property but also the unequal distribution of property that divides society into the two major classes of capitalists and wage laborers. In so defining economic relations, Marx is rejecting the central concepts of classical and neoclassical theory: production conceived as the relation of labor activity to the objective means of production, in classical theory; and need conceived as the relation between the human psyche and objects that satisfy needs, in neoclassical theory. The premise underlying both these concepts is that economic relations are determined by natural laws, independent of property ownership. Property is held by both classical and neoclassical theory to be social and to vary historically; but for both, all historical differences are only variations on private ownership. Thus neither sees a necessary connection between private ownership and the distribution of property that establishes the classes of capitalist society. Marx denied that need and production are determined independently of property relations, as these theories maintain. Capitalist property in its complete form, including the distribution of property, is the use of the elements and results of production by society as a whole in such a way as to maximize the monetary gain of the owners of property. Because production and consumption are means for realizing the overriding goal of profit maximization, these economic activities are determined by this goal. Linking Marx's redefinition of economic relations to the method of *Capital*, Campbell argues that Marx overcomes the separation of production and need from property relations by beginning *Capital* with the commodity. As the bearer of value, the commodity expresses the specifically capitalist property relations under which it is produced.

The final two chapters present a reexamination of the long-standing controversy over Marx's theory of prices of production in Volume 3 of *Capital*. Fred Moseley argues that the widespread criticisms of Marx's theory of prices of production (for example, that Marx failed to transform the inputs of constant capital and variable capital from values to prices) are erroneous because these criticisms presume a logical method, the method of linear production theory, that is fundamentally different from Marx's own logical method. Two main differences between Marx's method and the method of linear production theory are discussed: (1) the order of determination between aggregate magnitudes (total prices and total profit or surplus value) and individual magnitudes (individual prices and profits), and (2) the quantitative "givens" or presuppositions with which each theory begins. It is argued first that Marx's theory is based on the methodological premise that aggregate magnitudes are determined prior to and independent of individual magnitudes. These aggregate magnitudes are then taken as given in the subsequent analysis of the determination of individual magnitudes. Marx expressed this methodological premise in his distinction between "capital in general" and "many capitals." Linear production theory interpretation is based on the opposite methodological premise: that aggregate magnitudes are determined subsequent to the determination of individual magnitudes, as the sum of the individual magnitudes. It is argued further that the fundamental givens in Marx's theory are sums of money that are invested as capital, namely the *M* in the general formula for capital, M-C-M′. The main objective of Marx's theory is to explain how this given amount of money increases its magnitude. Linear production theory, on the other hand, takes as given "real" physical quantities of inputs and outputs, the technical conditions of production, and the real wage. It is argued finally that Marx's theory of prices of production is logically consistent and complete in terms of Marx's own logical method. Marx did not fail to transform the inputs of constant capital and variable capital. These inputs are taken as given in terms of prices of production; there is nothing to be transformed. The criticisms that have been made of Marx's theory do not in fact apply to Marx's theory; they apply only to the misguided attempt to interpret Marx's theory in terms of linear production theory.

Guglielmo Carchedi presents a largely complementary interpretation of Marx's theory of prices of production, with emphasis on other aspects of Marx's method. Carchedi emphasizes the distinction between Marx's method of inquiry and his method of presentation. He begins with a discussion of the basic principles of Marx's method of inquiry, which include the distinctions between determinant and determined instances and between determination in the last instance and concrete determination.

Carchedi defines a dialectical relation as a process in which determined instances, potentially existing within the determinant one, become the actual conditions of reproduction or supersession, and thus take on concrete features through a process of mutual interrelation and modification. This process is understood as a dialectical movement in which (1) potentially present instances realize themselves, and other realized instances go back to a potential state; (2) all instances change their concrete form; and (3) some conditions of reproduction of the determinant instance become conditions of supersession, and vice versa. These methodological insights are then used to discuss the criticisms of Marx's theory of prices of production. Most important, Carchedi argues that the neo-Ricardian critique of circularity (that in Marx's transformation, commodities as inputs are bought at their value) is based on a misunderstanding of the distinction between individual values as potential values and social values as actual, realized values. The only way to understand the transformation of individual into social values is to consider the real sequence of production processes as a chronological sequence of dialectical processes in which individual values realize themselves as social values and become again individual values only to realize themselves again as social values, in an endless chronological sequence of dialectical transformations. (Carchedi 1991 presents a more complete discussion of both Marx's dialectical method and its application to the determination of prices of production and other issues.) An important similarity with Moseley's paper is that Carchedi also argues that the inputs of constant capital and variable capital are taken as given in terms of already transformed prices of production. This point is extended to cover the important case in which technological change occurs between the time of purchase of inputs and the sale of outputs.

There are a number of important points of agreement among the contributors to this volume, but also significant disagreements. Not all the agreements and disagreements discussed below are evident from the essays, although most of them are. This summary is also drawn from other published works of these authors and from the discussions at the Mount Holyoke conference.

To begin with the more general issues, all the authors except Mattick and Carchedi agree that an understanding of Hegel is necessary for a full understanding of Marx's logical method, although there is considerable disagreement concerning the precise significance of Hegel's logic for Marx's theory (see Chapters 1–4). Smith (Chapter 1) interprets Marx's theory as a largely successful application of Hegel's dialectical logic. Reuten (Chapter 4) argues that Marx should have employed Hegel's logic (and perhaps attempted to), but did not fully succeed in doing so. Murray (Chapter 2) and Arthur (Chapter 3) argue that Marx's employment of Hegel's logical notions was intended as a simultaneous critique of Hegel's logic and of capitalist economic forms. It is interesting to note in this regard that, while Marx was working on the *Grundrisse*, he wrote to Engels that a review of Hegel's *Logic* "has been of great service to me as regards the *method* of dealing with the material" (Marx and Engels 1975b, 93; emphasis in the original). Marx went on to say that he would like someday to write an introduction to Hegel's method that would be accessible "to the ordinary human intelligence." Unfortunately, this introduction was never written, and we are now forced to try to figure out for ourselves the precise nature of Marx's critical appropriation of Hegel's method. An important clue that should be explored in future research is that just before the sentence in the letter quoted above, Marx said that in his recent work he had "overthrown the whole doctrine of *profit* as it has existed up to now" (emphasis added). These remarks suggest that a consideration of Hegel's method should clarify Marx's theory of profit, the centerpiece of Marx's theory of capitalism.

Related to this emphasis on Hegel, all the authors except Mattick agree that Marx employs some form of dialectical logic in *Capital*, although again there is considerable disagreement over the precise meaning of dialectical logic (see Chapters 1–4 and 8). It remains a question for further research whether these differences are only a matter of emphasis or are more substantial. The most important common element of these different interpretations of dialectical logic is that they all agree that dialectical logic involves the demonstration of *necessary connections* between the different constitutive categories of capitalism, such as commodities, money, capital, wage labor, and so on. According to this logic, later concepts are derived as the "necessary conditions of existence" of earlier concepts. In other words, it is argued that the phenomena to which earlier concepts refer could not exist without the phenomena expressed by the later concepts (for example, the commodity as Marx defined it could not exist without money, or without capital). The precise interpretations of these derivations differ somewhat among the different authors,[5] but they all emphasize that the demonstration of these necessary connections is a very important aspect of *Capital* that is overlooked by all three of the prevailing interpretations of Marx's theory discussed above.

A related point of disagreement among the authors is over the relative significance of the qualitative and quantitative aspects of Marx's economic theory. Reuten, Arthur, and Smith emphasize the qualitative aspects of Marx's theory,[6] by which is meant the derivation of the economic forms that are characteristic of capitalism and the demonstration of the necessary connections between these economic forms, as in the previous paragraph.[7]

The other authors generally do not disagree with the importance of these qualitative aspects of Marx's theory, but they also argue that the quantitative aspects, especially the determination of profit, are at least as important and should also be emphasized. The most important quantitative question of Marx's theory is whether the profit of capitalists is due to the exploitation of workers. Without a quantitative theory of profits, this question cannot be answered.

Most of the authors—not including Reuten, Smith, and Murray—agree with Moseley's interpretation of Marx's methodological distinction between capital in general and many capitals, according to which aggregate economic magnitudes are determined prior to individual magnitudes (most importantly, the aggregate amount of surplus value is determined prior to its distribution among individual branches of production and its further division into industrial profit, merchant profit, interest, and rent). As discussed in Moseley's chapter, this methodological principle has important implications for Marx's theory of prices of production and for the prevailing interpretation of the "transformation problem."

We turn now to specific parts of *Capital*, discussed roughly in their order in *Capital*. The interpretation of the commodity as the starting point of *Capital* is probably the strongest point of agreement among the authors. All the authors agree that the commodity with which Marx begins is assumed to be a product of *capitalist production*, not of a precapitalist simple commodity production. In other words, all agree that the logical-historical interpretation of Marx's method is mistaken on this, its most important point.[8]

All the authors also agree that Marx attempted in section 1 of Chapter 1 to derive abstract labor as the "substance of value," which exists prior to exchange—although it is not observable—and which determines the exchange values of commodities. But there is significant disagreement over the validity and the necessity of Marx's derivation. Indeed this disagreement is probably the most significant one among the authors. This controversy has a long history, beginning with Boehm-Bawerk. Smith, Arthur, and Reuten reject Marx's derivation of abstract labor as the substance of value for two main reasons (which have been cited by many others): the lack of an adequate reason given for selecting labor as the common property of commodities that determines their exchange values, and the unresolved problem of reducing different kinds of skilled labor to equivalent quantities of simple abstract labor. Reuten also criticizes the type of abstraction that Marx makes in this derivation—an analytical or reductive abstraction rather than a dialectical abstraction. Furthermore, these authors also argue that the important qualitative conclusions of Marx's theory, such as the necessity of money, can be derived without recourse to Marx's concept of abstract labor as the substance of value (such a derivation is carried out, for example, in Smith's chapter in this volume and in Reuten and Williams 1989, 59–66). Murray is undecided about the validity and necessity of Marx's derivation of abstract labor as the substance of value. The remaining authors largely accept Marx's derivation not as a "logical proof" but rather as a plausible hypothesis, the validity of which should be evaluated based on the extent to which it can explain the important phenomena of capitalism. They also argue that the main advantage of the assumption of abstract labor is that it also provides a quantitative theory of profit, which is the main question of Marx's theory.

All the authors also agree that money plays a much more significant role in Marx's theory than is generally acknowledged. All agree that Marx derived money in section 3 of Chapter 1 as the "necessary form of appearance" of abstract labor, although the specific interpretations of this derivation differ somewhat for different authors (see Chapters 1–5).[9] All the authors also agree that money continues to play a central role throughout Volume 1, as well as in the two later volumes. The significance of money in Volume 1 is most clearly expressed by the "general formula for capital," which is introduced in Chapter 4 of *Capital* and is expressed symbolically as M-C-M′—money that becomes more money. This formula poses the main question with which Volume 1 is concerned: What is the origin of the increment of money that is the characteristic feature of capital? Thus the Sraffian interpretation of Marx's theory, according to which Volume 1 is only about labor values, is incorrect.

Finally, all the authors agree that the prevailing interpretation of Marx's theory of prices of production is erroneous, since it is based primarily on the Sraffian interpretation of Marx's theory, which all agree is mistaken. The authors do not fully agree with the (broadly similar) interpretations of Marx's theory of prices of production presented in this volume by Moseley and Carchedi, but they all agree that the "transformation problem" should be thoroughly reexamined in light of the fundamental methodological differences between Marx's theory and Sraffa's theory.

There are also a number of important questions related to Marx's logical method that are hardly addressed in this volume and should be the subject of future research. Indeed, the main general lesson we learned from the conference was how much more we need to learn about Marx's logical method and related methodological issues.[10] Perhaps the most important of these remaining questions is the relation between subjects and objects in Marx's economic theory. Are Marx's conclusions derived from the objective characteristics of capitalism, or are they instead derived from the choices of individual agents in capitalism, or perhaps some combination of the two, as Smith suggests? This question obviously relates to the rational-choice interpretation of Marx's theory and to the question of a need for "microfoundations" for Marx's theory (see Roemer 1982; Elster 1985). (Mattick, Jr. 1986b discusses this question at length, and Smith 1990a and his chapter in this volume also address this question.) A second remaining question is a further exploration of the distinction between Marx's method of inquiry and his method of presentation, as emphasized by Carchedi. Finally, after all the various pieces of Marx's logical method discussed above have been explored, there should also be renewed attempts to forge a comprehensive synthesis of the overall logical structure of the three volumes of *Capital*, incorporating all these various aspects.

The insights gained from a better understanding of Marx's logical method should also be applied to the ongoing controversy over Marx's theory of the falling rate of profit. In recent years, this controversy has been discussed almost entirely in terms of Okishio's theorem.[11] However, Okishio's theorem presumes the Sraffian interpretation of Marx's theory, which all the authors in this volume agree is erroneous. Thus this important controversy should also be reexamined in light of the methodological insights gained from this line of research. In general, the research represented in this book suggests that a thorough reexamination of all aspects of the logical consistency of Marx's theory should be undertaken.

I would like to express appreciation to Mount Holyoke College for its generous financial support of the conference. Part of the funds for the conference came from a grant to Mount Holyoke by the Mellon Foundation for the purpose of encouraging new initiatives in interdisciplinary research; this grant is also gratefully acknowledged. I also thank various members of the Mount Holyoke staff, especially Dawn Larder, who assisted in the logistical arrangements for the conference. Finally, I would like to thank Cindy Kaufman-Nixon, our production editor at Humanities Press, and her capable assistants for their excellent editorial work in bringing our book to publication.

FRED MOSELEY
MOUNT HOLYOKE COLLEGE

Notes

In writing this Introduction, I have benefited greatly from substantial written comments and suggestions from all the authors in this volume, although they do not necessarily agree with the views expressed. The process of writing this Introduction and the discussions at the conference at which the papers were first delivered have been invaluable learning experiences for me.

1. Smith and Carchedi do not consider the method of successive approximations to be erroneous, but only one aspect of Marx's method that ignores many other important aspects.
2. Marx is partly to blame for the lack of understanding of his logical method, since he did not provide a clear and definitive statement of his method. In the Postface from which the above epigraph comes, Marx went on to quote a number of conflicting interpretations, with very little comment, and then to quote at length and approvingly a review of *Capital* by a Russian economist named Kaufmann. However, this review is subject to different interpretations and does not adequately address most of the important methodological issues identified above. The most complete discussion of Marx's method is in the Introduction to the *Grundrisse*, but this Introduction is also ambiguous (for example, see the debate between Echeverria [1978] and Carver [1980]) and does not address all the important issues.
3. Important recent works that should be useful in this reexamination of the methodological foundations of Marx's economic theory include: Backhaus 1980; Eldred and Roth 1978; Echeverria 1978, 1980; Banaji 1979; Zeleny 1980; Carver 1980; Eldred and Hanlon 1981; Arthur 1986; Mattick, Jr. 1986b; Murray 1988b; Williams 1988; Reuten and Williams 1989; Smith 1990c; and Carchedi 1991.
4. The criticism of methodological confusion in *Capital* is also made by Backhaus (1980) and other members of the value-form school, including Eldred and Roth (1978) and Eldred and Hanlon (1981).
5. Smith argues in terms of "necessary structural tendencies" rather than "necessary conditions of existence." According to this view, social agents operating within the social forms defined by the earlier concepts would necessarily tend to act in a manner that brings about a new social form, which is defined by the later concepts.
6. Smith notes that his emphasis on the qualitative aspects of Marx's theory is due to his own philosophical background and interests, not because he considers these qualitative aspects to be more important than the quantitative aspects of Marx's theory.
7. The meaning of *qualitative* here differs from that of Sweezy (1968) and others who discuss the qualitative aspect of the labor theory of value in terms of the specification of the unique social relations of capitalism, not the derivation of the necessary connections between commodities, money, and so on.
8. Earlier works that have presented similar arguments include Banaji 1979; Smith 1990b; and Campbell, forthcoming.
9. As mentioned in the previous paragraph, the main disagreement is over the extent to which Marx's derivation of the necessity of money depends on the assumption of abstract labor as the substance of value.
10. Other general lessons included how deeply these methodological issues affect the interpretation of the full range of concepts and issues in *Capital* (e.g., value, money, capital, profit, prices of production); how valuable the interaction between philosophers and economists can be on these issues; and how effective a small intensive working conference can be as a vehicle for advancing our understanding.
11. See Moseley 1992, 20–24, for a nontechnical discussion of the controversy over Okishio's theorem.

1

Marx's *Capital* and Hegelian Dialectical Logic

Tony Smith

This chapter reexamines the old issue of the relation between Marx and Hegel. I believe that future research work in Marxian theory requires a proper understanding of the relationship between Hegel's dialectical logic and Marx's *Capital*. The chapter concludes with a sketch of a research agenda for future work in Marxian theory based on such an understanding.

Our first task is to distinguish two different types of dialectical theory in Hegel. The first concerns the dialectics of history. Hegel believed that there is a logic of development underlying both world history and the history of art, religion, and philosophy. *Dialectics* was the term he used to refer to this logic of development. However, the second sort of dialectical theory, found in writings such as *The Science of Logic* and *The Philosophy of Right*, is our sole concern here. This may be termed *systematic* dialectics and is concerned with the ordering of categories from the simple and abstract to the complex and concrete. This ordering does not coincide with the order of events in history:

> What we acquire [in dialectical social theories] is a series of thoughts and another series of existence shapes of experience; to which I may add that the time order in which the latter actually appear is other than the natural order. (Hegel 1942, 233)[1]

What was Marx's attitude toward this second sort of dialectical theory? In an 1858 letter he stated, "I leafed through Hegel's *Logic* again and found much to assist me in the *method* of analysis" (Marx and Engels 1983, 50). Marx elsewhere asserted that his goal was to trace "the intrinsic connection existing between economic categories or the obscure structure of the bourgeois economic system" (Marx 1968b, 165). Since the entire focus of systematic dialectics in Hegel is "the tracing of intrinsic connections between categories," it would appear that Marx took over the project of constructing a systematic dialectical theory from Hegel. This judgment is reinforced when we recall that Marx also insisted that the ordering of categories does not correspond to historical stages: "It would be unfeasible and wrong to let the economic categories follow one another in the same sequence as that in which they were historically decisive" (Marx 1973, 107).

All this strongly suggests that in his major economic writings, Marx's method has its roots in Hegel's systematic dialectic. Yet in the Preface to the second edition of *Capital*, Marx vehemently insisted that he had merely "coquetted" with Hegelian terminology in the first edition (Marx 1978, 29). This, along with many other equally unflattering references to Hegel, suggests strongly that Marx did *not* make use of Hegelian method. What are we to make of this apparent paradox?

I believe that in *Capital* and elsewhere Marx did indeed make use of a systematic dialectical method similar to that found in Hegel. I also believe that this fact is of both theoretical and practical importance. In my view, Marx was led to deny this as a result of a somewhat uncharitable reading of Hegel, a reading that has been repeated uncritically by generations of Marxists. I attempt to make these theses plausible by considering three responses to Hegel found in the Marxist tradition. The first radically rejects Hegelianism in toto; the second grants a Hegelian legacy in Marxism, while insisting that it involves only superficial matters; the third holds that Hegelian method is of crucial importance to Marx's position, due to a number of perverse features that this method shares with capitalism.

The Case against Hegelian Dialectical Logic

Four Objections

A great many objections to Hegel's systematic dialectical method have been proposed by Marx and his followers. Four of these criticisms are examined here.[2]

First, with Marx, theorizing begins with the "method of inquiry," that is, the close empirical study of the object realm under investigation as well as previous theoretical work in this area. Any concern with the systematic ordering of categories is limited to the subsequent "method of presentation." In contrast, Hegelian dialectical logic proceeds from category to category in a completely a priori manner: "Hegel fell into the illusion of conceiving the real as the product of thought concentrating itself, probing its own depths, and unfolding itself out of itself, by itself" (Marx 1973, 101).

A second and closely related point is that Hegelian dialectical logic in social theory seems to impose the categories of *The Science of Logic* on the social realm in an external fashion. Marx expressed this criticism in the course of a comment on Lassalle's Hegelianization of political economy: "He will learn to his cost that to bring a science by criticism to the point where it can be dialectically presented is an altogether different thing from applying an abstract ready-made system of logic to mere inklings of such a system" (Marx and Engels n.d., 123).

Third, the term *dialectical logic* has struck many Marxist thinkers as utterly nonsensical. *Logic* implies the necessary deduction of one proposition from another. Ordinary formal logic shows how this can be done in a fairly straightforward manner. But practitioners of dialectical logic claim to provide a completely different sort of necessary derivation, without offering any adequate account of either the terms they use or the methods they employ (Elster 1985).

Fourth and finally, Marxist theory is materialist in the sense that it centers on material practices in the social world. A method such as Hegel's that centers on a progression of thought determinations seems to eradicate this essential dimension of the Marxist position (Suchting 1986).

If these points are accepted, the only possible conclusion is that Hegelian dialectical logic has no legitimate place in social theory. However great their other differences, this conclusion is shared by most neo-Ricardians, analytical Marxists, Kantian Marxists (e.g., Colletti), Habermasians, and many others. It is certainly possible to find passages in Hegel that appear to substantiate this hostile view. However, the reading of Hegel upon which this conclusion is based is questionable in a number of important respects. It is possible to read Hegel in a quite different fashion, one that makes him a much more interesting and plausible thinker.[3]

The first objection, which asserted that Hegel completely ignored the need for empirical study, loses much of its force in the face of passages such as the following:

> The knowledge of the particular is necessary. This particularity must be worked out on its own account; we must become acquainted with empirical nature, both with the physical and with the human. . . . Without the working out of the empirical sciences on their own account, philosophy could not have reached further than with the ancients. (Hegel 1955, 175–76)

As if in anticipation of Marx's criticism that for Hegel thought unfolds itself out of itself, by itself, Hegel insisted that:

> In order that this science [Hegel's philosophy] may come into existence, we must have the progression from the individual and particular

> to the universal—*an activity which is a reaction on the given material of empiricism in order to bring about its reconstruction. The demand of a priori knowledge, which seems to imply that the Idea should construct from itself, is thus a reconstruction only*. . . . In consciousness it then adopts the attitude of having cut away the bridge from behind it; it appears to be free to launch forth in its ether only, and to develop without resistance to this medium; but it is another matter to attain to this ether and to development of it. (Hegel 1955, 176–77; emphasis added)

Hegelian dialectical logic thus should be read as a method for the *reconstruction* in thought of a given realm, not as an a priori creation of thought out of itself.

On this reading, Hegel's systematic theory, like Marx's, begins with the method of inquiry, the empirical appropriation of the given area of investigation. Few if any philosophers have incorporated the empirical natural and social sciences of their day to the extent Hegel did. Recent research on Hegel's intellectual development (Petry 1970, 1978) documents how Hegel was completely willing to revise his analysis and ordering of categories when developments in the natural and social sciences showed that this was warranted. The picture of Hegel trying to deduce the content of nature and spirit from his logical categories is a myth that caricatures what we now know of his actual working procedures.

Turning to the second objection: Hegel did not generate his social theory by externally imposing the categories of the *Logic* on this realm. There is no one-to-one correspondence of the categories from the *Logic* and the categories of the social theory presented in *The Philosophy of Right*. There is no algorithm that when applied to a logical category automatically generates a social category. If Marx is correct in asserting that this is Lassalle's approach to political economy, it does not follow that Hegel is to be blamed for the faults of his epigone. Hegel's own approach to political economy began with many decades in close study of both political economists (Steuert and Smith especially) and the dominant tendencies of the modern economy (mechanization, overproduction crises, and so on).

Even if Hegelian dialectical logic is to be seen as a reconstruction in thought of a given subject matter rather than as an a priori procession of categories externally imposed on the subject matter, two other questions remain. What could the term *logic* possibly mean in this context? And what does any of this have to do with material practice? The best way to approach these issues is to examine in detail a paradigmatic example from Hegel's social theory.

The Philosophy of Right is an attempt to reconstruct in thought the categories that capture the modern epoch.[4] It begins with the category "property." In Hegel's view, one of the defining characteristics of the modern era is the manner in which the principle of individuality is acknowledged. In property the wills of individual subjects are manifested objectively, and for Hegel this is the most simple and abstract manner in which the principle of individuality can be institutionalized. Individual subjects can also assert their personality by withdrawing their will from an object, allowing the thing to become the property of another. Hegel here introduces the category "contract."

On this level of the theory we have abstracted from all other features of the modern epoch. Specifically we have abstracted from the presence of an apparatus to adjudicate competing claims regarding the objects of possession. Given this, Hegel asserted, it inevitably follows that even well-intentioned social agents will regularly disagree, each claiming that a specific object is his rightful property. It also inevitably follows that some social agents will make claims that they know to be fraudulent. Eventually we will have a situation in which it is impossible to distinguish rightful claims to property from those that are not. Such a situation, in which the concept of "right" is without any practical force, is what Hegel termed "crime."

It is not possible to derive "contract" from "property," or "crime" from "contract," with the deductive necessity of formal logic. Claims of deductive necessity can be undermined by a single legitimate counterexample. Many counterexamples can be imagined in which subjects hold property without engaging in contractual exchange. And many counterexamples can be imagined in which a number of subjects externalize their wills in contractual exchange without conflict. Nonetheless, to say that these notions are only contingently related is far too weak. Hegel's point, I believe, can be put as follows. Given the social form defined by the category "property," it is *necessarily* the case that social agents acting within the social form will tend to act in such a way that the social form defined by the category "contract" would come about. Likewise, given the social form defined by the category "contract," it is *necessarily* the case that social agents acting within that social form would tend to act in such a way that the social form defined by the category "crime" would come about. We have the following framework:[5]

Category 1: Social Form → Necessary Structural Tendency re Social Agents → Category 2: New Social Form[6]

I do not wish to discuss whether "property" is the correct category with which to begin a systematic reconstruction of the modern social world, nor will I consider whether the derivations of "contract" and "crime" are warranted. However, I do want to stress that there is an underlying plausibility to Hegel's general framework. In principle there may indeed be cases in which a given social form necessarily generates structural tendencies leading social agents to institute a different social form. If this is granted, then it follows that in principle it is possible to assert that one category (that defining the second social form) can be derived from another (that defining the first) with "necessity." The dialectical logic underlying Hegel's systematic social theory has to do with claims of necessity in this sense.

In the contemporary intellectual context it is certainly unusual to use the term *logic* to describe the methodological procedure of moving from one category to another in the systematic fashion just described. Of course if one wishes to restrict the term to formal deductive systems of propositions, one is free to do so. However, the term *logic* has typically been used in the history of thought to refer to claims of necessary derivations. It therefore seems legitimate to employ the term here, although the necessity underlying the derivations in dialectical social theory rests on the necessity for a structural tendency to arise (and not on the necessity with which one proposition follows another without exception within an axiomatic system).

Given the above reading, the connection between dialectical logic and material practice is straightforward. One category is derived from another precisely because the social form defined by the initial category necessarily would lead social agents operating within that form to tend to act in ways that would lead to a new social form. This provides the warrant for the introduction of a new category defining that new social form. From this perspective we can go so far as to define dialectical logic in social theory as the logic of material practices.[7]

Of course, establishing that there is a necessity for structural tendencies to arise within a given social form is a difficult task. No doubt Hegel failed at this task in many sections of his social theory. However, I can see no reason to deny that the construction of a systematic dialectical social theory is a theoretical project that is fully intelligible, inherently interesting, and possible in principle. I also hold that dialectical logic in the above sense provides the underlying architectonic of Marx's *Capital*, a claim I now attempt to substantiate.

DIALECTICAL LOGIC IN *CAPITAL*

Capital is a complex work in which a great variety of topics are discussed and a great variety of methods are employed. However, *Capital* is not merely an aggregate of separate studies. Underlying its complexity is a unifying thread: the systematic progression of socioeconomic categories reconstructing the capitalist mode of production in thought. A very abbreviated reconstruction of the categorial progression in Volume 1 follows.

Marx began with the method of inquiry, that is, the empirical appropriation of both relevant data regarding the capitalist mode of production and earlier attempts by political economists to comprehend this mode of production theoretically. He then moved to what he regarded as the simplest and most abstract categorial level,[8] from which he systematically progressed in a step-by-step fashion to ever more complex and concrete categorial levels.[9]

Marx termed the initial stage *the commodity form*. The social form presented on this categorial level defines a specific manner of structuring the social division of labor. Production is undertaken privately by isolated units of production without any prior social coordination. This private labor is undertaken in the hope that it will produce commodities that are socially validated through being sold in the marketplace.[10] The aim, in other words, is not just to produce use values, but to produce exchange values. If exchange does not occur, then the labor in question may be termed "socially wasted concrete labor." If successful exchange does occur, then the commodities can be said to possess value, or to instantiate the *value form*.[11] The private labor that has been validated as social labor in this manner is termed by Marx "socially necessary abstract labor."[12] The socially necessary abstract labor of producers is the essential social reality underlying all commodities with value.[13] It is the manner in which the collective nature of the social division of labor is shaped under a social form in which production is disaggregated.

The commodity form is historically specific (it is a stage in the reconstruction in thought of the capitalist mode of production) as well as simple and abstract (it is the first stage of that reconstruction). Corresponding to this we have a notion of social agency on this categorial level that is at once historically specific and extremely "thin." All cultural, sociological, and psychological features essentially connected to social agents within noncapitalist modes of production can be dismissed at once. We have to deal with social agents only insofar as their cultural, sociological, and psychological features are a function of the structures that make up capitalism. And we must also dismiss all features of social agency that are connected with more concrete and complex social forms within capitalism. If the labor of producers under the commodity form is socially wasted, they will be unable to exchange their products for other goods and services to satisfy their wants and needs. This leads social agents operating under the commodity form to develop a strong sense of private self-interest. It follows that the major motivation of producers under the commodity form is that their labor prove to be socially necessary.

How would self-interested social agents operating within the structure defined by the commodity form tend to act? Clearly they would generally attempt to find other agents with whom they could exchange commodities. When so many units of one commodity are exchanged for so many units of another (x commodity A = y commodity B), we have an instance of what Marx termed the *elementary form* of commodity exchange. Since there are, in principle, many other commodities besides commodity B that could be employed to satisfy the direct and indirect needs and wants of the holder of commodity A, a somewhat more complex tendency arises at once. Here the exchangeability of commodity A is evaluated in terms of the specific use values of many other commodities (x commodity A = y commodity B, m commodity C, n commodity D, and so on). Marx termed this the *expanded form*.

Given the disaggregated nature of social production here, the social dimension of production can appear only in an indirect form. The value of a commodity, the fact that the labor that produced it has proved to be socially necessary abstract labor, *must* appear in something other than itself (Murray, Chapter 2, this volume). In both the elementary form and the expanded form, the value of the initial commodity appears as something other than itself; it appears in the shape of the commodity for which it is exchanged. The social nature of production could appear directly only if there were a direct social coordination of production in order to fulfill social needs and wants.

If we simply reverse the expanded form, we obtain what Marx termed the *general form*. Here the value of commodities B, C, D, and so on is expressed in commodity A, which thus serves as the universal commodity. Of course it does not matter which commodity is selected to serve as an instantiation of the general form; B or C or D would do just as well as A.

The move from the expanded form to the general form strikes me as a straightforward logical deduction rather than as a dialectical derivation of a necessary structural tendency. If the value of commodity A can be expressed in commodities B, C, D, and so on, then the values of commodities B, C, and D can be expressed in commodity A. However, Marx goes on at once to derive from this final stage of the commodity form a necessary structural tendency for social agents operating within that form to select a single commodity to serve as the universal commodity in this sense. Generalized commodity exchange is continually subject to severe breakdowns if a generally accepted measure of the value of commodities is lacking. And so social agents operating in this context would necessarily tend to introduce such a general measure. With this the necessity of making the transition to a new social form is derived, and with it the necessity for introducing a new categorial level, the *money form*.

Money provides a specific shape in which the social nature of privatized production can be universally expressed; the most general definition of money is that it serves as the universal commodity. Money does not play this role as a result of any particular use value it may claim. Precisely this abstractness from any particular use makes money a more adequate expression of the universality of abstract labor. It allows money to be a more adequate manifestation of the abstractness and universality of the value of commodities.[14]

After developing money as the measure of value, Marx noted a structural tendency for money to be used in order to facilitate exchange in a C-M-C circuit. In this manner Marx derived the category "money as means of circulation." However, the social form defined by this category includes the possibility of interruptions in the circuit. There is no guarantee that social agents will be able to find someone to purchase their commodities so that they will then be able to use the money received to purchase needed commodities. Social agents who make money an end of exchange will be able to survive these interruptions in the circuit of commodity exchange. From this Marx derived the necessity of the C-M-C circuit to be transformed into a new social form, the M-C-M circuit. This new form is expressed in the category "money as end of exchange."

Self-interested agents seeking to acquire a store of money are hardly going to be content to conclude economic transactions with a sum of money identical to that with which they began. There is thus a further structural tendency for the M-C-M circuit to give way to an M-C-M′ circuit, in which economic agents aim at a sum of money exceeding the initial sum. With this we have moved to the capital form, for the simplest definition of capital is "money which begets money."

As we progress from the commodity form through the money form to the capital form, the relevant notion of social agency becomes progressively less thin. Once we have attained the M-C-M′ circuit we are no longer dealing with individuals simply as commodity and money holders. Within the M-C-M′ circuit we must consider social agents in terms of their position within a *class structure*. Not all who aim at attaining an excess above the original investment will be successful. Whether through superior luck or energy or ruthlessness, some will attain more money reserves than others; this in turn heightens their opportunities when engaging in the next series of transactions. Those who end one cycle of transactions with fewer reserve funds are less likely to be successful in the next. Corresponding to this is an inequality regarding access to productive resources. Those with extensive reserve funds, capitalists, are able to purchase the inputs required for production. Those without sufficient reserve funds are not. This inequality forces the latter to sell their labor power to the former in order to attain the money funds necessary to purchase the means of subsistence.[15] There is a systematic connection between the capital form and the wage relation in which labor power has become a commodity bought by capitalists. The latter necessarily follows from the former in a dialectical ordering of socioeconomic categories.[16]

Those lacking sufficient money reserves to survive must sell their labor power within the short to medium term, but those who are to purchase that labor power have sufficient reserves to wait until the terms of agreement are favorable to them. This asymmetry underlying the wage relation leads to another structural tendency necessarily arising under the capital form, the tendency for the wage contract to lead to the *exploitation* of wage laborers. Those forced to sell their labor power are forced to accept a situation in which (1) they produce an amount of economic value that exceeds what they receive back in the form of wages, and (2) this surplus is controlled by those who hired them. There also is a further structural tendency for the owners of capital to transform the production process in order to maximize the amount of surplus they appropriate. (This can be done by extending the working day or by increasing its intensity through technical change and the reorganization of the labor process.)[17]

Under the value form, socioeconomic power is generally a function of economic resources. From this Marx derived a final structural tendency for a portion of the surplus to be accumulated and reinvested in another capital circuit. It is then used to purchase new means of production and labor power in order to produce a surplus that can once more be appropriated. If the surplus that is accumulated is reinvested so as to replace used-up means of production and labor power while keeping the level of production the same, this is termed *simple accumulation*. If a level of surplus is produced and reinvested that allows for an expansion of production, we have *expanded accumulation*.

From a systematic standpoint, this completes Volume 1.[18] We have sketched the following systematic progression of categorial levels:

1. Commodity form
    - simple form
    - expanded form
    - general form
2. Money form
    - money as measure of value
    - money as means of circulation
    - money as end in itself

3. Capital form
    - class division
    - exploitation
    - transformation of the labor process
    - accumulation

This ordering is not at all arbitrary. It proceeds in a systematic fashion, moving from the most simple and abstract to the most complex and concrete determinations. And there is a systematic necessity underlying it. Dialectical logic in this context is simply the procedure of progressing from one level of abstraction to the next in a systematic fashion, based on the necessary derivation of one categorial level from another. This necessity is not that which is found in the deductive systems of formal logic. Nor does it involve some quasi-mystical generation of one idea from another. The necessity of the derivation is materially grounded in the practice of social agents. Derivations are justified if and only if we can show that social agents operating within one social form would necessarily tend to act in a manner that leads to the introduction of a new social form.

Let me note once again that I recognize that *Capital* is a complex work. It includes many dimensions that cannot be reduced to the systematic progression of economic categories. Even further, I am persuaded by Geert Reuten (Chapter 4, this volume) that elements actually incompatible with a systematic approach can also be found in *Capital*, primarily due to the fact that Marx's break from classical political economy was incomplete. The systematic dialectical reading does not incorporate the whole of the book. However, I believe that it does capture the work's unifying thread, its underlying architectonic.

This claim faces one major difficulty. In the above account of systematic derivations, the key element in a transition from one categorial level to the next involves the behavior of social agents. This appears to make subjective psychological dispositions the ultimate theoretical foundation of *Capital*. But Marxian economics is based on the radical *rejection* of the subjectivism and psychologism found in most bourgeois economics. Marx insisted vehemently that his concern was with the objective nature of the capitalist mode of production, whatever the subjective beliefs and dispositions of agents within that mode of production might be. It would seem that the above reading is fundamentally incompatible with this crucial aspect of Marx's position.

Three points can be made in reply. First, the main problem with most bourgeois economics in this context is that they universalize features of human subjectivity that are historically specific, treating dispositions unique to generalized commodity production as if they were transhistorical features of human nature. (Adam Smith's assumption of a transhistorical propensity to "truck and barter" provides one example.) In contrast, in dialectical social theory the starting point is a set of historically specific social forms. The relevant subjective features of social agents are evoked by these particular social forms. In the above reading of *Capital*, for instance, "self-interest" is recognized as a dominant disposition of social agents under the commodity form. Its dominance is *not* posited as a transhistorical feature of human nature.

Second, it is true that in the above account of dialectical social theory transitions from one categorial level to another are justified through arguments regarding how social agents operating within a given social form would act. However, it does not follow that this grants explanatory primacy to the conscious intentions of those agents. The behavior, as well as the dispositions, of these social agents is structured by social forms. When these social forms are given, the behavior of social agents necessarily tends to go in certain directions rather than others. In this sense explanatory primacy resides with the objective social forms. For example, given the objective asymmetry underlying the wage contract under the capital form, social agents necessarily tend to accede to wage contracts formalizing exploitation. It is the objective asymmetry, not the subjective intentions of the social agents, that has explanatory primacy here.

Finally, I do not see how a reading of the categorial progression in *Capital* that does not make reference to the behavior of social agents can avoid being guilty of tautology or reification. One alternative is to argue that since our theoretical starting point (i.e., the object to be reconstructed) is capitalism, and since we already know that commodities, money, and the like are essential features of capitalism, then we can simply go from "commodities" to "money" to "capital" without having to refer to social agents. I have already noted (see note 6) that this sort of "backward" justification for progressing from one categorial level to another does indeed have a role to play in dialectical social theory. However, when it becomes the sole warrant for transitions, then the theory is reduced to one big tautology. This does not undermine the validity of the theory, but in my view it does limit its theoretical interest.

Another alternative is to attempt to account for the transitions in a "forward" manner without providing "microfoundations" in the behavior of social agents. I do not see how this can be done without reification. Commodities do not "beget" money, nor does the C-M-C circuit turn into the M-C-M and M-C-M′ circuits of its own accord. "Commodity," "money," and "capital" have indeed become alien social forces dominating the human community. But they are not things. They are constituted in and by social relations, however alien from social control these social relations have become. In themselves they lack both independent metaphysical status and any causal powers. The above emphasis on social agency remains true to this crucial thesis of Marxism.

This concludes the response to the viewpoint that Hegelian dialectical logic has no role whatever to play in Marxist theory. The next perspective to be considered asserts that dialectical logic merely provides one among a series of possible "methods of presentation" available to Marxist theorists.

Dialectical Logic and the Method of Presentation

Let us grant that it is legitimate to present Marx's theory in *Capital* in terms of dialectical logic in the sense of that term discussed above. In *Capital* Marx does move from simple and abstract determinations to complex and concrete ones. This parallels the path taken in Hegelian systematic theory. We may grant as well that in making these transitions Marx makes use of a method that also has its roots in Hegel. Does the fact that some aspects of Hegelian dialectical logic have seeped into Marx's position have any great significance? The discussion thus far has been concerned solely with the method of presentation. Although systematic dialectics may provide a convenient way to proceed, is not this the most that can be said for it? Surely this is just one option of presentation among many others. Why should Marxists submit to the theoretical straightjacket of being restricted to any one method of presentation?[19]

We can distinguish at least four different sorts of theoretical projects within Marxism: (1) theories regarding transitions from one mode of production or social formation to another, (2) theories regarding the individual events and processes that occur within a given mode of production or social formation, (3) theories regarding the particular epochs within a given mode of production, and (4) theories regarding the general nature of a given mode of production. Each of these theory types requires its own method of inquiry and its own method of presentation. All Marxist theorists, including the defenders of systematic dialectical logic, thus must be methodological pluralists.

The method of systematic dialectics is appropriate only for the fourth type of theory. Dialectical logic in *Capital* concerns the universal nature of the capitalist mode of production, the essential features that capture how this mode of production is distinct from others. The question can now be restated. Is not dialectical logic merely one among a number of possible methods of presentation appropriate to this theory type? I believe that it is more than this for two reasons—one theoretical and one practical.

What is the theoretical alternative to attempting to reconstruct the essential features of the capitalist mode of production in a systematic fashion, moving from the abstract and simple to the concrete and complex in a step-by-step fashion? It can only be to consider first this feature and then that, following an order fixed by the interests of the theorist in question. The great danger here is that some essential features will be overlooked. Proceeding in a systematic manner does not eliminate this danger, but it surely minimizes it. If our goal is to construct a comprehensive theory of capitalism, this is a significant advantage.

The practical importance of systematic dialectics for Marxism has to do with the distinction between revolutionary politics and reformist politics. Revolutionary politics are oriented to the long-term goal of changing the fundamental structures of society (however necessary it is to be concerned with transitional goals in the short and medium term). Reformist politics are concerned exclusively with changing less than fundamental structures. This distinction can be made only if we have some way of distinguishing fundamental structures from nonfundamental ones.

Typical reformist projects include rent control and the regulation of the financial sector. In contrast, revolutionary Marxists struggle for a society that is not governed by the commodity form, the money form, or the capital–wage labor relation. The foundation for this practical commitment is found in *Capital*. Insofar as the commodity form, the money form, and the capital–wage labor relation are principles for the derivation of further categories in the systematic reconstruction of the capitalist mode of production, they articulate structures and structural tendencies that essentially define this mode of production. This implies that transforming other tendencies, thematized in the systematic reconstruction by later, more concrete categories,[20] leaves the heart of this system intact. In this sense a systematic dialectical ordering of social forms is a necessary condition of the possibility of revolutionary politics, even if most activists have not explicitly reflected on the systematic ordering their politics implies. There are thus strong theoretical and practical reasons for considering dialectical logic as more than just one arbitrary method of presentation among others.

THE "LOGIC OF THE CONCEPT" AND CAPITALISM

The final position on dialectical logic to be considered here approaches the issue from a quite different perspective. Defenders of this view insist that

Hegelian dialectical logic does indeed play a significant role in the method of *Capital.* It provides a method uniquely suited to the object of Marx's investigations. In capitalism, human creations such as commodities, money, and capital have taken on a reified form and lord over their creators. An automatic logic generating determinations out of itself is appropriate to such a reified reality. Capital itself is shown by Marx to be a self-moving subject, a totality that posits and then supersedes its own conditions. Capital forms a relatively self-subsistent whole that is continuous and self-reproducing. In this sense it appears to be an instantiation of what Hegel termed "the Concept" (*Begriff*), the culmination of his *Logic.* In both cases we have alien pseudosubjects that subjugate real individuals. From this perspective dialectical logic is a perversion of thought, but this is what makes it a suitable method for understanding the perverted reality that is capitalism (Arthur, Chapter 3, this volume).

There is no need to repeat the above reading in which the dialectical ordering in Hegel's social theory is based on material practices rather than some automatic logic generating itself out of itself. However, I would like to comment on the connection between Hegel's "logic of the concept" and capitalism.

I believe that Hegel did not deduce the nature of capitalism from his logic of the concept. But Hegel's studies did lead him to assert that the logic of the concept is exemplified in the capitalist order. Marx, taking this claim at face value, rejected Hegel's logic of the concept in the course of his critique of capitalism. However, it is possible that Hegel's position stems from a mistaken application of his own framework. If this were the case, then rejecting the application would not imply abandoning the framework. My own view is that the social forms constituting capitalism are exemplifications of the ontological structures discussed in the second section of Hegel's *Logic* under the heading of essence (*Wesen*). Hegel's logic of the concept provides the framework for comprehending socialism, not capitalism. Unfortunately this cannot be spelled out without a somewhat involved digression on the content of Hegel's *Logic.* (Readers who have already had their daily recommended dosage of Hegelianism may skip the remainder of this section.)

I begin with a brief examination of Hegel's section on the concept (*Begriff*). This part of the *Logic* is divided into the subjective idea, the objective idea, and the absolute idea. Those who go to the chapter on the absolute idea looking for some sort of metaphysical supersubject will be disappointed; it consists entirely of an account of the dialectical methodology used in the *Logic* as a whole. The section on the objective idea discusses types of object realms. Adequate explanations of these realms take a syllogistic form: "Everything rational is a syllogism" (Hegel 1969a, 664). *Therefore, any adequate account of Hegel's logic of the concept must make his theory of the syllogism central, the culmination of the subjective idea.*

As a principle of explanation the syllogism connects three moments: universality (U), particularity (P), and individuality (I). Now the central point Hegel insists on is that no single syllogism is sufficient to capture the intelligibility of objects falling on the level of the concept. Any attempt to conclude that there is a connection between I and U through premises asserting a connection between I-P and P-U leaves these latter assertions unjustified. Likewise, any attempt to derive P-U from P-I and I-U leaves the latter two premises unmediated, and any attempt to connect I-P through I-U and U-P treats those premises as simply given immediately. For syllogisms to operate as explanatory principles, a system of all three sorts of syllogism is required: I-P-U, P-I-U, and I-U-P. In other words, each determination takes in turn the role of the middle term, whose function is to mediate the extremes into a single totality. On the one hand, "the true result that emerges . . . is that the middle is not an individual Notion determination but the totality of them all" (Hegel 1969a, 684). On the other hand, "the extremes also shall be posited as this *totality* which initially the middle term is" (Hegel 1969a, 696). In this manner each determination is thoroughly mediated with the other two. "In the consummation of the syllogism . . . the distinction of mediating and mediated has disappeared. That which is mediated is itself an essential moment of what mediates it, and each moment appears as the totality of what is mediated" (Hegel 1969a, 703). It is this system of syllogisms as a whole that forms the culmination of Hegel's logic of the concept.[21]

It follows that self-reproduction is a necessary but not sufficient condition for the applicability of Hegel's logic of the concept. If we want to locate the category of a self-reproducing totality in Hegel's *Logic* it does not fall on the level of the concept. It falls on the level of essence, specifically the last determination on that level, "substance." To not see this is to conflate Hegel and Spinoza. Spinoza's substance is an essence that is manifested in its modes and attributes. It is a self-reproducing totality. But it does not fall on the level of the concept because these modes and attributes are subsumed by substance as an alien force above them. Particularity and individuality are not allowed to develop on their own terms, but are immediately reduced to the imperatives of substance. "When Spinoza passes on to individual things, especially to self-consciousness, to the freedom of the 'I,' he expresses himself in such a way as rather to lead back all limitations to substance than to maintain a firm grasp of the individual" (Hegel 1955, 269). "There is, in his system, an utter blotting out of the principle of subjectivity, individuality, personality" (Hegel 1955, 287). We can see clearly that the mere fact that a structure is self-reproducing is not sufficient for it to count as an instance of the logic of the concept in Hegel's view. The logic of the concept is instantiated only in a structure that can be comprehended in terms of a system of syllogisms in which the moments of individuality and particularity are equiprimordial with universality. Only this allows subjectivity, individuality, and personality.

In Marx's account, capital is manifested in the M-C-P-C′-M′ circuit. All the social agents that play a role in this circuit (wage laborers, consumers, even individual capitalists themselves) must submit to the imperatives of capital accumulation. Marx's description of capital, then, roughly parallels Hegel's description of the relationship between substance and its modes and accidents in Spinoza.[22] And, as we have seen, this falls on Hegel's logic of essence, not that of *Begriff*. The Marxist critique of this structure is that the capital is an alien force externally imposing itself on the social agents, preventing them from democratically controlling social life themselves. In more Hegelian jargon, the Marxist critique is that the moments of universality, particularity, and individuality are not allowed to develop freely when all social life must submit to the drive for capital accumulation. This critique is formulated in terms that echo Hegel's critique of Spinoza. Marx's critique of capital, then, is undertaken from the standpoint of Hegel's logic of the concept, with its insistence that the moments of individuality and particularity vis-à-vis the universal be equiprimordial. Marx is not content with a self-reproducing totality (even if capitalism could attain this in the long run, which it cannot). He too wants a totality that does not blot out the principle of subjectivity, individuality, personality. And this is what he termed *socialism*.

Hegel's *Logic*, then, is not of importance to Marx's method because it shares the same perversions as Marx's object, the capitalist mode of production. The second part of the *Logic*, the logic of essence, does provide categories that help us comprehend the social forms making up capitalism. But the third part, the logic of the concept, provides a categorial framework for the anticipation of socialism.

New Directions

The Hegel-Marx connection is a very old issue in Marxist studies. However, I believe that more is at stake here than a mere issue in the history of ideas. I have already argued that a familiarity with Hegelian dialectical logic minimizes the theoretical danger of overlooking essential social forms. It also provides a grounding for the practical distinction between revolutionary and reformist politics. A third place where familiarity with Hegelian dialectical logic can aid in the pursuit of new directions in Marxism follows directly from the previous section.

With the collapse of the Soviet model it is more imperative than ever that socialists attempt to spell out in detail the institutional framework they advocate. Alex Nove (1987), Ernest Mandel (1988), and Diane Elson (1988) conducted an extended debate on the nature of socialism in *New Left Review* that provides a helpful beginning. Familiarity with Hegel is certainly not a precondition for engaging in this debate. However, it does provide assistance regarding both the ultimate goal of the debate and the means to attain that goal. The implicit goal of the debate is to decide whether market socialism (Nove) or workers' councils (Mandel) or socially regulated markets (Elson) best allow the dialectical mediation of universal, particular, and individual. The debate in effect aims at discovering which social forms provide an institutional framework instantiating Hegel's logic of the concept.

In order to approach this goal, the systematic relationships among the specific social forms making up socialism must be explored. For example, in Elson's perspective there are definite form relationships that hold among households, public enterprises, public regulatory bodies, public coordinating bodies, and so forth. Hegelian dialectical logic does not provide the only procedure for exploring form relationships, and Marxist social scientists can surely discuss these matters without a knowledge of it. However, in my view it does provide the most comprehensive procedure for exploring form relations systematically, and is surely a legitimate direction to be taken by Marxist philosophers.

I close by mentioning one final area in which dialectical method holds the promise of significant new directions in Marxist theory. This can be introduced by means of a few additions to the illustration introduced earlier:

Category 1:	Social Form	—	Social Agents	→	Structural Tendencies (1)	—	Structural Tendencies (2)	—	Social Policies
					↓				
					Category 2				

In principle it is possible that two distinct sorts of structural tendencies necessarily arise from a given social form. We are familiar with the first already. Certain tendencies result in new social forms. These are the tendencies of most interest in the reconstruction in thought of the social forms that make up capitalism. But there may be other tendencies that involve some specific issue. These may warrant consideration in their own right. In principle it is possible to proceed through each categorial level in a step-by-step fashion, deriving on each level the tendencies relevant to this issue. At the conclusion we would have a dialectical ordering that applied the systematic dialectical method of *Capital* to this area.

From this perspective the research agenda defined by Marx's systematic dialectical method has hardly been explored, let alone exhausted. There are an indefinite number of theories that can be constructed along the lines just sketched. One example should suffice to make the point. It should be possible to construct a systematic theory of technology in capitalism using Marx's dialectical method. In this theory the progression of social forms that provides the unifying architectonic of *Capital* would be taken as given. Then on each categorial level one would ask what tendencies regarding technical change necessarily tend to arise. For example, given the commodity form, there are systematic tendencies for social agents to introduce technologies that ignore external social costs and respond to effective demand rather than social need. Given the capital–wage labor social relation, there is a systematic tendency for capitalists to introduce technologies that control the work force. If we proceeded in a step-by-step fashion, asking this question on each categorial level in all three volumes of *Capital*, at the conclusion we would have a complete Marxist theory of technology and social forms in capitalism.

Finally, it is also possible to derive basic social policies from a systematic dialectic of social forms. For every structural tendency that is derived in the dialectical ordering, there are general strategic objectives that follow for different groups of social agents.[23] For instance, it should be possible to derive a set of policies for agents to pursue regarding technology. Given the points discussed in the previous paragraph, it follows that wage laborers ought to organize themselves to struggle against the imposition of external social costs, the neglect of pressing social needs, and the loss of control of the labor process. In this manner dialectical social theory can show why these policies are medium- and long-term strategic objectives for the working class, not mere short-term tactical goals. This approach provides a new direction to the most fundamental dimension of Marxism, the unity of theory and practice.

Notes

1. For further discussion of the relationship between historical dialectics and systematic dialectics, see Smith 1990b.
2. Others are considered in Smith 1990a, 20ff.
3. A parallel point can be made regarding Marx. It cannot be denied that there are passages in Marx that suggest a crass technological determinist position. Critics who reject Marx on the grounds of his alleged technological determinism are

not to be faulted for pointing to such passages, for they are there. However, they are to be faulted for ignoring the fact that a reading making Marx a much more interesting and plausible thinker can also be easily provided. I believe that most Marxist critics of Hegel are to be faulted on similar grounds.

4. Hegel is quite explicit regarding the historical specificity of his social theory: "Philosophy is its own time apprehended in thoughts. It is just as absurd to fancy that a philosophy can transcend its contemporary world as it is to fancy that an individual can overleap his own age" (Hegel 1942, 11).
5. It should be kept in mind that this holds only for dialectical *social* theory. It is my belief that Hegel's dialectical method takes into account the specificity of its object realm. It will operate differently in the realm of "objective spirit" than it does in the realm of purely logical determinations or in other parts of the *Realphilosophie*.
6. This illustration captures the "forward" impulse of Hegel's systematic dialectical theory. The reconstruction of the given object realm in thought progresses step-by-step through the derivation of necessary structural tendencies. However, there is a second, "backward," impulse at work as well. We know that we want to end up with a reconstruction in thought of the given totality. Whenever the forward progression stops short of this, the fact that we are not yet where we want to be provides another sort of justification for introducing a new categorical level. Ideally both the forward and backward justifications for transitions from one stage to the next operate simultaneously. However, there are places in both Hegel's systematic theory and in Marx's as well where a forward justification is not provided and a backward one must do all the theoretical work. See Smith 1990c.
7. From this perspective, transitions in dialectical social theory demand "microfoundations," a point completely missed by analytical Marxists hostile to dialectical logic. See Smith 1990a.
8. In Marx's methodological remarks in the *Grundrisse* he wrote that after beginning with the "real and concrete"—but uncomprehended—experience, "I would then, by means of further determination . . . move analytically towards ever more simple concepts, from the imagined concrete towards ever thinner abstractions until I had arrived at the simplest determinations" (Marx 1973, 100).
9. Having arrived at the simplest determinations, Marx continued, "from there the journey would have to be retraced until I had finally arrived at the population again [i.e., the concrete], but this time not as the chaotic conception of a whole, but as a rich totality of many determinations and relations. . . . The abstract determinations lead towards a reproduction of the concrete by way of thought" (Marx 1973, 100–101).
10. In successful exchange, "the labour of private individuals takes the form of its opposite, labour directly social in its form" (Marx 1978, 64). Obviously "socially useful" in this context is judged from the standpoint of the exchanging parties and not from that of the needs of society as a whole.
11. The value form is not itself a stage in the categorial reconstruction of the capitalist mode of production. It specifies the general structure of generalized commodity production, which is then instantiated in a progressively more concrete and complex fashion in the commodity form, the money form, and the capital form.

12. The term *abstract* in the phrase "socially necessary abstract labor" designates that the commodity produced by the labor in question has a value that can be considered in abstraction from its concrete features as a use value. This must be distinguished from the sense of the term in the phrase "abstract labor" *simpliciter*, which refers to the amount of physiological exertion going into any labor process, in abstraction from the concrete content of that labor process. I do not think that the latter sense of the term has any essential role in a dialectic of the social forms making up a specific mode of production. It is a transhistorical category having application to labor occurring under *any* mode of production. In contrast, "socially necessary abstract labor" refers to labor that has been socially validated within the historically specific system of generalized commodity exchange.
13. Note that on a single categorial level (e.g., the commodity) a number of different categories may be introduced in the course of explicating that level (use value, exchange value, value, concrete labor, socially necessary abstract labor, and so on).
14. Simultaneously, however, the presence of money makes it more difficult for social agents to grasp socially necessary abstract labor as the source of value. A tendency for money fetishism can be derived here.
15. In *Capital* Marx simply took the existence of wage labor as historically given. This suffices for a "backward" motivation for introducing the category of wage labor (see note 6 above). I have attempted to provide a "forward" motivation that is consistent with Marx's theory.
16. Strictly speaking, we could also derive a creditor relation here instead of a wage labor relation. See Roemer 1982. However, this has no effect on the present discussion.
17. We thus have an M-C-P-C′-M′ circuit. Money capital is initially invested in the purchase of commodities (means of production and labor power); the production process (P) leads to new commodities (C′), which can then be sold for a profit (M′).
18. The concluding chapters of Volume 1 discuss the process of "original accumulation." They provide a historical account of the genesis of the mode of production that the earlier chapters have begun to reconstruct systematically. Other parts of Volume 1 provide historical digressions illustrating one or another categorial stage. The long sections on manufacturing and big industry, for instance, provide concrete historical illustrations of the general tendency for capitalists to transform the labor process. The reader wishing to trace the dialectical ordering in more detail, including the second and third volumes of *Capital*, may consult Smith 1990c.
19. This view has been argued forcefully by G. Carchedi (see Chapter 8, this volume).
20. Both "rent" and "bank capital" are categories discussed by Marx in Volume 3 of *Capital*.
21. This interpretation of Hegel's doctrine of the syllogism contrasts sharply with Marx's (Murray, Chapter 2, this volume). On Marx's reading, Hegel's logic of the concept starts with two terms in fixed opposition and then introduces a third term in order to displace that opposition (e.g., the state goes beyond the oppositions of civil society). On this reading, Hegel's logic of the concept is really reducible to his essence logic, in which initial oppositions are retained. In

Marx's supposedly alternative logic of the concept, the initial opposition is truly overcome through the revolutionary transformation of the initial elements. I reject Hegel's account of the move from civil society to the state in *The Philosophy of Right*; Hegel's state does indeed retain the basic contradictions of capitalism. However, I do not think that this is sufficient to justify the general rejection of Hegel's *Begriffslogik*. When Hegel moves to the level of the concept in the *Logic* he does *not* retain the oppositions of essence—ground/existence, correlation/actuality, substance/modes and attributes—and then merely add some "third thing" to overcome these oppositions. Instead each pole of the oppositions is completely transformed. "Ground," "correlation," "substance," and so on, are replaced by the category "universal." Similarly, "existence," "actuality," "modes/attributes" disappear, and in their place we have the categories "particular" and "individual." After this radical transformation of the elements has taken place there is no need to introduce some external principle to reconcile universal/particular/individual. The reconciliation of *these* elements is an immanent one.

22. Marx does speak of capital as a "subject"; however, the fact that he uses the same word as Hegel does not imply that he uses it in the same sense as Hegel.
23. It is, of course, impossible to derive tactics from a general theory of social forms. The formulation of tactics requires insight into the contingencies of specific situations (Smith 1991, ch. 1).

2

The Necessity of Money: How Hegel Helped Marx Surpass Ricardo's Theory of Value

Patrick Murray

Marx's theory of value has long been confused with Ricardo's labor theory, and, in the wake of Piero Sraffa's revival of Ricardian thought, we now discover a whole school of Marxist (or post-Marxist) economics operating on neo-Ricardian assumptions.[1] However, Marx's theory of value is cut from different cloth than Ricardo's, a point to which Marx called attention in the very first chapter of *Capital*. There he emphasized the centrality (and originality) of his distinction between concrete and abstract labor, further characterized the abstract labor that constitutes value as "socially necessary," described value as a "social substance" and a "ghostly objectivity," and introduced a seminal yet seldom acknowledged innovation into political economy—the analysis of the *value-form*. In this chapter I hope to make plainer the dialectical logic of the value-form as Marx presents it. To aid in this I trace the history of Marx's engagement with Hegel's philosophy—his logic in particular—showing how Marx acquired the conceptual resources that enabled him to overcome Ricardo's theories of value and capital. Unless the distinctive logic operating in Marx's theories of value and capital is appreciated, his unique achievements go unrecognized. Contrary to Joan Robinson's complaint that smatterings of "Hegelian stuff and nonsense" botch up *Capital*, I argue that it is precisely the lessons learned from Hegel that make *Capital* great.

Marx's critical engagement with Hegel's logic, particularly his logics of essence and the concept—both as pure theories and as Hegel put them into practice (notably in *The Philosophy of Right*)—was an early and decisive element in his intellectual development. Hegel characterized the study of logic as "the absolute education and breeding of consciousness" (Hegel 1969b, 58), and Marx's was a "well-bred" consciousness. Hegel pointed to the lack of this logical education as the chief shortcoming of scientific empiricism:

> The fundamental illusion in scientific empiricism is always this, that it uses the metaphysical categories of matter, force, those of one, many, universality, also infinity, etc. Furthermore, [it] extends *implications* along the thread of such categories, whereby [it] presupposes and applies syllogistic forms, and in all this [it] does not know that it itself carries on and contains metaphysics and uses those categories and their connections in a fully unconscious manner. (Hegel 1975a, 62)

Marx has this "fundamental illusion" in mind when, in a footnote to his treatment of the value-form in the first edition of *Capital*, he levels against the economists just that complaint:

> It is hardly surprising that the economists, wholly under the influence of empirical [*stofflicher*] interests, have overlooked the content of the form of the relative expression of value, when before Hegel, professional logicians even overlooked the content of the form of the paradigms of judgment and syllogism. (Marx and Engels 1966, 274; translation by the author)

By concentrating on certain episodes in Marx's development of a logically "well-bred" consciousness in the first part of the chapter, I seek to identify what Marx learned from Hegel, as well as the criticisms he made of Hegel, in ways that will illuminate his mature critique of political economy, which is the focus of the second part.

I believe that Hegel's philosophy functioned as a heuristic guide as Marx worked out his critique of capitalism, a point best made by reference to the Paris manuscript critique of Hegel. Hegel surely aided Marx in understanding capitalism, but conceiving of him as the logician of capital may not have made Marx a more accurate interpreter of Hegel.[2] My purpose, however, is to explicate Marx's use of Hegel *as he understood him*, not to judge this interpretation.

Since the Hegelian essence logic, whereby the *essence necessarily appears as something other than itself*, is the pivotal conceptual resource funding Marx's theory of value—value necessarily appears as something other than itself, namely money (price)—it is the center of attention in much of what follows.

MARX'S CRITIQUE OF PHILOSOPHY

THE STANDARD ESSENCE-APPEARANCE MODEL AND ITS HEGELIAN CRITIQUE

The standard essence-appearance model mistakes essence for a real but strangely unobservable thing hidden behind the curtain of appearances, and it admits of no logical relationship between essence and appearance. (This is just the model operative in Ricardo's theory of value: Value is something real and independent, "embodied labor" secreted in commodities, and no thought is given to showing any logical connection between value and its appearance, price). In fact, these two features of the standard model amount to much the same thing. If the essence is reified, it stands alone, logically free of the appearances. The relationship between essence and appearances is conceived on the model of two types of things: one, sensuously manifest yet dispensable (appearances); the other, real yet unobservable, except to pure reason (essence). In this model of essence and appearance, science must be a one-way street, externally (since there is no internal relation between independent entities) relating the appearances to their real basis in the world of essence. Just why *this* essence should have *these* appearances is never raised.

A prime example of this thinking is provided by Descartes' analysis of the bit turned blob of wax in his *Meditations*. After wondering how we know a bit of wax to be the same thing after all its sensuous appearances have been altered, Descartes concludes:

> The truth of the matter perhaps, as I now suspect, is that this wax was neither that sweetness of honey, nor that [pleasant] odor of flowers, nor that whiteness, nor that shape, nor that sound, but only a body which a little while ago appeared to my senses under these forms and which now makes itself felt under others. (Descartes 1960, 87–88)

Descartes attributes the primary qualities (extension, flexibility, duration, and movability) to the body of the wax. In making this famous distinction between primary and secondary qualities (color, touch, taste, smell, sound), Descartes engages the standard model of essence and appearance that accounts for differing appearances by referring them to a common underlying essence.

In the Cartesian model, Hegel recognizes a classic case of Enlightenment reification and forgetfulness. Hegel objects that Descartes recasts primary qualities into the logic of secondary qualities, that is, into the logic of immediacy (the logic of being). Hegel takes his clue from Descartes' own words:

> But what is here important to notice is that perception [or the action by which we perceive] is not a vision, a touch, nor an imagination, and has never been that, even though it formerly appeared so; but is solely an inspection by the mind. (Descartes 1960, 88)

According to Descartes, perception is not a matter of (sensuous) imagination, but the activity of pure understanding. In one respect Descartes' observations do not differ from Hegel's, for Hegel recognizes in Descartes' statements the admission that the distinction between essence and appearance—primary and secondary qualities—posits a distinction between two logics of thought: intuition and understanding. Descartes errs by reifying the concepts of the understanding (primary qualities), forcing them into the same mold as immediate intuitions or secondary qualities.[3] But primary qualities are—by Descartes' insistence—in principle nonobservable, nonsensuous. Likewise Descartes forgets that the concepts of the understanding arise only by abstracting from sensuous intuitions. In terms of Francis Bacon's witty metaphor, in thinking that he knows the wax solely by means of the understanding, Descartes the bee absentmindedly mistakes himself for a spider.[4]

In this light we see why Hegel writes that "the essence must appear." Essence must show itself in something that is not immediately itself, precisely because it has no immediate existence—its is not the logic of being. Essence must appear because it is a being of reflection, and it pertains to the logic of reflection that something be given for reflection. That something is appearance. (How far, after all, would Descartes have gotten in knowing the wax without having sensed it?)[5] Under this dialectical conception of essence and appearance,[6] science is no longer a one-way street that externally relates appearances to essence; it works both from the appearances to the essence and from the essence to the appearances.[7] Appearances are no longer viewed as extraneous to the essence. Hegel's dialectical conception of essence thus overcomes the one-sidedness of the standard view, which overlooks the nature of reflection. Essence, for Hegel, includes the complete logical figure, the appearances (which are appearances only by being reflected) and that which is reflected in them. It would be a terrible mistake to conclude from Hegel's statement "the essence must appear as something other than itself" that we should ignore the appearances precisely because they are not the essence. Rather, the appearances *belong* to the complete concept of the essence; they are interdependent. This is precisely the logic that must be understood in order to grasp what sets Marx's theory of value off from the Ricardian.

MARX'S CRITICISMS OF HEGEL'S LOGIC

Though he draws heavily on Hegel's criticisms of conventional categories, Marx has a less optimistic understanding of the dialectic of essence than the one he attributes to Hegel. According to Marx, Hegel believes that the oppositions inherent in essence can be reconciled through the mediation of a third party: For example, the state can reconcile the antagonisms provoked by civil society. For Marx, however, the very opposition of essence and appearance needs to be uprooted, not mediated; the logic of essence poses irreconcilable conflicts rather than a necessary differentiation that pushes on to higher unity. Third parties, such as heaven, the state, or money, signal submerged conflict, not achieved harmony. Marx's perceived differences with Hegel regarding the logics of essence and the concept are best examined in the context of two early works, namely his *Critique of Hegel's "Philosophy of Right"* and the essay on Hegel's philosophy among the Paris manuscripts.

The Philosophy of Right

In Hegel's political philosophy, the incarnation of mediation in the state is the law-making power, where monarch and bureaucracy come into contact with the people, the atoms of civil society, to reconcile diverse and opposed interests. Marx assembles a host of empirical arguments against Hegel's theory of the law-making power as mediator, but we are after the *logical* implications of the discussion. Marx states them as follows:

> The rational relation, the *syllogism*, appears then to be complete. The *law-making power*, the middle term, is a *mixtum compositum* of both extremes: the sovereign principle and civil society, the empirical singularity and empirical universality, the subject and predicate. In general Hegel conceives of the *syllogism* as mediator, as a *mixtum compositum*. One can say that in his development of the rational syllogism the whole transcendence and mystical dualism of his system comes to the surface. The middle term is the wooden sword, the concealed opposition between universality and singularity. (Marx 1970b, 85)

Here Marx traces the inadequacy of Hegel's conception of the law-making power back to a fundamental inadequacy in Hegel's logic of mediation, typified by the rational syllogism. The logic of the concept's promise of reconciliation proves an empty boast, a wooden sword.

For Marx, Hegel's is a logic of accommodation, for it passes beyond a given level without revolutionizing it. The relation between civil society and the state is a case in point. Hegel's state transcends the inadequacy of civil society without transforming its logical atom, the abstract, egoistic individual. The contradictions of the political sphere result from not addressing the unreconciled contradictions of civil society.

The Paris Manuscript

The Paris manuscript on Hegel pursues the theme that his philosophy provides a faulty reconciliation of particular and universal, of thought and nature: Hegel fails to escape the antinomies of the logic of essence as Marx construes it. Moreover, in this essay, Marx merges the logic of Hegel's philosophy with that of capitalist economic forms, thus anticipating the roles that his criticism of Hegel's logics of essence and the concept will play in *Capital*.

Marx explicitly associates Hegel with classical political economy:

> Hegel shares the standpoint of the modern national economists. He grasps labor as the essence, as the self-confirming essence of man; he sees only the positive side of labor, not its negative side. Labor is man's coming-to-be for himself within externalization [*Entausserung*] or as externalized man. (Marx 1964, 177)

This passage is deceptive because as yet Marx lacks a differentiated use of the term *labor*. As it reads, Marx seems to say that labor is by nature both positive and negative, that it always involves externalization. To interpret labor in that way would make Marx's critique of Hegel unintelligible. By labor Marx means alienated labor, the specific social form of labor that exists under capitalism.

Marx's remark, then, is no more a naive congratulation of Hegel for celebrating human self-creation in the *Phenomenology* than is Marx's theory of value an uncritical echoing of Ricardo's. The barb is that Hegel captures the essence of humanity under the conditions of alienated, abstract labor. The double character of capitalist society permeates both classical political economy and Hegel's philosophy; both achieve undeniable scientific insights, but always "within the framework of externalization [*Entausserung*]."

In *Capital* Marx develops the dialectic of the value-form to demonstrate the necessity by which value has an external expression that is not identical with it. That expression is money. In Hegel's philosophy, logic is the external expression of abstract thinking, the money of spirit. The appearance of logic as a sphere of its own is for Marx a necessary consequence of the activity of abstract (alienated) thought:

> The positive thing that Hegel achieved here—in his speculative logic—is [to show] that the determinate concepts, the universal, fixed thought-forms in their independence over against nature and spirit are

> a necessary result of the universal alienation [*Entfremdung*] of the human essence, hence also of human thinking. (Marx 1964, 189)

Hegel's system of absolute idealism demonstrates for Marx the *necessary* connection between abstract, alienated thinking and a freestanding logic, just as Marx's later analysis of the value-form demonstrates why, under the conditions of abstract, alienated labor (value-producing labor), we need money.

We can now see how Marx views the path of Hegel's system as a whole: The idea externalizes itself as nature and spirit, only to return to itself as absolute in the end. The idea's story of externalization (*Entausserungsgeschichte*) parallels the dialectic by which money is transformed into capital: Money externalizes itself in commodities (means of production and labor power) and returns to itself (with a surplus) in the valorization process (*Verwertungsprocess*). The logical idea externalizes itself in nature and (human) spirit, but it recognizes nature and (human) spirit only as representations of itself. "Thus the whole of nature [and we could add "spirit" here] only repeats for him [Hegel] the logical abstractions in a sensuous, external form" (Marx 1964, 191).

When money is transformed into capital, it is externalized into natural objects, labor power, and products of human labors on natural objects. In so doing, capital posits the earth and labor power (nature and human spirit) as values. At the end of its valorization process, capital returns to the fixated abstraction of its starting point—money. To the eyes of capital, the earth and human labor are valueless in themselves, just as in absolute idealism's scheme of things, "*Nature as nature . . . is senseless*" (Marx 1964, 190). By forgetting their sources, both the idea's course of externalization, which treads the logical path of the negation of the negation on a grand scale, and capital's cycle of negations (buying, producing, selling) in the process of valorization condemn themselves to a hellish running in spirals.

These last considerations set up an observation about *Capital* to which we will return, namely, that Marx frames the logic of capital in terms of his own construal of Hegel's logic of the concept, according to which it fails to break free of the antinomies of the logic of essence.

THE IMPORTANCE OF HEGELIAN LOGIC TO MARX'S EARLY WORK

We now have the background to appreciate how decisive Marx's attention to Hegel's logic was for much of his early work. Already in his dissertation and associated notes, that logic plays an important role. Thus, Marx argues that Plato's transcendence, his creation of a world of ideas, the Absolute paralleling the sensible world, stems from his uncritical acceptance of the given. Moreover, this acquiescence leads Plato to create a mythology that uses given sense images as symbols and as myths for the Absolute. Thus, an unreconciled dualism necessarily expresses itself in a third party: Plato's myths. As for the central figure of his dissertation, Marx construes the Epicurean declination of the atom, its swerving from the regular path, as the necessary manifestation of the (defective) principle of the free, subjective individual that Marx identifies as the essence of Epicurus' philosophy.

"On the Jewish Question" is an extraordinary example of Marx's logic of essence set to work: Heaven is the necessary expression of the unreconciled divisions within Christian society; the modern state is the necessary expression of the unreconciled contradictions of civil and political life; and money is the necessary expression of the antinomies of the capitalist economy.

Marx's criticism of Feuerbach, and of the Young Hegelian approach to religion generally, is informed by his distinctive logic of essence. Feuerbach regarded religion as alienation precisely because it is the appearance of the human essence in something other than the human, namely, the divine. Marx, however, criticizes Feuerbach for not seeing that alienation was the necessary result of the contradictory character of the human essence that is driven to religion:

> Feuerbach starts out from the fact of religious self-alienation, the doubling of the world into a religious one and a secular one. His labor consists therein, to dissolve the religious world into its secular foundation. But the fact that the secular foundation lifts itself up from itself and fixates itself as an independent realm in the clouds is only to be explained out of the self-rupture and self-contradicting of this secular foundation. This [foundation] must itself therefore be understood in its contradiction as well as be revolutionized in practice. (Marx 1967c, 401)

It is the divisions among humans that necessarily give rise to religion: to eliminate the gods is not to eliminate those divisions. This insight, which encapsulates his logic of essence, sets Marx off from the program of the Young Hegelians. Attacking religion will not address the more fundamental problem of which religion is only the necessary expression. Analogously Marx later rejects the Proudhonian analysis of the relationship between value and price and, consequently, rejects Proudhonian (and left-Ricardian) socialism.[8]

Let us take stock of Marx's thinking about the logic of essence:

1. An essence logic is in place in situations involving unreconciled dualisms, as, for example, between the private and the social aspects of labor in capitalism.
2. The dualism involved in an essence logic is not only unreconciled but

unreconcilable until that dualism is overturned. Thus, Marx rejects Hegel's conception of the way the concept purports to reconcile the oppositions inherited from essence.

3. The essence must appear as something other than itself, as, for example, abstract labor (value) must appear as exchange-value (money, price) and surplus-value must appear as profit.
4. Because essence must appear as something other than itself, efforts to establish the identity of appearances with essence are necessarily one-sided. (This point comes into play in Marx's criticism of Proudhonian "time-chit" proposals and generally with regard to value-price issues.) Appearances are indispensable to the essence; they belong to it. Thus, a scientific account moves not just from appearance to essence (as does Ricardo in his theory of value) but from essence to appearance (as Marx does in his account of the value-form). Even this kind of talk can be misleading, for *the essence is really the whole logical figure, the appearances and that which necessarily does not appear ('essence').* Thus, value-producing labor and price belong to a logical whole.
5. That the essence *must* appear as something other than itself tells us of its defects. So, for example, the analysis of the value-form reveals something defective about value. Thus Marx consistently associates essence's "logic of the third party" with religion and alienation.
6. As Tony Smith points out in his book *The Logic of Marx's "Capital,"* "an individual moment within an essence structure is thoroughly subordinate to the essence lording over it" (Smith 1990c, 51). Essence logic is characterized by relations of domination, domination by abstractions—a theme that lies at the heart of *Capital.*

MARX'S CRITIQUE OF POLITICAL ECONOMY

I now want to show that Marx's attention to the logic of categories is just as vital to his critique of political economy as it was to his critique of philosophy. I begin with a few examples from his early work on political economy, then I show it in detail in some mature contributions to the critique of political economy.

MARX'S EARLY WORK IN POLITICAL ECONOMY

Toward the end of the unfinished Paris manuscript called "Alienated Labor," Marx looks back over the course of his engagement with political economy:

> *Private property* is thus the product, result, and necessary consequence of *externalized labor,* of the exterior relationship of the worker to nature and to himself. . . . We have, of course, obtained the concept of

> *externalized labor* (*externalized life*) from political economy as the result of the *movement of private property*. But it is evident from the analysis of this concept that, although private property appears to be the ground and reason for externalized labor, it is rather a consequence of it, just as the gods are *originally* not the cause but the effect of the aberration of the human mind. (Marx 1964, 117)

In these passages we find rudiments of Marx's mature view that value-producing labor (essence) necessarily appears as something other than itself, namely, exchange-value (appearance). Moreover, Marx here connects essence logic to religion as he later does in his critique of Feuerbach.

Two paragraphs later, Marx links his construal of externalized labor to a preliminary but telling criticism of Proudhon:

> Political economy starts from labor as the veritable soul of production, and yet it attributes nothing to labor and everything to private property. Proudhon has drawn a conclusion from this contradiction that is favourable to labor and against private property. But we can see that this apparent contradiction is the contradiction of *alienated labor* with itself and that political economy has only expressed the laws of alienated labor. (Marx 1964, 117)

What Marx here brings home is the futility of trying to eliminate private property without upending the dualism that pervades externalized labor, just as the Young Hegelians failed to rout the holy family without revolutionizing the earthly family. Externalized labor necessarily appears as private property. The essence logic operating in this early critique of Proudhon recurs in Marx's critique of Proudhonian time-chits in the *Grundrisse*.

Marx's comments on James Mill contain striking glimpses of his mature treatments of the value-price relation (more specifically, the price of production-market price relation) and of the value-form.[9] The passage on the value-price (price of production-market price) relation offers a remarkable early example of Marx's essence logic at work in his reception of political economy:

> Mill makes the mistake—generally like Ricardo's school—of giving the *abstract law* without the variation and continuous suspension by which it comes into being. If it is an *independent* law, for example, that the costs of production ultimately—or rather with the periodic and accidental coincidence of supply and demand—determine price (value), it is equally an *independent* law that this relationship does not hold and that value [I take it that "price" is what Marx actually has in mind here] and production costs have no necessary relationship. . . . This *actual* process, in which this law is only an abstract, accidental, and

> one-sided factor, becomes something unessential with the modern economists. (Marx 1967b, 265–66)

Marx could hardly be more explicit in directing his own dialectical logic against the standard version operative in Ricardian value theory: The law whereby costs of production determine value does not exist independently; it comes into existence only by virtue of the actual oscillations of prices, the "*actual* process," which the Ricardians neglect as unessential.[10]

Here is the prefiguration of Marx's value-form analysis in *Capital*:

> Thus, on both sides private property appears as representing private property of a different nature. It appears as the equivalent of another natural product, and both sides are interrelated in such a way that each represents the being of the other and both relate to each other as substitutes for themselves and the other. The being of private property has therefore as such become a substitute, and an equivalence. Instead of possessing a direct self-identity it is only a relation with something else. . . . Its existence as value is different from its immediate existence; it is exterior to its specific being, an externalized aspect of itself; it is only a relative existence of the same. (Marx 1967b, 274)

Marx immediately comments: "We must keep for another time a more precise definition of the nature of this value and also of the process by which it turns into a price" (Marx 1967b, 274). This is a date Marx kept in *Capital*, but only a few pages later Marx indicates that the end point of this early exploration of the value-form lies in money: "The complete domination of the alienated thing *over* man is fully manifested in *money*" (Marx 1967b, 276). The essence logic of value that culminates here in money is clearly identified by Marx as involving the domination of those persons who perform value-producing labor by abstract things: "What was the domination of person over person is now the general domination of the *thing* over the *person*, of the product over the producer" (Marx 1967b, 276).

ESSENCE LOGIC AT WORK: MARX'S THEORY OF VALUE

Though the thought that Marx simply takes over Ricardo's labor theory of value still has currency, it is a profound misconception. The fact is, Marx overtakes Ricardo's labor theory. Appreciating Marx's distinctive logic of essence enables us to see how. In the following passage Marx draws our attention to his differences with the Ricardian labor theory of value:

> It is one of the fundamental failings of classical political economy that it was never granted to it to discover from the analysis of the commodity, and especially of the commodity-value, the form of value, which precisely makes it exchange-value. Even in its best

> representatives, such as A. Smith and Ricardo, it handles the value-form as something entirely indifferent or external to the nature of the commodity itself. (Marx 1977b, 174)

In addressing the value-*form*, Marx's theory moves beyond classical theory's dependence on the traditional model of essence and appearance, which fails to show that essence (value) must appear (as money).

Another clue toward distinguishing Marx's dialectical theory from the Ricardian one comes at the beginning of the section of *Capital*'s first chapter entitled "The Value-Form or Exchange-Value":

> Here, however, it is a matter of performing what was not once attempted by bourgeois economy, namely, to establish the genesis of this money-form, thus to follow the development of the value-expression contained in the value-relationship, from its simplest, least visible shape up to the blinding money-form. Therewith disappears likewise the riddle of money. (Marx 1977b, 139)

Marx declares his intention dialectically to bring the category of money within the extended scope of the theory of value. Not only is exchange value the necessary form of value's appearance, money is the necessary end form of exchange-value.

Marx presents his theory of value in two movements: First he moves from exchange-value to value, that is, from appearances to the underlying essence that explains their behavior; then, in the analysis of the value-form, Marx shows why it is necessary that value appear as something other than itself, as exchange-value, a thing—money. Bridging the two movements—found in sections 1 and 3 of *Capital*'s first chapter, respectively—is the exposition in section 2 of the double character of the labor that produces commodities.

There is nothing particularly dialectical about the first movement. Marx starts out from the ordinary exchange relationship:

> Let us furthermore take two commodities, e.g., wheat and iron. Whatever their ratio of exchange, it is always presentable in an equation in which a given quantum of wheat is set equal to some quantum of iron, e.g., 1 quarter of wheat = *x* cwt. of iron. What does this equation purport? That a common element of the same magnitude exists in two different things, in 1 quarter of wheat and likewise in *x* cwt. of iron. Both are therefore equal to a third thing which is in and of itself neither the one nor the other. Each of the two, insofar as it is an exchange-value, must thus be reducible to this third thing. (Marx 1977b, 127)

What is this "third thing"? It is value, the "mere congelation of undifferentiated human labor," a "social substance":

> Now if one leaves the use-value of the commodities out of consideration, they retain only one property, that of being products of labor. However, the product of labor has already changed in our hands. If we abstract from its use-value, we abstract also from the material components and forms which make it a use-value. It is no longer a desk or a house or yarn or any other useful thing. All of its sensuous qualities are extinguished. . . .
>
> Now let us consider the residue of the products of labor. There is nothing of them remaining other than the same ghostly objectivity, a mere congelation of undifferentiated human labor, that is, the expenditure of human labor power without respect to the form of its expenditure. . . . As crystals of this their common social substance, they are values—commodity values. (Marx 1977b, 128)

There is a striking, nonaccidental resemblance between this passage and the one in which Descartes draws his conclusion about the bit turned blob of wax.[11] Descartes and Marx face similar conundrums: How can two objects totally dissimilar in their sensuous qualities—the bit and the blob of wax—be the same? How can two qualitatively dissimilar commodities be identical in terms of value? Descartes resolves his difficulty by appealing to the primary qualities of material substance: nonsensuous, nonimaginable qualities cognizable only by the pure understanding. Marx turns to the "ghostly objectivity" of that "social substance" value of commensurate commodities. So for Descartes the residue of the wax, that which remains after we abstract from all the secondary qualities and that which makes the wax what it is, is something altogether abstract and intellectual—nothing at all sensuous or intuitive. Likewise for Marx: The way in which two commodities are identical, namely value, is something utterly abstract—the product of an actual social process of abstraction—and contains not a whit of concrete use-value or useful labor.

This first movement captures the nondialectical thinking about essence and appearance to which Ricardian value theory is confined. Not so for the second movement, which answers the question never raised in Ricardian theory: Why does value appear in the form of exchange-value? Marx prepares his answer to this question by digging deeper into the nature of the labor whose "congelation" is value. The crux of this preparation lies in recognizing that value and value-producing labor are abstractions, "beings of reflection," rather than anything immediate, natural, or sensuous.

Just as the commodity has a double character, use-value and exchange-value, the labor that produces commodities is double:

> Tailoring and weaving are constituent elements of the *use-values*, coat and linen, precisely through their *different* qualities; they are *substance* of

> coat-value and linen-value only insofar as one *abstracts* from their specific quality and both possess *equal quality*, the *quality of human labor*. (Marx and Engels 1966, 224; translation by the author)

Already in section 1, Marx had investigated the nature of this abstract, "human labor." The labor that congeals as value is abstract labor in the "physiological" sense that it is the expenditure of human labor power without regard to any definite end. But for an hour's labor to count as an hour's worth of value it must meet several conditions:

1. It must be an hour of "simple average labor"; hours of complex labor count for more. And what counts as simple average labor is historically variable, not naturally determined.
2. To be "socially necessary," the hour of labor must produce the number of commodities equal to the number produced in an hour averaged across all producers of that commodity. An hour's labor that produces more commodities than the average counts as more value, and conversely.
3. An hour of labor that is socially necessary in sense (2) is socially necessary in a further sense—*one that builds demand into the very concept of value*—only if the demand for that type of commodity matches the supply. If the supply of a commodity exceeds demand, an hour's labor on that commodity that is socially necessary in sense (2) produces less than an hour's value, and conversely. This third consideration, involving as it does a co-constitutive relationship between value and price,[12] is a deeply non-Ricardian element of Marx's value theory.[13] According to Ricardo's theory, prices are to be the variable completely dependent on labor inputs construed in a technical sense. There is no room in Ricardian theory for a dialectic of value and price.

What these three considerations mean is that Marx's theory of value cannot be construed as a labor theory in any ordinary or naturalistic sense. The labor that goes into the production of any particular commodity, the "labor embodied," does not determine the value of that commodity[14]—for the three reasons just specified.[15] Value is not a concept appropriate for all human labor—as in naturalistic theory. It applies only when conditions (1) through (3) above are in force, that is, in competitive, market societies where all goods are produced as commodities. *Value* is Marx's term for the specific, puzzling, and self-obscuring form that social labor takes under capitalism. He could hardly be more explicit than in this passage from *A Contribution to the Critique of Political Economy*:

> Since the exchange-value of commodities is indeed nothing but a mutual relation between various kinds of labor of individuals regarded

> as equal and universal labor, i.e., nothing but a material expression of a specific social form of labor, it is a tautology to say that labor is the only source of exchange-value and accordingly of wealth in so far as this consists of exchange-value. (Marx 1970a, 35)[16]

As an account of the specific social form of labor under capitalism, Marx's theory of value is definitely cut from different cloth than the classical labor theory culminating in Ricardo.

Marx describes his characterization of the double character of commodity-producing labor as "the linchpin [*Springpunkt*] to the understanding of political economy" (Marx 1977b, 132). His recognition that value and value-producing labor are abstractions that depend on the *actual* process of abstracting that transpires in capitalist production and distribution—not anything naturally, sensuously occurring—parallels Hegel's claim that Descartes' secondary and primary qualities are not logically similar: The former are immediate, the latter, reflective. Hegel teaches us that matter is not some substance underlying appearances that just *happens* not to be observable, rather it is no thing at all on the model of sensuous things. Matter is a being of reflection, an essence in the dialectical sense, that is, the kind of being that must appear as something other than itself. Marx's counterpoint to Ricardian value theory runs along just these lines: *Value-producing labor differs logically from concrete labor.* The latter is immediate, sensuous, particular; the former is reflective, abstract, universal. Because it is an abstraction, a being of reflection, value cannot appear immediately; it must appear as something other than itself.[17] Money proves to be the necessary form of value's appearance—and to be necessary for value's existence—yet money is not value. Indeed, there is no physically existing, *fixed measure of value*—and there cannot be one.[18]

Marx says of the turn from the first movement to the second in his exposition of value theory: "The progress of the investigation will lead us back to exchange-value as the necessary mode of expression, or form of appearance, of value" (Marx 1977b, 128). Here we have an incontrovertible assertion of necessity on Marx's part. It is one of many.[19] The necessity involved here is neither the tautology of deduction nor causal necessity. Dialectical claims are of this nontautological, noncausal sort.[20] What justification does Marx offer for this particular assertion of necessity? The answer lies in section 3, on the value-form. There Marx reveals exactly how the exploration of the double character of commodity-producing labor prepares the way for the presentation of the value-form.

> Not an atom of matter enters into the objectivity of commodities as values; in this it is the direct opposite of the coarsely sensuous

> objectivity of commodities as physical objects. We may twist and turn a single commodity as we wish; it remains impossible to grasp it as a thing possessing value. However, let us remember that commodities possess an objective character as values only in so far as they are all expressions of an identical social substance, human labor, that their objective character as values is therefore purely social. From this it follows self-evidently [*so versteht sich auch von selbst*] that it can only appear in the social relation between commodity and commodity. (Marx 1977b, 138–39)

Once we recognize what value is, namely, an abstract, reflective, "social" objectivity, it is evident that it can have no immediate appearance. The necessity here lies—as in Hegel's criticism of Descartes—in recognizing the different *logics* of immediacy and reflection.

Marx begins the analysis of the value-form with its simplest form: "x commodity A values at y commodity B." The seminal feature of this value expression is its polarity. Commodity A expresses its value in commodity B; A is active and B is passive. Commodity B is the mirror in which commodity A first recognizes itself as a value. The value of A cannot appear in A itself; it can only be expressed relative to A in another commodity.[21]

> I cannot express, e.g., the value of linen in linen. 20 yards of linen = 20 yards of linen is no expression of value. The equation says much more reversed: 20 yards of linen are nothing other than 20 yards of linen, a specific quantum of the useful object, linen. The value of linen can then only be expressed relatively, i.e., in other commodities. (Marx 1977b, 140)

Hence, Marx speaks of commodity A as in the relative value-form. Commodity B, in which the value of A is mirrored, is in the equivalent-form. Acknowledging these two as necessarily polar is crucial in analyzing the value-form.

The value-form is a social magnet: Relative value-form and equivalent-form are extremes that belong to one another yet shut the other out. To say that the expression of value is necessarily polar means that the expression of value requires a reflective relationship. Marx's repeated use of "mirror," or "value-mirror," to characterize the commodity in the equivalent-form highlights this feature. The polarity of the value-form signals the essence logic. As the essence of exchange-value, value must appear in something other than itself.

To appreciate fully Marx's account of the value-form, we must be mindful that essence involves alienation. Essence appears only by giving itself over to something that is not itself—through alienation. Value recognizes itself only in its reflection in another object. The labor that produces value is alienated labor. Fitting the pattern of alienation, the logic of value is inherently religious in Marx's critical sense. In discussing the relative value-form, Marx refers explicitly to his critique of Feuerbach.

> Its [that of the linen, which is in the relative value-form] existence as value appears in its equality with the coat as the sheep-nature of the Christian [does] in his equality with the Lamb of God. (Marx 1977b, 143)

The Christian achieves fullness only mirrored in the Lamb of God, but the nature of the Christian thereby revealed is that of a sheep. For Marx, the religious alienation of the Christian is the necessary expression of the Christian's sheepish nature. Likewise, the fact that a commodity expresses its value only through another commodity manifests the alienation of the labor that produced it.

In this context we should emphasize the "must" in Hegel's statement "the essence must appear." Essence is constrained to appear because it harbors within itself an unreconciled contradiction between immediacy and reflection. The practical point is this: Change must be effected by recognizing and resolving the contradiction immanent to the essence.

In the *Grundrisse*, Marx contraposes the essence logic of value production to the quite different logic of communist production:

> On the foundation of exchange-value, labor is first posited as universal through exchange. On this foundation [communist society] labor would be posited as such before exchange, i.e., the exchange of products would not at all be the medium through which the participation of the individual in the general production would be mediated. Mediation must of course take place. In the first case, which starts out from the independent production of the individual—no matter how much these independent productions determine and modify each other *post festum* through their interrelations—mediation takes place through the exchange of commodities, exchange-value, money, all of which are expressions of one and the same relationship. In the second case, the presupposition is itself mediated, i.e., communal production, the communality as a foundation of production, is presupposed. The labor of the individual is from the very beginning posited as social labor. The product does not first have to be converted into a particular form in order to receive a universal character for the individual. (Marx 1973, 171–72)

In production governed by value, the particular is mediated by the universal, but only after it has been produced privately. The two determinations fall asunder and must be wrenched together by the price system. Mediation takes place in communist production as well, but the "middle man" is avoided by the fact that the particular and universal determinations coincide. Particular use-values produced communally are already universals inasmuch as they are decided upon by society as a whole. There is no further need to impose, at the level of exchange, a social determination on communally produced use-values.[22]

VALUE AND PRICE IN *CAPITAL*

It is sometimes assumed that in the first volume of *Capital* Marx simply identifies values with prices and that divergences between value and price turn up first with the third volume's discussion of prices of production. But in the first volume of *Capital*, as well as in related treatments in the *Grundrisse*, Marx insists on the necessary nonidentity of value and price, a claim he explicates in terms of his dialectical logic of essence.

Before delving into the theory of price presented in Volume 1, its relationship to the discussion of market value, prices of production, and market prices in Volume 3 should be aired. Boehm-Bawerk's famous critique that Marx's theories of value and price in the first volume were contradicted by the third displays several misconceptions. One is that the theories of value and price developed in the first volume are intended to apply to just any commodity. When Marx theorizes about commodities and capital in the first volume, he assumes that an individual capital is an aliquot part of the aggregate capital and that an individual commodity is the product of such an average capital. When these qualifications are kept in mind, we realize that Marx did not forget to bring in market value and prices of production in Volume 1; *they do not belong there.*

Notice that even though the category of price of production, which generally deviates from those of individual and market value, can have no place in Volume 1, a discrepancy between value and price remains. Why? The nonidentity of value and price in the chapter on money picks up the discrepancy not between values and production prices—under the assumptions of Volume 1, that cannot enter in—but between production prices and market prices in the third volume. Despite its name, production price is not a price at all, for prices are the money expression of value, whereas production price, like market value, is a value category. As such, production price must appear as something other than itself, namely market price. This is the necessity that is registered in the first volume's theory of price.

Marx's theory of price in the first volume insists that the difference between value and price is not nominal.[23] To call the distinction between value and price nominal is to obliterate, or leave unexplained, the differences between these two forms. Marx's theory of price explains the discrepancies by carefully examining the logic of the forms themselves.

We have seen the first, and decisive, phase of Marx's antinominalist theory of price in his theory of value, which shows the logical necessity for value to express itself in money. Since the value of a commodity is expressed through an alien, independent object (money), value and price are not, and cannot be, immediately identical. Their identity arises only in the gravitational pull that value exercises over the oscillations of price. The nominalist theory of price concentrates only on the identity of price and value; it disregards the fact that the *reflective identity* of price and value in the law of price operates only on the unavoidable presupposition of the *immediate nonidentity* of price and value. Marx's theory, on the other hand, recognizes both as equally essential.

In terms of Hegel's logic of essence, we can say that both the oscillation of price and the law of that oscillation are on the logical level of essence and that the proper comprehension of essence recognizes the necessary unity of the two. Hegel writes in the section of his *Science of Logic* entitled "The Law of Appearance":

> The law is therefore not on the other side of appearance, but rather immediately present in it; the realm of laws is the stable reflected image of the existing or appearing world. But even more so are both One Totality, and the existing world is itself the realm of laws, which, as the simply identical, likewise is identical with itself in positedness or in the self-dissolving autonomy of existence. (Hegel 1969b, 503–4)

If we substitute "law of price" for Hegel's "law of appearance," "the actual oscillations of price" for Hegel's "existing or appearing world," and "the constant negation of . . . itself [price] as the negation of the real value" for Hegel's "the self-dissolving autonomy of existence," we have the basics of Marx's critical theory of price. Hegel's emphasis on the immanence of the law of appearance to the appearances themselves carries over into Marx's theory of price.

Like his critical theory of value and the value-form, Marx's theory of price does not hypostatize value. As the law of price, value is not something beyond or outside of the actual movement of price, rather it is the tethering of price. Value does not exist as an actual, observable thing, but as the reflection of actual things. So Marx's theory of price reconfirms the nonmetaphysical character of the theory of value he puts forth in the first chapter of *Capital*, just as it underlines his debt to Hegel's logic.

Marx reminds us, in the third chapter of Volume 1 of *Capital*, not only that the distinction between price and value is a logical necessity but also that it indicates the social relations within a society characterized by these categories.

> The possibility of quantitative incongruence between price and value-magnitudes, or the deviation of the price from the value-magnitude, lies therefore in the price-form itself. It is no defect of this form, but rather, quite the opposite, that makes it the adequate form of a mode of production in which the rule can push itself through only as the blindly operating law of averages of irregularity. (Marx 1977b, 196)

The divergence of price and value is not a surd, as in the nominalist theory; rather, it is identified as the necessary consequence of the commodity mode of production. By attending to the moment of nonidentity of price and value, rather than abstractly fixating on their reflective identity in the law of price, Marx discloses the price-form as a determinate and crisis-laden category of capitalist production.

To disregard prices, then, as "mere appearances," or to set them aside on the grounds that, after all, they are something other than the essence, is the wrong consequence to draw from Marx's invocation of an essence-appearance model to conceive of the relation between value and price. The model of essence and appearance that Marx employs is dialectical. Appearances are necessary to the essence: There can be no value without price.

Since Proudhonism was such a powerful force within European socialism, Marx was particularly pleased with the polemical points his theory of price scored. Writing to Engels on 22 July 1859, Marx lists as the first outcome of *A Contribution to the Critique of Political Economy* "that Proudhonism is eradicated." Moreover, the body of the *Grundrisse* begins with an extensive critique of Alfred Darimon, a follower of Proudhon who wanted to supplant money with time-chits issued on the basis of how many hours an individual actually worked. If price were just a label for the labor embodied in a good, the proposal should work. But Marx links the problem with time-chits to a misunderstanding of the price-form:

> The first fundamental illusion of the time-chitters consists therein, that by annulling the *nominal diversity* between real value and market value, between exchange-value and price—thus expressing the value in the labor-time itself instead of a specific objectification of labor-time, say, gold and silver—they also put aside the actual difference and contradiction between price and value. (Marx 1973, 138)

Along with Proudhon, Darimon takes the nominalist view of money, claiming that as the mediator of commodity exchange, money is a troublesome but removable contrivance rather than a logically necessary third party. Such theorists resent the interference of money at the same time as they champion commodity production and the egalitarianism found in the exchange of equal values. Marx takes to mean that the utopian or "bourgeois" socialists want to have their cake and eat it too, or, as he puts it with respect to John Gray, "The products are supposed to be produced as commodities, but are not to be exchanged as commodities" (Marx 1970a, 85). These "unscientific socialists" simply fail to grasp the logical relations linking the categories of commodity, value, and price.

THE LOGIC OF CAPITAL

The logic of simple commodity circulation, which we have just examined, conforms to Hegel's logic of essence as well as to Marx's. I now argue that Marx deliberately presents capital in terms that evoke his early treatment of Hegel's logic of the concept and thereby reinforce his early criticism that Hegel's logic of the concept is a "wooden sword," a defective reconciliation that leaves the opposed elements standing in their opposition to one another.[24]

When Marx speaks of value in the sphere of simple circulation, he speaks of (social) "substance." But Marx describes capital with the phrases "automatic subject," "here value becomes the subject of a process," "the encompassing subject of such a process," and "itself, self-moving substance." In the concept of capital, substance reveals itself as subject, albeit an automatic one. Marx here recalls Hegel's criticism of Spinoza for conceiving of the Absolute as substance but not subject.

A comparison of the following two passages—the first, Hegel's description of the infinite as conceived on the logical level of the concept; the second, a description of capital from Marx's *Urtext*—brings out what was in Marx's mind in identifying the logic of capital with Hegel's logic of the concept.

> Only [*erst*] the veritable infinite, which posits itself as finite, reaches at the same time beyond itself as an other and remains therein, because it is its other, in unity with itself. (Hegel 1962, 183)
>
> Its [money's] going into circulation must itself be a moment of its remaining-with-itself, and its remaining-with-itself must be a going into circulation. (Marx 1939, 931)

Marx underlines the identification of simple circulation with Hegelian essence logic and capital circulation with the Hegelian logic of the concept (as he conceived of it) by appealing to the association of Judaism with the former and Christianity with the latter. At the same time these associations bring home the point that, for Marx, the Hegelian concept is just as "religious" as is essence. The association of capital with Christianity could not be more explicit than in this passage:

> It [value] differentiates itself as original value from itself as surplus-value, as God the Father from Himself as God the Son, and both are of the same

> age and constitute in fact only one person, for only through the surplus-value of 10 pounds sterling do the advance 100 pounds sterling become capital, and as soon as they have become this, as soon as the Son is created and through the Son, the Father, their difference disappears again, and both are one, 101 [*sic*] pounds sterling. (Marx 1977b, 256)

Just before this passage Marx contrasted the logics of simple circulation and capital circulation with those of Judaism and Christianity, respectively.

> The capitalist knows that all commodities, no matter how raggedly they always look, or how bad they always smell, are in faith and in truth money, innerly circumcised Jews, and moreover wonder-working means to make money out of money. (Marx 1977b, 256)

The fact that, in *Capital*, Marx endeavors to associate the logic of capital with Hegel's concept and with Christianity demonstrates the continuing relevance of his early writings to his mature critique of political economy, in particular to his theory of capital.

Recall Marx wrote that Hegel's logic is the necessary result of his whole philosophy being governed by abstract thought: Logic is the necessary form of appearance of abstract thinking—just as money is the necessary form of appearance of the abstract labor performed under the conditions of capitalism.[25] "Logic is the money of spirit." Following the consequences of these associations sheds light on the significance of the dialectical logic of the value-form for Marx's theory of capital. As he criticized Hegel in the last of the Paris manuscripts, Marx simultaneously explored the logic of value, including, of course, the logic of capital. As we saw earlier, Marx associated the logical idea's externalization in nature and spirit with the valorization process whereby money is transformed into capital. Notice, now, that in both cases, the cycle begins—and ends—not with abstract thought or with value, but with their necessary forms of appearance, logic and money. What this tells us is that the dialectical logics of essence and of value are already integrated into Marx's conception of Hegel's philosophy of spirit and his theory of capital. As value striving to expand itself in an endless spiral, capital is not money, nor any production process, nor any commodity. What our exploration of Marx's theory of value has taught us is that as a category of value, capital is itself necessarily nonapparent, nonobservable, *and* it must appear as something other than itself. What distinguishes capital from the logic of value at the level of simple commodity circulation is that, though it is identical to none of them, capital recognizes itself in money, in production, and in commodities. The formula M-C-M′ (or more fully, M-C . . . P . . . C′-M′) is the necessary form of capital's appearance.[26]

This embedding of the dialectical logic of the value-form in Marx's introduction of the concept of capital implies that his theory of capital is at least as profoundly post-Ricardian as is his theory of value. Unaware of the significance of social form, the Ricardian theory of capital depicts capitalist production as "the production of commodities by means of commodities," or C . . . P . . . C′. The givens in Marx's theory of capitalist production are not the physical quantities of the technical conditions of production and the real wages, as they are in Ricardian theory, but sums of money—value's necessary form of appearance—which are invested as capital.[27] Thus the logical lessons Marx learned from Hegel are central to his surpassing of Ricardo's theory of value whether at the level of simple circulation or of capital.

Notes

1. I have treated topics of this chapter as well as related ones in my *Marx's Theory of Scientific Knowledge* (Murray 1988b) and "Karl Marx as a Historical Materialist Historian of Political Economy" (Murray 1988a).
2. The fact that Marx read Hegel so much in the light of various Hegelians, including amateurs like Szeliga and Proudhon, may have blurred his outlook on Hegel himself.
3. Descartes writes: "But when I distinguished the real wax from its superficial appearances, and when, just as though I had removed its garments, I consider it all naked . . ." (Descartes 1960, 89–90).
4. In aphorism XCV of *The New Organon*, Bacon writes: "The men of experiment are like the ant, they only collect and use; the reasoners resemble spiders, who make cobwebs out of their own substance. But the bee takes a middle course: it gathers its material from the flowers of the garden and of the field, but transforms and digests it by a power of its own" (Bacon 1960, 93).
5. Descartes states that imagination (taken here to include sensation) is nonessential to his thinking: "I notice that this ability to imagine which I possess, in so far as it differs from the power of conceiving, is in no way necessary to my nature or essence, that is to say, to the essence of my mind" (Descartes 1960, 127).
6. I have no closing arguments for the notion of necessity operative here, but it is a fact of our use of language that noncausal claims of necessity are common, e.g., without property there can be no theft. A good deal of philosophical energy has been spent—notably by David Hume and Immanuel Kant—to account for these claims of necessity. The analytic-synthetic distinction put forward by Kant explains many such claims in terms of analyticity, that is, as tautologies. It took him most of a long, hard book to try to explain necessity of a nontautological sort. It is fair to see in Hegel a forerunner of Quine in rejecting the analytic-synthetic distinction, and with it the nominalist effort to reduce all necessity to a matter of human conventions for the use of terms. Dialectical logic extends ordinary judgments about how concepts are connected, without either the "dogma" of the analytic-synthetic distinction or any sweeping philosophical prohibitions against our ordinary attributions of necessity.

7. Marx pursues this double movement in his accounts of value and capital in *Capital*. See the treatment of value in the second part of this chapter.
8. H.-G. Backhaus pursues this analogy in detail (Backhaus 1980, 108).
9. Toward the end of the chapter I consider the relationship between the value-price issue as it comes up in *Capital*'s third chapter and the discussion of market value, price of production, and market price in the third volume.
10. When Marx writes that prices and production costs have "no necessary relationship," it might appear that he directly contradicts my claim that there is a necessary connection between the law of value and the oscillations of price. However, I take him to mean that there is no necessity for an individual product with a certain production cost to have a certain price. On the contrary, non-identity of price and the monetary expression of production costs is the rule.
11. See the passage already cited (Descartes 1960, 87–88).
12. Paul Mattick, Jr., writes: "'abstract labor' in Marx's sense is undefined except in relation to a system of prices" (Mattick, Jr. 1981, 777). In a similar vein Guglielmo Carchedi writes: "prices are not determined by values but rather are their concrete form of existence" (Carchedi 1986, 201).
13. As Carchedi writes: "The basic difference between the Marxian and the neo-Ricardian notion of value is that for the latter value is embodied labor and is determined by the technical relations of production, independent of demand" (Carchedi 1988, 96).
14. That Marx's is not a "labor embodied" theory is made plain in his polemics against Proudhon and the "time-chitters." This is discussed below.
15. Geert Reuten, who distinguishes essence-appearance models along the lines I do, between the "ontological" and the "conceptual dialectical," worries that some "abstract labor theorists" may still subscribe to a "labor embodied" theory. This can happen if one thinks that value-producing labor is "abstract labor" in the "physiological sense," of which Marx writes: "all labor is an expenditure of human labor-power, in the physiological sense" (Marx 1977b, 137). If one thus characterizes value-producing labor, setting aside the three considerations examined above, one could end up with an abstract labor embodied theory that sticks to the standard, or ontological, essence-appearance model and falls not far from the Ricardian tree. As Paul Mattick, Jr., observes, even the neo-Ricardian advocate Ian Steadman insists that it is "abstract labor embodied" that neo-Ricardians sum in calculating labor values (Mattick, Jr. 1981, 776–77). Thinking through the consequences of the three features of value-producing labor just considered forces upon us the dialectical model of essence-appearance and therewith the abandonment of labor embodied thinking. See Reuten's Chapter 4 in this volume.
16. Two pages later Marx writes, simply: "the labor which posits exchange-value is a specific social form of labor" (Marx 1970a, 36).
17. Chris Arthur likewise connects Marx's theory of the value-form to his rejection of the standard essence-appearance model: "If the necessity of a material form of appearance of value is not recognized then value theory becomes nothing but metaphysical essentialism" (Arthur 1979a, 68).
18. As Geoffrey Pilling puts it: "All those who think there can be some invariable measure of value in fact completely misunderstand the nature of capital" (Pilling 1980, 194). Pilling places Ricardians among those who do: "It is no accident that there is no trace of the notion of fetishism in the work of what might be called

the 'Sraffa School' which has returned to Ricardo for some answers to the current crisis in economic theory. For it is precisely this school which has grappled with what we have tried to show is a quite mistaken problem—namely the search for some abstract standard of value—be it a 'standard' or 'composite' commodity" (Pilling 1980, 195–96).

19. See, for example, the first footnote to Chapter 3 of *Capital*. Later in that chapter Marx writes: "The price-form entails the exchangeability of the commodity against money as well as the necessity of this exchange [*Verausserung*]" (Marx 1977b, 198). Claims of such necessity may be found in many passages from Marx already cited in this chapter.
20. Tony Smith is right to insist that "Marx's theory, like Hegel's, includes claims of systematic necessity" (Smith 1990c, 38).
21. Samuel Bailey, with whose critique of Ricardian theory Marx was in certain respects impressed, observed this necessary polarity in the expression of value: "It is impossible to determine or to express the value of a commodity except by a quantity of some other commodity" (Bailey as quoted in Backhaus 1980, 106).
22. See also Marx's first footnote to Chapter 3 of *Capital*, in which he favorably contrasts Owen to Proudhon (Marx 1977b, 188–89).
23. As Weeks writes: "For Marx, the essence of the value-price relationship is their non-equivalence" (J. Weeks as quoted in Carchedi 1988, 99).
24. As Jeanne A. Schuler, Tony Smith, and Geert Reuten have pointed out to me, there are very good reasons for doubting that Hegel's logic of the concept actually applies to capital. I am very suspicious about this myself, but here I restrict myself to what Marx saw himself doing with Hegel in *Capital*, not whether he was justified.
25. See the discussion under "The Paris Manuscript" above.
26. This is a natural extension of the connections I pointed out regarding Marx's Parisian critique of Hegel, but it was Martha Campbell who helped me see that.
27. See Moseley's Chapter 7 in this volume.

3

Hegel's *Logic* and Marx's *Capital*

Christopher J. Arthur

Marx said that a science must adopt the logic proper to the peculiar character of the object under investigation (Marx and Engels 1975a, 91). The question arises, therefore, what is the appropriate logic for the critique of political economy? We know from numerous sources that Marx characterized his presentation in *Capital* as "dialectical." Unfortunately, he never wrote his promised work on dialectic. But we know that he found rereading Hegel's *Logic* a great help in "the method of treatment" (to Engels [16] January 1858). Furthermore, in *Capital* itself he openly avowed himself to be "the pupil of that mighty thinker" (Marx 1976b, 102–3).. In the first section of this chapter, therefore, I show just how Hegel's logic, in spite of his avowed idealism, is indeed relevant—precisely to the peculiar character of a money economy. The bulk of the chapter offers a reconstruction of the analysis of the value-form initiated by Marx. This is prefaced by an account of the Hegelian method of systematic exposition employed. In concentrating on the value-form I leave aside initially any labor content—in this way departing from Marx, who analyzed both together. However, I conclude by providing a novel proof that Marx was indeed right in giving central importance to capitalistically produced commodities.

HEGEL'S LOGIC AND THE VALUE-FORM

The starting point of my discussion is the belief that we need to take absolutely seriously the question of how Marx's critique of political economy benefited, in its presentation at least, from his appropriation of Hegel's logic. It is my belief that Marx himself was not clear about the answer to this question; the relatively sketchy and enigmatic methodological remarks in his prefaces may be a sign of this. Although Marx acknowledged the influence of Hegel's dialectic on his *Capital*, he failed to explain how an idealist logic could assist a materialist science. He left the impression that one could preserve a logic while inverting its ontological presuppositions. This introduces a dichotomy between form and content that is itself undialectical. My view is that there is indeed an "elective affinity" between Hegel's "Concept" and the structural relations of commodities, money, and capital, but only because of certain very peculiar properties of a money economy.

Hegel's logic treated the fundamental categories of thought as pure categories independent of any contingent empirical instantiation. He presented them as systematically ordered, from simple abstract ones to more complex and hence more concrete ones. This system of categories was said to be "self-moving" in that meditating on one category drives us to introduce another contrary, or more comprehensive, one. Hegel was an idealist in that he seemed to think that he had thereby shown the necessity of such relationships arising and developing in the real world.

In order to establish the relevance of Hegel's logic to the critique of political economy, it is necessary to grasp the ontological foundation of the capitalist system. We must take absolutely seriously the *reality* of abstraction in exchange. This material abstraction has a substantive reality quite independent of any methodological points about abstraction in theory construction. It produces an inverted reality in which commodities simply instantiate their abstract essence as values, and concrete labors count only as lumps of abstract labor (see Arthur 1979b). In the value-form there is not only a split between form and content, but the former becomes autonomous and the dialectical development of the structure is indeed form-determined. Because of this, I argue that capital is both real and ideal. Hence Hegel's logic can be drawn on in a critical way.

In order to explain further why Hegel's logic is relevant to value theory, I provide a brief preview of the presentation to come. Goods are brought to market because they are believed to be use-values required by others, and if they are eventually consumed this actualizes their original positing as use-values. But along the way they are in a different phase of being, for while they are being exchanged they are not being used; furthermore, this power of exchangeability has no evident basis in their use-value as such. Occasionally such a comparison might occur if, say, two half-bottles of wine were exchanged for one full one, but in the main the commodities exchanged are incommensurable as use-values because their particular qualities are adapted to different uses. What seems to be going on is an abstraction from such particularity and the negation of this difference of use-value.

What is of great interest here is that this abstraction is not a mental operation; it is a *material abstraction.* As Alfred Sohn-Rethel (1978) forcefully pointed out, before the positing of labor as abstract there is the positing of commodities themselves as bearers of their abstract identity as values. (It is implicit in this purely material process of abstraction that it is not necessary for the parties to the exchange to know what they are doing in this respect or the logical form posited in their practical activity.)

As a consequence of this material abstraction from the specificity of the use-values concerned, which is suspended for the period of exchange, the commodities acquire as a new determination the character of exchange-values, and the particulars concerned play the role of bearers of this determination imposed on them while passing through this phase of their life cycle. They become subject to the value-form. Conversely, in actualizing their use-value, their exchange-value is suspended or vanishes altogether (although in productive consumption it may reappear in "transferred" form).

When goods are reduced to moments of a unifying form in commodity exchange they are taken as identical instantiations of their abstract essence (value). But in such an identity their particularity drops away and remains as such excluded from the further advance of the dialectic of forms. The value-form of the commodity posits a split between value as the identity of commodities premised on an abstract universal posited through equivalent exchange and their enduring particularity, differentiating them from one another as use-values.

This is the key to our argument for the relevance of Hegel's logic, for he too starts with an abstraction from everything particular and determinate in order to reach the category of pure being. It is my contention that Being, and the categorial dialectic arising from it, is paralleled by Value and the dialectic of forms of value. The point is that there is a strong parallel between Hegel's pure thoughts—that is, the evacuation of contingent empirical instantiations to leave the category as such—and the same process in practical terms when a commodity acquires a value that disregards its natural shape. Thus our exploration of the latter can draw on the parallel found in Hegel's presentation of his logic. The movement from exchange to value parallels his Doctrine of Being; the doubling of money and commodities parallels the Doctrine of Essence; and capital, positing its actualization in labor and industry, as absolute form claims all the characteristics of Hegel's Concept. Hence we will find that, just as Hegel's logic follows the self-movement of thought as it traverses the categorial universe, so the dialectic of exchange sets up a form-determined system. Here the formal structures are indeed self-acting, not just in the sense of being categorially connected by our thought process.

Immediately, such form-determination posits a content that amounts to nothing more than the abstract possibility of place, a pure algebraic variable, a determinable with no particularly necessary determinate content. So anything and everything can in principle be posited as a value. At the same time, the universal needs the particulars it subsumes. Whereas Hegel's pure thoughts posit merely potential extensions, the economic forms must be constituted materially in the relation of exchange. Thus all the way through its analysis we will find that a doubling into the abstractly universal, and the materially particular, is characteristic of the value-form.

I think that the relationship between Hegel's logic and the value-form is much closer than that of an external identification of its logical structure, or a methodologically motivated application of its norms of adequacy, or an expositional strategy that finds it convenient to move from simpler to more complex structures. I believe that in some sense the value-form and Hegel's logic are to be identified; we are not simply applying Hegel's logic to an independent content. It is not that the value-form happens to generate structures of a complexity mapped by Hegel in his logical categories; the forms are in effect of such abstract purity as to constitute a real incarnation in the world of the ideas of Hegel's logic.

Marx's claim (to Lassalle, 22 February 1858) that the presentation of the commodity-capitalist system is at the same time a critique of it (it is so in itself—apart from the bringing to bear of any external criteria, such as the rather dubious one of justice) makes sense in our context when we observe that it is precisely the *applicability* of Hegel's logic that condemns the object as an inverted reality systematically alienated from its bearers, an object that in its spiritualization of material interchange and practical activities into the heaven of pure forms virtually incarnates the Hegelian "Idea."

To sum up: The secret of the structure and development of the capitalist economy is to be found right at the start when the material abstraction of commodity exchange creates the reality of pure forms, which then embark on their own logic of development (as in Hegel), and the entire system has to be grasped (within limits yet to be specified) as form-determined.

Hegelian Method

Given my argument thus far, it can be understood why in what follows I feel able to draw on Hegel's method of exposition in analyzing the value-form and the *form-determined* totality arising from it.

The presentation of the analysis presupposes that we are concerned with articulating the inner structure, and law of motion, of a (relatively) self-subsistent whole. The problem of presentation is in large measure a problem of (1) the starting point, and (2) the nature of the argumentative advance. My method of presentation of the forms of value below is purely Hegelian in character. Since this method is unique to Hegel (albeit partially employed by Marx, especially in section 3 of Chapter 1 of *Capital*), it may be unfamiliar to many. It is therefore worth spelling out.

What it is not: It is not an inductive method generalizing from perceived instances a hypothetical law of the phenomena, to be further tested in experience. It is not a hypothetico-deductive system in which an axiom is made the basis of a sequence of inferences that formally follow from it, the result being, as it is said, already contained in the premises. It is not a transcendental argument for the conditions of possibility of a form of experience taken as established.

It is the logical development of a system of categories, or forms of being, from the most elementary and indeterminate to the richest and most concrete; it is self-evident that the result cannot be contained in the premise, for the latter is poorer in content than the former. But this is precisely the key to the argument; the impulse to move from one category to the next is the insufficiency of the existing stage to prove its necessity and prevail against the contingencies to which it is subject. Upon examination, it is seen that the form under consideration is not able to sustain itself on its own basis; it depends on conditions of existence that seem to be contingent, such that it could easily vanish.

The movement of thought is thus from the conditioned to the unconditioned; each stage takes care of, with a minimum of new elements, the problem perceived with the previous stage, but in turn is found insufficient. The presentation ends when all the conditions of existence needing to be addressed are comprehended by the entire system of categories developed. The forms incorporate within themselves, and produce through their own effectivity, these conditions. This means that the totality so grounded is judged self-sufficient. The starting point is not an axiom or an empirical given upon which all else depends; rather the originating form gains actuality and truth only when grounded in the totality to which it gives rise through the dialectic outlined. A number of points about this Hegelian method need to be added. First, because the development is from the poorer to the richer form, a transition cannot be so formally necessary that a computer could predict it. Rather a certain openness and creativity are present. Hegel speaks here of "an upward spring of the mind" (Hegel 1975b, §50). This allows Hegel to present what he takes to be a logically necessary development as at the same time a free self-production of spirit.

A second point is that for Hegel's absolute idealism the major point of reference is not the individual thinking being. Instead of the ordinary mind solving problems with this method of advance, Hegel likes to think of the categories arising and dissolving out of their own instability; insofar as they are thought, it is by some "objective mind." This objectivist tendency of his logic is further strengthened because its truth is meant ontologically as much as logically. The coherence of the logic is at the same time the coherence of reality. We, of course, are dealing from the start with forms of reality, of which the logical equivalents in Hegel are always to be interpreted in terms of a real system of commodity exchange.

Another point that needs to be mentioned at the outset is that we have no confidence that the capitalist system can become secured in the harmonizing of all its determinations. But Hegel's method, besides being good for exhibiting the inner articulation of a self-sufficient system, is equally good for indicating the central contradiction that will bring down a system.

So the method of presentation follows a Hegelian procedure in ordering categories according to their relative abstractness and motivating transitions according to the criterion of the relative insufficiency of the currently established categorial framework to guarantee on its own basis the self-reproduction of the system.

Essentially, then, the presentation is of a system of categories. These may be picked up from everyday discourse or from existing bourgeois ideology, but some categories will have to be newly evolved because of the confusions of existing thought. The most general guideline in evolving these new categories, and in the presentation of the whole system of categories, is that the presentation should be able to establish a clear order of succession, from the simplest to the most complex, from the most abstractly indeterminate to the most concretely specific. Each category will unify a manifold. But insofar as it appears external and imposed on the elements, and they, conversely, appear only contingently available to it, the category is not securely grounded, and hence the real that is grasped under this aspect appears unstable and liable to dissolution.

Insofar as the real is self-reproducing, the presentation should be able to exhibit its categorial articulation in such a manner as to show how this is achieved through certain inner necessities of its structure, in other words, how the logic of the system tendentially ensures its reproduction. It should also be possible to indicate the degree of dependence of the system on empirically given contingencies. Thus that money is a necessity for capitalist development may be demonstrated, but the role historically played by gold in this connection clearly presupposes the contingencies of its existence and suitability.

The most notable category we pick up from everyday consciousness is that of commodity exchange. Like Marx we begin from the perception that the wealth of bourgeois society presents itself as "an immense accumulation of commodities." But I differ here from Marx in that I refuse to find it necessary to come to labor until after conceptualizing capital as a form-determination. Bringing in labor too early risks giving the appearance of model building and committing the exposition to a stage of simple commodity production.

Incidentally, it is not a matter of starting with a discussion of exchange systems in general and then further specifying the system we face as a species called general commodity production. It is a matter of demonstrating how the inner logic of exchange itself gives rise (systematically—although often historically as well) to capitalist production, given certain historically contingent conditions. We zero in on the historically determinate through a process of specifying at each level a more adequate shape of existence of the abstract indeterminateness of the origin.

But this does not mean that such a development gives us the dynamic of several modes of production (as Mandel [1990] seems to think Marx's *Capital* does with both simple commodity production and general commodity production), because the abstractness of the stages means precisely that there is a lack of actuality to any supposed empirical instantiation of them. Mandel seems to think, along with many other commentators (see, for example, Sweezy [1968] on the method of successive approximations), that what we are given by Marx is a series of models each more complex, but each equally workable.

The whole point of my procedure (and to some extent Marx's) is that each stage *lacks* self-subsistence, and hence there is the impulse to transcend it. If it *were* self-sufficient there would be no immanent dynamic in the presentation, and the shift from one model to another would be due to *our* decision to add a further determination, e.g., let money be invented, let labor-power be a commodity, let different organic compositions prevail. The starting point itself is inadequate and hence provides for movement because it has been abstracted from the whole, and the presentation is thus impelled to reconstruct the whole precisely through negating the starting point.

To begin with, we analyze the commodity-form itself, and only at the end give grounds for picking out as systematically important those commodities that are products of labor. In this way, by exploring to the full the dialectic of form and letting the form itself reach the content it demands, we are doing something very different from the bulk of the Marxist tradition, which is always in a hurry to address the material content.

I hold that under definite historically emergent conditions the value-form comes to acquire substance, or, conversely, labor comes to express itself in value. But in the space allowed in this chapter, I am concerned solely with the derivation of the forms of value; I indicate only in a general way where and why the reconstruction will explore the category of labor.

The presentation itself covers value, money, and capital, in that order. The ultimate object of Marxist theory is the capitalist form of social material production, but it does not follow that in the presentation it is necessary to evolve general categories of production and then further specify these in terms of the form of capital. It is proposed here that, because of its importance in shaping the character and direction of social material production, the value-form (as the germ of capital) should be analyzed first and the transition made to production in accordance with the determinations immanently required for the reproduction of capital according to the necessity of its concept. In other words, the question of form is so crucial that the presentation starts with the form of exchange, bracketing entirely the question of the mode of production, if any, of the objects of exchange.

The advantage is that we begin with the same perception as that of everyday consciousness, namely, that in the bourgeois epoch nearly everything is capable of taking on commodity-form, and we avoid an appearance of arbitrariness in concentration from the outset only on products of labor. My approach has the advantage of starting with commodities in general and arriving through the dialectic of the systematic presentation itself at the justification for a focus on production as the prime site of economically significant relationships.

Before embarking on the argument proper, let us contextualize it further by giving a general characterization of the social form of the bourgeois epoch.

Preliminary Notions

It is agreed by all intelligent Marxists that the question of social form is the key to the Marxian understanding of economic systems. It is only by virtue of differences in social form that Marx can insist that there is no such thing as economics in general, but that each mode of production has its specific and peculiar laws of motion. Unfortunately, the laconic opening sentence of *Capital* ("The wealth of society in which the capitalist mode of production prevails appears as an immense accumulation of commodities.") is far too brief a gesture toward the necessity of spelling out just what is peculiar about the social form of the bourgeois economy. He goes immediately into the double determination of the commodity; only in the last section of the chapter, in the interests of highlighting the uniqueness of the fetishistic form of the commodity, is there a fuller discussion of social form.

Marxist theory needs a science of form. It is true that Marx himself has a superb analysis of the forms of value in sections 3 and 4 of Chapter 1 (and this is where we see the influence of Hegel most clearly). He has a critique of form (fetishism) as well as a critique of content (exploitation), but in his anxiety to relate value to production he had already jumped—far too hastily—to labor as its substance. This permits some to read into the text an embodied-labor theory of value; at its worst this last approach asserts baldly, "labor *is* value" (Mandel 1990), collapsing the form completely into the content. Yet contrary to Mandel, Marx stresses that "labor . . . creates value, but is not itself value" (Marx 1976b, 142). It is so only in objective form, namely as a determination of the commodity form of the product.

Only in recent years have some begun to appreciate how significant the role of form-determination is in the theory of value, and how useful a resource Hegel's *Logic* is in construing Marxian theory. Those writers who have endeavored to relate Marx's work to Hegel's logic include Banaji, Sekine, the Konstanz-Sydney group (Eldred and others), Smith, and Reuten and Williams. In terminology, I draw on the language of Reuten and Williams (1989), although I do not pretend to follow their definitions exactly, and employ the triad of categories: sociation, dissociation, and association.

By *sociation* is meant the universal, ahistorical reality that in order to be active economically, people engage in social relationships and social practices. Outside of a Robinson Crusoe situation, production and consumption are immediately, or mediatedly, socially contextualized.

By *dissociation* (the negation of sociation) is meant the historically specific reality of the separation between economic agents predominant in the bourgeois epoch; *separation* here does not mean a geographical distance of course, but a social barrier. Dissociation has three dimensions: first, that useful objects are held by persons as their private property and hence are not immediately available for satisfying the needs of others; second, that production is carried out in enterprises likewise in the hands of private owners; and third, that labor power is separated from its object in that the most important means of production are held as the property of members of the capitalist class.

By *association* is meant that the opposition of sociation and dissociation is mediated in the form of exchange whereby consumers acquire the objects they require, production units acquire inputs and dispose of outputs, and through contracts of labor people find work and capitalist enterprises find workers. It is important to understand that when dissociation is negated through association this is on the same ground; that is to say, the basic element of privatized appropriation of goods is retained, but a form of mediation (properly called here sublation—*Aufhebung*) is found. Thus association does not replace dissociation; rather it replicates it through developing its conditions of existence. Sociation now takes the contradictory form of their unity. I agree with Reuten and Williams (1989) that dissociation is the conceptual starting point of the presentation of the bourgeois epoch and that the exchange relation provides the first moment of association. The presentation proper thus starts with exchange.

Since *exchange* is understood to mean a voluntary transaction that is not indicated by any central authority and is rooted solely in the private purposes of the agents concerned, it is on the face of it extremely unlikely that any coherent system of economic order could emerge at all—still less one characterized by the beneficent "hidden hand" of Smithian faith. Our problem is to determine the conditions of existence of a system in which goods take the form of commodities offered for exchange on the market. What is the form of social cohesion in a system in which all decisions to produce and to exchange are private? It is the forms of unity of this system that it is our task to explore, with a view to seeing just how much integration is possible.

Although the form of capital will turn out to be the overriding moment in the system, the drive that provides the impulse for reproduction, we could not possibly start with it right away, because it is far too complex a determination. Rather the presentation deliberately starts with the most indeterminate characterization of the whole (exchange). The argument develops precisely because of the need to overcome the inadequacy of this characterization, measured either immanently (e.g., by its self-contradictory implications) or by reference to its failure to be self-subsistent. In this way thought is impelled onward to reach a more concrete totality; only when the presentation reaches the whole is the starting point grounded in its connection with the whole and thereby validated as a true determination in this relative sense of being inadequate on its own but valid as one of the multiple determinations that come together in a mutually grounding interchange to constitute the concrete whole. The whole is grounded in its elements, and these elements mediate themselves in the whole. Commodities are the starting point; we do not at first raise the question of where commodities come from, whether they are produced or nonproduced goods, and, if they are produced, under what relations of production. But the development of the argument itself eventually grounds them as results of capitalist production (see Marx 1976, Appendix, "Results of the Immediate Process of Production" and Banaji 1979).

To sum up this introductory material: The sociation-dissociation contradiction is the presupposition of the entire epoch, and hence our presentation. It is association through exchange that gives this contradiction "room to move." The first concrete category is therefore this mediation, and we study its further development; this first category of movement determines goods as commodities, and hence the first object of analysis is the commodity, a unity of use-value and exchange-value. This doubling is a relation in which the form, the abstract universal, dominates the matter, the particular use-values; the value-form is therefore the theme of our categorial dialectic.

THE PRESENTATION OF THE VALUE-FORM

We have said enough to establish a general case for appropriating Hegel's logic in our value analysis. The following presentation works through this in detail. As a preliminary, let us lay out our plan (compare Hegel 1975b, §83):

1. Commodity exchange in its immediacy—value implicit in commodities.
2. The mediation of exchange in money—the reflection and showing forth of value.
3. Exchange in its unity with itself (circulation)—value in and of itself as capital.

A more detailed comparison of Hegel's logic and Marx's logic of the value-form is summarized in the Appendix to this chapter (see p. 87).

EXCHANGE

This first section thematizes the commodity. This is a form of Being—a category of Hegel's *Logic*—and the determinations below will also follow those in the *Logic*, namely, quality, quantity, and measure. These correspond in our domain to exchangeability, the bargain, and value in exchange. The dialectical exposition proper begins with the most abstract indeterminate notion, but nonetheless the essential and originating one, which initiates the process of social synthesis in the bourgeois epoch, that of exchange. The only presupposition made at the outset is that dissociation is overcome through commodity exchange. (The need for this form of association depends, we have explained, on historical contingencies beyond the scope of the systematic presentation itself.) Goods therein take the form of commodities, namely the value-form.

Given exchange, we can speak of goods in terms of the elementary opposition between Being and Nothing treated by Hegel at the beginning of his *Logic*. Goods appear as beings in the circuits of exchange and pass into nothingness as they disappear from it, perhaps to be consumed. Their being, made determinate and fixed in this sphere (as *Dasein*), is that of exchangeable commodities. Commodities are distinguished from being goods in general by the quality of being exchangeable. (The denotation of the category is of course historically variable. Water was once a free good; now it is an increasingly expensive commodity.) At the same time, exchangeability is still rooted in the commodity's utility. At this level the immediate motor of exchange appears to be the exchange of one commodity for another of a different kind having a different use. There is no conceivable point in exchanging for the same good. We do not exchange iron for iron, but iron for corn. Thus a condition of existence of exchange is the universe of use-value. For the moment, this condition of existence is bracketed; we come back to it later.

The quality of exchangeability requires further determination. If exchange is to be possible, it is not enough for the goods to be specified as having properties that make them exchangeable in a general indeterminate sense. A determination is required that allows for discrete exchanges to occur; in other words, a commodity must be specifiable as an item (a bakery does not in truth sell bread, it sells so many loaves of such and such weight). The good has to take on a determinable shape and be able to specify itself in discrete items, each of which announces itself as an instantiation in delimited form of the good concerned. Through this notion of limit we make the transition to the category of quantity.

To be commodities, goods offered for sale must be delimited quantitatively. The striking thing about this quantification is that, although each good has its own index of amount (weight or whatever) in terms of which haggling goes on, these amounts seem unable to refer to any common index because, *ex hypothesi*, as naturally diverse goods, their index of amount differs absolutely (no one would exchange two pounds of gold for two pounds of iron). Hence the quantum, the unit of exchange, does not appear as a unit of anything common; it is a pure number: I'll give you six of these for four of those. This is the quantitative form of the bargain.

Being incommensurable as natural bodies, the commodities are bargained over in the abstract, where the haggling is in terms of pure quantitative variation. The contradiction is that the properties that give them the quality of exchangeability—their use-values—are too particular to form the basis of a common measure. Yet in a bargain a pure quantitative relation must be fixed in spite of such absolute difference. There appears no ground for such determinacy. This is no mere theoretical contradiction, but a practical incoherence. Perhaps, as Aristotle feared, we must accept its theoretical absurdity in the interests of practical expediency; or maybe we must accept the subjective approach of the neoclassicists; or, as here, we must press the objective tendency of the logic further.

As it stands, the relation is unstable and insecure; there seems no reason why any particular pair of numbers should form the basis for the striking of a bargain. Given this, it may well turn out that any particular offer is always rejected. There is no necessity yet granted to this form in its character as quantitatively determinate. Someone, sometime, for some reason, might be prepared to accept a certain amount of one commodity for a certain amount of another. Even if a commodity does achieve social recognition in an exchange, the ratio of exchange, the bargain struck, seems purely accidental—arising ad hoc, it may be varied on the next occasion.

Yet the abstraction of quantity and quality from each other is not absolute. They are as much in unity as opposed. For, after all, one is not in the bargain settling for six, one is settling for six *something*; there is a qualitative determinant present as much as suspended in the haggling over amounts. But the something varies in material terms with every transaction as much as the numbers quantifying it. It could be anything. Can all these somethings represent the same thing?

Exchangeable commodities can actualize themselves only in a bargain, that is, in quantitative form. Conversely, the quantitative ratio practically uniting them in the bargain actualizes their common character as exchangeables, as having the potential to draw other commodities in exchange for themselves. The ratio of exchange is thus implicitly a measure of this potentiality, their value in exchange.

This is probably the most important turning point in the whole theory of value, and by far the most controversial. For, as we see from Hegel's *Logic* (Hegel 1975b, §111), the notion of measure leads us to "the essence": that which is measured externally in the ratio of exchange is an inherent dimension of the commodity, just like its volume.

Marx skips over this transition astonishingly quickly. He simply declares that in the exchange relation of iron and corn there is a quantitative identity. This identity is clearly not to be assimilated to the natural properties of iron and corn and must represent some third thing present, if not visible, in both: their value. Critics have been vociferous in denying the necessity for any such inference: from Bailey (1967; against the Ricardian version) and Boehm-Bawerk (1975) to Cutler and colleagues (1977) and Moore (1963) today.

The meaningfulness of this transition therefore needs thorough elucidation. It involves grasping the relation with the other as mediately a self-relation. In the terms of the discourse of bargaining, it is marked by a shift from the simple demand, "offer me more of that other commodity," to the proposition that "this is worth more than what you are offering" or, even more precisely, "this is worth twice that." Such formulas show the consciousness of "this" being immediately, in itself, of worth, that value has an identity with itself, and thereby grounds some immanent measure that is merely expressed or reflected externally in a satisfactory bargain, one in which no one loses anything. The relation of exchange between A and B is now grasped as no longer a conjunctural external relation but a self-relation in which each, in referring to the other as an embodiment of its value, is indirectly referring to its own value as reflected in something equivalent to itself. Thus we now say, "A is worth B" or "as values A = B."

If the quantitative determination established in an exchange is not to be purely conjunctural, determined extrinsically in the contingencies motivating the agents bearing the goods to market (preference schedules, for example), it requires a dimension intrinsic to both commodities yet distinguishable from their appearance as immediately different. This dimension is such that it obviously varies for each commodity in proportion to its own index of amount, but it is itself, insofar as it no longer has anything to do with the particularity of use-value, a single quantitative determination—that is, value in itself. Thus the *essence* of being a commodity is having value.

It is just this notion of an intrinsic value that Bailey (1967) and others have objected to. For them, the value posited in exchange is illusory. There is, in truth, nothing lying behind the visible relation. "A table is worth four chairs" resembles in grammatical form "This shoe is as long as two of those put together." But it is not the same, because extension is an inherent dimension of the shoes, whereas exchange value is a purely relative matter, an accidental external relation. Tomorrow, or in the next town, a table might be worth three chairs. We should not be misled by such relations into postulating any identity in the substance of the goods. There is no such thing as intrinsic value, only conjunctural correlations of different amounts of use-values.

It seems to me that this argument has much more force than most Marxists allow. At this point we have only the *postulate* of identity in essence and of common measure. If the system is to be grounded on itself, rather than being prey to external contingencies, this essence must be actualized. The main point here is that for there to be unity of commodities in a common identity, and determinacy in their relations, they must exist in the same universe and their measure must be predicated on a common dimension that actualizes their commensurability as values.

Although each commodity could embody a unique need and a unique supply (e.g., payment for a blackmailer's negatives), for the system of exchanges to be grounded on itself (rather than each transaction registering a specific externally determined conjuncture), the plurality of commodities must be instances of a universal type. There need not, however, *be* any such identity or resulting immanent determination of exchange ratios. So the further presentation, although it seems to assume that we already know value exists, is really an exploration of its conditions of existence through the development of more concrete concepts, which will eventually provide sufficient grounds to set aside any skepticism and at least validate a research program based on value.

Before proceeding I would like to call attention to the fact that nothing has been said yet about a labor theory of value. People have rightly complained that labor is not common to everything in commodity-form. But in any case it should be noted that—to use an analogy—it is one thing to undertake a number of experiments and conclude that material things each have an intrinsic, definite weight that regularly expresses itself in ratios such as so much of this balances so much of that, which justifies our speaking of weight, as such, independent of its expression in such ratios. It is another thing to determine that weight arises from the effect on masses (m) of a gravitational field (g) and that its immanent magnitude is mg.

Before we can even address the Marxian question of the substance of value, it is necessary to establish what we mean by the value dimension. Can there be such a thing? Many have thought not. Its meaning is all the more doubtful when we remember that, unlike weight, value has no connection with anything inherent to the commodity itself as a natural body. It is an alien determination that attaches itself to a good only when the latter is subject to commodity exchange. It does not seem possible to argue that value exists independently of exchange in the same sense as weight exists independently of weighings. It is true that *if* the market exists, one can anticipate that a value can be realized on it; but can one speak of value when there are no markets?

I argue that it is not the case that a preexisting material content merely takes on the value-form; rather, as the form-determined relationships develop, the value content is grasped as a result—it is demanded only when the form completes itself in capital. At this stage we have not yet established value—still less a labor content. Or rather value has not yet established *itself*. It is not merely that our presentation has not yet reached a proof of value; insofar as it does not preexist exchange, value itself only comes to be and gains any actuality in the fullest development of the form itself—in money, capital, and productive labor, as we shall see.

Value exists only when market exchange is more than an aggregation of accidental transactions, when it is a systematically unified and ordered process that is guaranteed some stability, permanence, and continuity. But at this stage of the presentation this is by no means secured. To speak of a commodity as a thing of value, or simply a value, and of things related to one another as values implies the existence of value in itself as a sort of homogeneous "matter" underlying the diverse bodily shapes of commodities. According to Hegel, it is an abstraction of the understanding to suppose that there is an underlying matter in things behind their phenomenal shape. But here it is not just that the fetishistic consciousness does this; the exchange abstraction itself posits value as this reified essence.

But as merely implicit, value is a vanishing semblance. To be really of the essence it must become posited for itself; it must gain actuality in its further developed forms of appearance. This is what makes money necessary. Hegel observes that Spirit is "not an essence that is already finished and complete before its manifestation, keeping itself aloof behind its host of appearances, but an essence which is truly actual only through the specific forms of its necessary self-manifestation" (Hegel 1971, §378). I would say the same of value. Thus its further concretizations up to market price are not merely more finished forms of value, they are themselves constitutive of its actuality.

MONEY

In comparison to the brevity with which Marx argues in the first two sections of Chapter 1 of *Capital*, most people find the third section over-elaborated. Why these dialectical minutiae, when all he is saying is that we need a measure of value analogous to the standard meter in Paris, which gives science a common basis for establishing lengths? Gold serves as an exemplar of value, as the standard meter does of extension. Value, however, unlike extension, is merely a virtual dimension; its actuality is posited only in the relations commodities bear to one another. Therefore, Marx is right to show how money, as the (external) measure of commodities, is evolved in those relations. So how is it to be derived?

Thus far the presentation has argued that the form of exchange posits value in itself. The distinction between use-value and exchange-value points to the possibility of overcoming the contingency implicit in mere barter; for, if there is a value dimension, order and determinacy will characterize exchange. The difficult thing to grasp here is that, although the possibility of determinate measure is grounded if value is of the essence of the commodity, this essence itself is actualized only in the development of the process of commensuration itself. It is that very process of commensuration that posits commodities as value masses in the first place. The actuality of value and its expression or measure develop together at the same time.

The exchange relation has to be grasped as simultaneously constitutive of value and serving as its expression. A commodity cannot express its value in itself, because value gains reality only in the relations of commodities to one another; Marx says that value "can only appear in the social relation between commodity and commodity" (Marx 1976b, 139), that is, as exchange-value. The value of linen cannot be expressed in linen. But if another commodity acts as its equivalent, a distinction is drawn in reality between the two aspects of the commodity—its use-value immediately present in its own shape, and its value present through the mediation of the equivalent commodity's shape.

In truth, the value dimension is constituted at the same time as its measure. This means that it is even more abstract than space, because extension is perceptible as such prior to the evolution of a unified measuring system. To say that this is equivalent in length to that by laying them side by side does not in itself give a measure of either (although it presupposes in its form of expression that such a measure is possible); nevertheless, extension is naturally inherent in both of the objects we see. The value dimension, however, has a purely virtual existence insofar as its reality is merely the ideality of the unity of commodities in their abstract identity as exchangeable.

The insight that value subsists only in relations of exchange opens up this question: What form of exchange relation could actualize a determination that is posited as identical in each commodity, yet subsists only through the mediation of a different commodity against which it exchanges?

In Marx's brilliant exposition of the dialectic of the forms of value, he calls our attention to the relevance of Hegel's logic of "reflection-determinations" in the "doctrine of essence" (Marx 1976b, 149). Essentially, something is (1) identical with itself, (2) different from itself, and (3) grounded in the unity of these moments. Through this dialectic, the category of identity in difference will be reached as the principle of the universal equivalent form of value.

In truth, we already had occasion to employ this dialectic earlier when we argued that, if value in exchange is to be a real measure, then value in itself must ground the truth of commensuration. The world of commodities then has a ground to which all difference falls. As soon as we reached that conclusion, however, through reflecting the commodity into itself, we thereby posited a realm of values wherein is distinguished the essence of value from its forms of appearance or exchange-values. Thus value must now reflect back on exchange-value, that is, make of it its appearance. Insofar as the reality of essence is accomplished only in its appearance, the latter is thereby just as much ground as grounded.

As we know already, taken in isolation a commodity exhibits only use-value; it can double into a use-value and a value only if the latter determination achieves independent expression. But does it not in every exchange? Certainly, of a single "accidental" exchange relation, Marx says: "The simple form of value of a commodity is the simple form of appearance of the opposition between use-value and value which is contained within the commodity" (Marx 1976b, 153). The "insufficiency" (Marx's word) of the simple form to establish this opposition explicitly is that the simple form logically posits symmetry; it can be read in either direction, between measure and measured, between the implicit value and its expression. Hence it is difficult to keep hold of the polar relation (Marx 1976b, 160); the relation collapses to an identity of immanence of value, not an articulated ground for it. Furthermore, although the implicit distinction between use-value and value is made manifest in every dyadic relation, an aggregation of barters does not constitute a unified homogeneous value system (see Marx 1973, 204–5).

Thus we move to a fuller relative form of value, the expanded form in which the commodity expresses its identity as a value in a whole array of different commodities. This establishes the commodity in that form as something with a value expression in this totality of relations. The very number of these expressions indicates the indifference of the value expression to any particular equivalent body; hence Marx says that we can suppose there is some continuing magnitude present unaltered through the series of exchange-values. The "defect" (according to Marx) is that there is "no single, unified form of appearance" of value because each excludes the others. Although no unified expression of value is thereby provided, the solution is implicit in this form, for the very same action in which the one commodity sets up its value in expanded form posits it as the single equivalent of the others.

In the reversed expression, the general form of value emerges. In this, the universal equivalent functions simply as the incarnation of the abstract identity of all the different commodities as values. As such a unity of the differences it articulates explicitly the value dimension we found necessary to secure the independent status of commodities from the idiosyncrasies of their owners. With this unifying form the inner identity of values gains outward expression. The point I want to restate is that this is not a superficial development of the essence of value. The actuality of these forms is the very condition of the category of value gaining any real meaning. Marx says: "By this [universal equivalent] form, commodities are, for the first time, really brought into relation with each other as values, or permitted to appear to each other as exchange-value" (Marx 1976b, 158).

This is also why Marx's theory of money is so different from both Ricardian and neoclassical conventionalisms. For Marxism the universal equivalent is no convenient *numéraire*, it is essential that it has actuality. The transition from the implicit immediacy of value in a commodity, and its mediation in the universal equivalent, to the reality of money is necessary because (as we must always remind ourselves) the forms we are concerned with are not pure thoughts but are borne by matter, namely commodities. Hence the unity in form of these commodities must be more than thought, it must be practically posited: thus the necessity for a material bearer of the universal equivalent, i.e., the necessity for money.

Measure is also made explicit because, as the universal equivalent, money is posited as value for itself, which is now distinguished from its implicit existence in the integument of the other commodities and is capable of being applied to them as their (external) measure. Money does not merely solve the quantitative problem of providing a measure common to values, it solves the qualitative problem of establishing the very commensurability of commodities by relating them to one another as values. Marx argues that goods do not confront one another as commodities (that is, as values) but as use-values only, until there exists *in practice* a universal equivalent. It is through the social action of commodities on one another that there is set apart a particular commodity in which they all represent their values. "Through the agency of the social process it becomes the specific function of the commodity that has been set apart to be the universal equivalent, it thus becomes—money" (Marx 1976b, 180–81).

The first function of money as the expression of value, as the existent appearance of the value dimension, is to serve as the measure of value. What exactly is measured? Analogies with other measures such as rulers or weights are very misleading here for the reason that I have been stressing: Money *constitutes* value in a unity rather than serving as an exemplar of some property the commodities possessed prior to their commensuration. Money is the external measure of exchangeability of which value is the immanent measure. But insofar as value is—as yet—determined as pure form, there is nothing substantial (analogous to mass or extension) to measure. (Commodities are not yet, we stress, determined as products in our presentation; hence we know nothing here of such an index of immanent measure as socially necessary labor time.)

Insofar as money unifies the world of commodities, it has the form of immediate exchangeability. Although having the same value in the abstract as a commodity it measures, money successfully actualizes the posited immanence of value, the essence lying behind the appearance of equivalent exchange, and thereby provides for value to appear in immediate existence, and with it determinate measure. Money, Marx says in his *Grundrisse*, is "value for itself" (Marx 1973, 459).

In a peculiar sense, in the money form, value measures itself against itself. Exchangeability is measured by exchangeability. For this self-identity to gain adequate form requires the doubling of the values into commodities and money, into value in itself and value for itself. Thereby, value measures itself *in* itself *by* itself *for* itself. As the immediate equivalent of all commodities, money solves the qualitative value problem through its pure ideality, creating a virtual space—the value dimension. Marx speaks of the price form of commodities as "like their form of value generally, quite distinct from their palpable and real bodily form; it is therefore a purely ideal or notional form" (Marx 1976b, 189).

Both rulers and money allow a unified commensuration. But, insofar as a ruler is itself extended, the relation of equivalence in length follows the logic of transitivity, symmetry, and reflexivity; and it is not too absurd to say that the standard meter measures one meter itself. But money cannot measure its own value because money is in effect measure as such. Money has no price: It is price.

CAPITAL

In the systematic development of exchange relations, the contradictory unity of form (value) and matter (use-value) is expressed by a doubling into commodities and money. In this doubling, value acquires different forms of existence. In the price-form its particular and universal moments are distributed between the commodity and money.

In thought we analyze concepts into moments, we distinguish within a thing the universal and particular determinations (my humanness on the one hand, and the man before you on the other). Empirically, these are not perceptible distinctions, being mere abstract moments of real being. But the self-development of the value-form analyzes the concept of value in reality; the universal moment is dominant in money and the particular in commodities. If we describe our investigation as value-form analysis, we now realize that we just "look on" (Hegel's words) while the restless movement of the value-form carries out the analysis itself!

With regard to the functions of money, the most immediate from a logical point of view is its function as a measure of value. However, it is clear that its immediate exchangeability opens up a more concrete determination, that of a medium of circulation. Money now is more than formally posited as a measure; it is a concrete mediator unifying commodities in their life process. In commenting on the contradictions of commodity exchange, Marx says that the distinguishing of money from commodities solves the contradiction by allowing it "room to move." He means that in the metamorphoses of commodities both the particular and universal determinations get expressed as moments in a unity insofar as money serves as a medium of circulation (Marx 1976b, 198–99).

The contradiction between the forms of appearance of value (commodities and money) is brought into motion and their unity established in the fluidity of circulation whereby each passes over into the other; the self-same value, doubled into different shapes of existence, appears now as commodity, now as money, now again as commodity. Here, a purchase has the shape of a simple exchange, but it realizes a universal, whereas a mere barter transfers particulars from one hand to another. But, as Marx points out against Say, the circulation of commodities, conceptualized as C-M-C′, has no necessity, because a producer may not find a market and a sale need not be followed by a purchase. In any case the motivation is external to the process in itself, in that the ends of the chain pass out of circulation. Hence the renewal of circulation depends on the continuance of demand and of supply.

The interesting point about the possibility of a temporary hiatus in circulation is that the determination of money as a store of value now emerges; with money in hand the possibility of renewing the circuit when required, or when conditions are favorable, is present. Marx gives a very thorough analysis of the development of C-M-C′ into M-C-M′, where, of course, the only motivation of the latter sequence is the possibility of $M' = M + \Delta M$.

With M-C-M the extremes are unified in a spiral of valorization. Money goes from a passive medium in C-M-C to a dynamic unifying and initiating role in M-C-M. Marx says:

> The path C-M-C proceeds from the extreme constituted by one commodity, and ends with the extreme constituted by another, which falls out of circulation and into consumption. Consumption, the satisfaction of needs, in short use-value, is therefore its final goal. The path M-C-M, however, proceeds from the extreme of money and finally returns to that same extreme. Its driving and motivating force, its determining purpose, is therefore exchange-value. (Marx 1976b, 250)

It should be remembered that, since our presentation here is systematic rather than historical, we cannot speculate on the form of capital arising out of these circuits from the impulse of greed or any other motive. We simply draw attention to the systematic advance that is made possible in the interweaving of money and commodities, namely that the M-C-M circuit has built into it greater possibilities of continuity and self-reproduction than the C-M-C circuit. Value is now immanent in the activity of exchange; it is its own end, not the effect and medium of other motives.

We now see that from the circulation of commodities and money emerges capital. The following passages are reminiscent of Hegel's doctrine of the concept:

> The simple circulation of commodities—selling in order to buy—is a means to a final goal which lies outside circulation, namely the appropriation of use-values, the satisfaction of needs. As against this, the circulation of money as capital is an end in itself, for the valorization of value takes place only within this constantly renewed movement. The movement of capital is therefore limitless. (Marx 1976b, 253)
>
> It is constantly changing from one form into the other, without becoming lost in this movement; it thus becomes transformed into the subject of a process in which, while constantly assuming the form in turn of money and commodities, it changes its own magnitude, throws off surplus-value from itself considered as original value, and thus valorizes itself independently. For the movement in the course of which it adds surplus-value is its own movement, its valorization is therefore self-valorization. (Marx 1976b, 255)

In investigating the form of capital, Marx speaks of M-C-M′ as being "value-in-process." But this self-moving substance does not merely assume the form of commodities and money, it enters into a relationship with itself, as it were, because it "differentiates itself as original value from itself as surplus value" only when both are united in the new capital, to supersede this difference, and become one again (Marx 1976b, 256). It is "absolute form" (Hegel 1975b, §164).

Capital makes value actual in the sense that it now has a form that posits itself as its own end. That is to say, with the form of capital, we have before us an individual "subject" (Marx's word) that expressly aspires to the totalization of its determinations and to include within its effectivity all its conditions of existence. The motive of our presentation so far in seeking to elucidate the conditions of existence of value has now become the motive of the form itself!

PRODUCTION

What, then, is the condition next required to grant necessity to the existence of capital as self-valorization? Capital is defined as self-valorizing value; but how can this form maintain itself? The main point here is that although capital has the form of self-realization it still lacks control over its bearers. It is here we remember that at the outset we stated that a primary condition of exchange is the world of use-values. With capital we reach a form of circulation of commodities that is its own end, but the self-valorization process still rests for its possibility on the emergence into being of the goods themselves from some external source.

Clearly, therefore, there is still a large element of conditionedness in the mere possibility of valorization. It is not self-grounded. Circulation in "its immediacy is therefore pure semblance" (Marx 1973, 255), a play of forms. Exchange could fade away (as during the decline of the Roman Empire), so capital must take charge of sustaining and developing the value circuit. The problem is solved if the goods are themselves produced by capital and reduced to moments in its own circuit. Only on this condition does value in and for itself pass from a mere formal potential to embed itself in a real material process.

To be self-grounded, value must be produced by value. This means that only those goods produced by capital itself count as values, as true commodities in both form and content. Only capitalistically produced commodities have adequacy in both form and content to value in and for itself. The activity of production is an activity of labor. Hence, capital must make that activity its own activity. Only now does the presentation find it necessary to address labor. The limitlessness of accumulation inherent in the form of capital is given a solid ground in productive labor.

Our presentation has reached the point at which nonproduced commodities are seen to retain the value-form but only the semblance of value; they are lacking in the substance of value because they do not originate within the value circuit itself as it is driven by valorization. They play no essential role in the dynamic of capitalist development (although two such nonproduced commodities—labor power and land—are materially essential inputs but cannot be treated in this chapter). Products, if capitalistically produced as commodities for sale, gain both determinations of value, being both produced as values and sold as values. Insofar as capital conquers the sphere of production, it gains reality and permanence instead of being dependent on external conditions to provide the values on which it feeds.

The fact that the presentation found it necessary to turn to productive labor only when the capital form required a ground implies that there are inadequate grounds for positing a labor theory of value at the level of commodity exchange alone. The fit between form and content would be too loose, the relation still too indeterminate.

Marx moves so quickly to the substance of value that we lose sight of the fact that value is actual only in the fully developed concept (namely, capital). Hence Marx sometimes gives the impression in his discussion that a prior content, labor, reduces the value-form to its mere phenomenal expression. The dialectic of commodity production is better presented, I think, as one in which the form sinks into the matter and then develops it as its own content (which, with Marx, we can analyze in terms of such categories as labor power and surplus labor). Within the value-form, instead of the content developing itself through the mediation of its form, the form seeks to secure and stabilize itself through subsuming the matter and turning it into a bearer of self-valorization. What we are arguing in relation to Hegel's work is that his speculation about an Absolute seeking to actualize and reproduce its entire conditions of existence has reality in capital, which has such a drive implicit in its form. Hegel's supposedly universal logic is also the specific logic of capital. At the same time, the logic of the development can issue only in tendencies, which in truth depend on material premises. Unfortunately for capital, it cannot actualize itself and conquer all its presuppositions of existence as easily as Hegel's Idea is supposed to. The true reality is material. As pure form, capital spins in a void. The logic of capital accumulation would run into the buffers pretty quickly were it not for the material fact that workers produce more than they themselves consume. Moreover, the laborers are liable to resist their incorporation as internal moments of capital's ideality, that is, the Idea of capital made real.

CONCLUSION

A general distinction may be made in dialectical argument between systematic and historical dialectics. On the whole, Marx is trying to use the former, as I do here. The relation between a systematic and historical dialectic is obscure. Certainly, any attempt to identify them may lead to the positing as real historical stages of forms that are in truth insubstantial phases of a dialectical presentation of an existing dialectically articulated totality.

The ontological presupposition of my argument is that commodity exchange creates an inverted reality in which abstractions, instead of being the pale efflorescence of matter, are the *demiurgos* of the world. With the ever-extending commodification of all material things and persons, and the inscribing of all relations within the value-form, mere abstraction is loosed upon the world. Pure forms that develop themselves and enter into relations with one another are objectively present in a realm other than thought. But their conditions of existence are material; hence capital drives to shape matter into a content penetrated through and through by the value-form.

As we said at the outset, insofar as the presentation traces the imposition of alien forms on the material content of economic life, it is itself immanently critical of the system. However, this is immaterial unless that system is itself immanently unstable and produces the contradiction that will overturn it. The germ of the diagnosis to this effect is seen in our identification of productive labor as a necessary ground for capital. The further development of this side of the matter can show that confronting the subject capital is another subject, the proletariat, emerging as its contradiction brought forth in the development of capital itself. To this extent it could be shown that, after all, capital cannot reach the infinite self-subsistence of Hegel's Idea, that no genuine unity in difference is achieved, and that the material and ideal sides of the economy remain estranged from one another no matter how much mediating complexes attempt to secure room to move for the contradictions.

Appendix

LOGICAL CATEGORIES (HEGEL)	THE VALUE-FORM (MARX)
Doctrine of Being	*Commodity*
Quality	Exchangeability (use)
Quantity	The bargain
Measure	Value in exchange
Doctrine of Essence	*Money*
Ground of existence	Value in itself
Appearance	Forms of value
Actuality	Money
Doctrine of the Concept	*Capital*
Subjectivity	Price
Objectivity	Metamorphoses of commodities
Idea	Self-valorization of capital

4

The Difficult Labor of a Theory of Social Value: Metaphors and Systematic Dialectics at the Beginning of Marx's *Capital*

Geert Reuten

Although the science of nature, it seems, first got off the ground from a social scientific impetus,[1] eighteenth- and nineteenth-century social scientists felt constrained to cast their theoretical innovations in terms of metaphors borrowed from the natural sciences, in particular physics (see Mirowski 1990). The birth of Marxist social science in the nineteenth century is no exception in this respect. This is remarkable because Marx was very aware of the naturalism of classical political economy. Borrowing metaphors from physics, it is true, need not be naturalistic. Nevertheless metaphors may be dangerous (as Hegel observed) if perhaps unavoidable. Within Marxist social science, I will argue, the metaphor *substance of value* as introduced by Marx (1976b) has played a very dubious role. It seems that this metaphor came to be taken for a real embodiment—at least within one important strand of Marxism. Of course, because our thinking is so tied to our language, it is always difficult to disentangle metaphoric language from what we really think. It is, however, important to try to be conscious of the metaphors and their purport.

Although the metaphor *substance of value* was used by Marx (1976b), not without a Hegelian undertone, his linking it to embodiment seems to derive from classical political economy. I argue that the combination of (1) the substance metaphor and the classical embodiment remnant with (2) the only implicit method of *Capital* and, in particular, the unclarity as to the type of abstractions used by Marx gave rise to an extensive period of birth of a true theory of social value (a theory of value as a purely social institutional phenomenon). I take such a theory to be in the spirit of Marx's theory in *Capital*. Despite Marx's explicit rejection of classical naturalism, the actual content of *Capital* often seems to bear the remnants of such a naturalism, which can be explained from his lack of clarity as to the extent of the break with his predecessors (which is a common occurrence among path-breaking theoreticians).

I examine to what extent Marx's theory may indeed be considered a labor embodied theory of value and to what extent labor is seen to be a substance of value. Then I consider how this has affected current Marxist theory of value, especially in its varieties of the labor embodied and the abstract-labor theories of value. These theories contain, in my view, a number of defects that may be traced back to the substance of value view. Finally, I provide an outline of how these defects might be overcome.

I hope to show that interpreting the type of abstractions that Marx uses is crucial to the examination of his value theory. Are these dialectical abstractions or some sort of analytical abstractions? An answer to this question is complicated by the fact that Marx is hardly explicit about his method. His attitude vis-à-vis Hegel's logic is an especially ambivalent one. First I briefly set out my view of this dialectical logic. This will be the vantage point for the examination of Marx's theory of value as well for my view on a possible reconstruction of the labor theory of value. I also make a number of general remarks on Marx's method in *Capital*.

SYSTEMATIC DIALECTIC

That Marx's method remains only implicit in *Capital* has always complicated the discussion of the work both among and between supporters and opponents. There seems to be no way out of this dilemma apart from making one's own methodological inclinations explicit: Inasmuch as empirical observations are theory laden (Popper), theoretical evaluations will be methodologically laden. My own methodological inclinations, however—as inspired by Hegel's logic—are not totally farfetched with respect to Marx. Marx has repeatedly stressed his own indebtedness to this dialectical logic. (See, e.g., Arthur 1986, Echeverria 1978, Murray 1988b, Smith 1990c, and the contributions in the collection by Schmidt 1969.) The Introduction to the *Grundrisse* (Marx 1973) provides a statement of a number of the characteristics of systematic dialectics. In other works, however, Marx often seems to distance himself from this approach. The brief outline of the method of systematic dialectic below may prove to be difficult when abstracting it from the content of the theory. In order to give a more complete picture, I include certain concepts that are less relevant for the issues discussed in the sections that follow (these paragraphs are starred [*] in case the reader wishes to skip them).

Systematic dialectic or *conceptual dialectic* refers to the dialectic as developed in Hegel's logic (Hegel 1985, 1989), which is a logic of dialectical conceptual development. This dialectic should be distinguished definitely from a theory of dialectical historical development (as in Hegel's philosophy of history) or a theory of historical development of concepts (as introduced in Hegel's history of philosophy).[2]

The starting point of the presentation of the dialectical theory (*Darstellung*) is an abstract universal notion—an abstract all-embracing concept. This starting point itself is the result of a process of inquiry, of critical appropriation of empirical perceptions and existing theories (of them). This abstract notion is the staring point of explicit theorization and its presentation (cf. Marx 1976b, 102; 1973, 100). Thinking cannot conceivably make anything of such an abstract universal notion, other than by thinking its abstract negation and its abstract particularization. In both cases (negation and particularization), opposed concepts are applied to the same thing or notion, and in this specific sense these opposites are contradictions. In this sense also, to think these things and notions is to articulate their doubling—that is, the universal doubles into the universal and an opposite universal, or into universal and particular. (The value–use-value opposition is an example of the former; the opposition of universal and particular labor [amplified upon below], or in simpler terms the animal-cat opposition, are examples of the latter.)

*Two further remarks concerning these oppositions should be made. First, it is precisely the purpose of the presentation to resolve the contradiction from which we start; it is this process of thought that should render comprehension of reality. "The essence of philosophy consists precisely in resolving the contradiction of the Understanding" (Hegel 1985, 71). Second, to immediately subsume single empirical phenomena as particulars under universals provides only empty abstractions. One reason for this is that such subsumption may indicate what such phenomena have in common, but not what, if anything, unites them, how they are interconnected. Another is that it is the difference between phenomena that determines them; but this difference also does not say what, if anything, unites them. As long as we have provided no difference *in* unity we have provided no concrete determination. It is this double determination (difference in unity) that systematic dialectical thinking seeks. As Hegel expresses it: "The truth of the differentiated is its being in unity. And only through this movement is the unity truly concrete." Whereas at first, at the starting point: "difference is still sunk in the unity, not yet set forth as different" (Hegel 1985, 83).

*The object of the presentation is to grasp the phenomena from which we start in our perception as concrete, that is, as the "concentration [*Zusammenfassung*] of many determinations, hence unity of the diverse" (Marx 1973, 101). But that may only be possible to the extent that these are phenomena necessary to the existent, rather than contingent ones. (For example, if we have established monetary policy to be necessary to the existent, then credit restrictions or open market policy may be only contingent). Contingent phenomena cannot be explained as codetermining the internal unity of many determinants—thus not as necessary—but only as an external determinant. (In this chapter, however, we will not reach this stage of contingency of phenomena.)

A further characteristic of the method of systematic dialectic is that the argument is not based on rules of axiomatic deductive nomological systems. All axioms are eschewed. Rather, anything that is required to be assumed, or anything that is posited immediately (such as the starting point), must be grounded. But it should not be grounded merely abstractly (i.e., giving the arguments in advance), because this always leads to regress. That which is posited must be ultimately grounded in the argument itself, in concretizing it. Therefore, the intrinsic merits of the presentation—and not some external criterion—have to convince the reader of the adequacy of the presentation. Thus the presentation moves forward by the transcendence of contradiction and by providing the ever more concrete grounds—the conditions of existence—of the earlier abstract determination. In this forward movement the conditions of existence of earlier abstract determination do not dissolve, but transcend the opposite moments (identity-difference, universal-particular) of the abstract determination. (A moment is an element considered in itself that can be conceptually isolated and analyzed as such but that can have no isolated existence.)

*Thus the previous conceptualization of abstract determinations as moments is not negated, but rather transcended in the ground; or the ground provides the unity of the opposed moments. But at the same time it is a further, more concrete determination of the difference, a difference previously posited only in itself (*an sich*, potentially, implicitly), as it now appears. So the differences that were previously not set forth as such now come into (abstract) existence. The ground at this new level itself then gains momentum; it is itself an abstract existent showing the contradiction that it cannot exist for itself (*für sich*, actually). The presentation has to move on in order to ground it in its turn, so as to provide its conditions of existence (Hegel 1985a, 120–24; 1985b, 81–83). And so on, until the presentation claims to have reached the stage where it comprehends the existent as actual, as actuality (*Wirklichkeit*), in the sense that its conditions of existence have now been determined such that it is indeed actual, concrete, self-reproducing, or endogenous existence, which requires no external or exogenous determinants for its systematic reproduction.

The presentation then is one of conceptual reproduction of the concrete in successive steps (levels of abstraction); if successful, the presentation is able to grasp the concrete as mediated by the theory (that is, to theoretically reconstitute the empirical "facts," which were at the basis of the initial inquiry). Such a process of inquiry and reconstruction can of course never be posited as definitive and completed.

*Levels of abstraction may further be characterized by degree of necessity versus degree of contingency of the elements theorized. It is the purpose of the theory to single out which elements of the object of inquiry may be theorized as necessary to the object, and which elements are (merely) contingent. Of course the more the presentation moves toward lower levels of abstraction, the more (historically) contingent elements have to be incorporated.

MARX'S METHOD IN *CAPITAL*

KINDS OF INTERPRETATION

I have indicated that Marx is hardly explicit about the method he uses in *Capital*. The scarce explicit remarks, moreover, are open to different interpretations. Of course such interpretations are linked to the understanding of the content. In this respect the history of Marxism has resulted not only in various fashions (such as those led by Bernstein or Althusser) but also in specific research programs (linked to minor groups, e.g., around Lukács and Korsch or Gramsci).

In general, interpretations can be of three sorts, and one can find all three within the Marxist tradition. The first allots authority to, in this case, *Capital* and sticks in an exegetic way to the text. In terms of the development of a scientific program this is not very fruitful. The second is historiographic, and for this critical approach one cannot normally stick to a single text. The third type of interpretation is heuristic. Under the heuristic approach, *Capital* has proved to be a fruitful source. (Indeed, this is what makes a work a classical text.)

Aspects of these three approaches, in general, cannot be kept separate. The historiographer, for example, will at some point be faced with exegetic questions, and good theoretical history will end up with either heuristically interesting questions or heuristically interesting loose ends. My remarks in the remainder of this section and the next derive primarily from the heuristic interest.

SYSTEMATIC DIALECTIC IN *CAPITAL*?

Is Marx's method in *Capital* systematic dialectic? And if not, what kind of dialectic is it? Even if I were able to answer this question, this is not the place to do so in a well-balanced and well-documented way. (One need only consult the scholarly works of Murray 1988b and Smith 1990c to see that the issue is quite complicated.) In the next section I consider, from a limited point of view, only one aspect of the question: How can we evaluate the very beginning of *Capital*, that is, the starting point, in terms of a systematic dialectic? However, these considerations do not provide an answer to the question of the systematic dialectical character of *Capital* as a whole. For several reasons, there cannot be a simple yes or no answer to this question.

Hegel's logic is not a philosophy of social science or of political economy in particular. It is propaedeutic to that philosophy, which needs to be developed on the basis of that logic. There are several ways to do this, and the choice is connected to one's view of the object realm of the science. However, the object realm is inseparable from the content of the science. Further, these ways are tied not only to the object realm but also to one's view (vision) of the state of the science in relation to the phenomena (although this is closely related to the object realm).[3]

It follows that the philosophy and methodology of a science cannot be developed in separation from the content of the science. Both Hegel and Marx seem to have been well aware of this point. (And I am very much aware of it from my own research experience.) Nevertheless, I believe that much of the trouble with Hegelian Marxism is due to an exaggerated puritanism in this respect. I want to make a plea for making the philosophy and methodology of systematic dialectical social science explicit. However, this can never be a once-and-for-all matter. It can never be more than a temporary state of the art since it is necessarily linked to (one's view of) the state of the science. Marx, for example, might have written such a treatise after the completion of the *Grundrisse* (i.e., more than the current Introduction) and a new one after the completion of Volume 1 of *Capital* and another new one after the completion of Volume 3 of *Capital*.

There are indeed several ways to proceed from Hegel's dialectical logic. For example, within an agreed movement from abstract to concrete categories, as well as an agreement that Hegel's *Begriffs* logic cannot be applied or developed immediately to the social science of capitalism, Murray (1988b) stresses general versus determinate abstractions and their development, Smith (1990c) a triadic development, and Reuten and Williams (1989) systemic necessity versus contingency as well as negation and particularization.[4] In their works these authors do not deny the importance of that which is stressed by the others; only the emphasis is different.[5]

In *The Philosophy of Right*, originally published in 1821, Hegel does develop *Begriffs* logic into social science (i.e., in his theory of the state). It is a social scientific work into which Hegel develops his own logic. Although *The Philosophy of Right* contains, in my view, a number of outstanding insights (especially in the Introduction), it does not live up to Hegel's logic. At least it can be highly criticized from the point of view of Hegel's logic. For example, it does not (cf. Smith 1990c) follow a strict triadic movement—even if the three parts do so, the movements within the parts definitely do not. Hegel leaves no room for the articulation of general versus determinate abstractions (cf. Murray 1988b), and the articulation of the necessary versus the contingent is far from sound (cf. Reuten and Williams 1989).[6]

I will not blame anyone for not seeing a systematic conceptual development in Marx's *Capital*. When I first read the work I knew little about dialectics and conceptual development, and my reading was a flat one. A later reading though—with some knowledge of dialectics—did not convey to me more than three broad levels of abstraction in line with the three volumes of *Capital*. Nevertheless, and perhaps paradoxically, certain moments in Marx's *Capital* contain a conceptual development. In general this applies to his concept of tendency and, in particular, that of the tendency of the rate of profit to fall. But in a recent reading of the first three chapters of Volume 1 (undertaken in writing this chapter), I once again found them very disappointing in terms of systematic conceptual development.

THE STARTING POINT OF *CAPITAL* AND THE THEORY OF VALUE

A SYSTEMATIC STARTING POINT

The opening sentences of *Capital* are:

> The wealth of societies in which the capitalist mode of production prevails appears as an "immense collection of commodities" [quoted from Marx 1971a]; the individual [*einzelne*] commodity appears as its elementary form. Our investigation therefore begins with the analysis of the commodity. (Marx 1976b, 125)

Is this the systematic starting point of a dialectical systematic presentation? It might be argued that the first section of Marx's chapter, as well as the very important second one on the double character, introduce a number of preparatory notions; therefore, the actual starting point would be the third section, which again starts off with the commodity (cf. Murray 1988b, ch. 12; see also Eldred and Roth 1978). But even so, is this, the commodity, the most abstract all-embracing concept for the capitalist mode of production? I doubt it. For example, does it embrace in itself a notion of the activity of creation of useful objects in capitalist form? The commodity is certainly a ubiquitous phenomenon. Marx certainly develops from it the form of capitalist production (from Chapter 4 onwards). Nevertheless, from a systematic dialectical point of view, this is not convincing.

I think that Marx does what he says he does (see the quotation above): analyze. In fact he repeats several times statements to that effect. What kind of analysis is this? It is certainly not the kind of axiomatic analysis that proceeds from definitions. Marx does not define. (At one place in the English translation the word occurs—"as it has just been defined"—but in German the word is *bestimmt*, i.e., determined.) What Marx seems to do, at least in Part 1, is conceptual analysis rather than dialectical conceptual development. Again, there is a process, but it seems to go from simple (rather than abstract) to complex concepts. Each time it seems to be the analysis of concepts that keeps the process moving. It is not an internal proceeding from contradictions and their transcendences (negation or particularization). (Note that the latter proceeding would not exclude the analysis of moments—but then moments would need to have been posited as such.)

I do not think that my interpretation in this respect is fundamentally different from either Smith's (1990c) or Murray's (1988b), although the emphases are somewhat different. Further, Marx's "Notes on Wagner" do not falsify such a reading. Smith quotes from this text:

> In the first place I do not start out from "concepts" hence do not start out from "the concept of value." . . . What I start out from is that simplest social form in which the labor-product is presented in contemporary society, and this is the "commodity." (Smith 1990c, 23; cf. Murray 1988b, xvii, 143)

In the next sections I further consider Marx's conceptual analysis, especially focusing on the type of abstractions that are being used.

ABSTRACT LABOR AND VALUE

In the first two sections of Chapter 1 of *Capital* Marx introduces the twin concepts of *abstract labor* and *value*. They seem to exist by way of a transformation whose character is hardly expanded upon.

Abstract Labor

When the term *abstract labor* is introduced for the first time, Marx refers to a transformation:

> If then we disregard the use-value of commodities, only one property remains, that of being products of labor. But even the product of labor has already been transformed in our hands. [*Jedoch ist uns auch das Arbeitsprodukt bereits in der Hand verwandelt.*] If we make abstraction from its use-value, we abstract also from the material constituents and forms which make it a use-value. . . . The useful character of the kinds of labor embodied in them also disappears; this in turn entails the disappearance of the different concrete forms of labor. They can no longer be distinguished, but are altogether reduced to the same kind of labor, human labor in the abstract. (Marx 1976b, 128)

Here abstract labor is not posited as universal labor in contradiction with particular labor (the universal-particular contradiction referred to above). Rather, the particular labor appears to be abstracted away. We have a transformation that seems to be established via a *reductive abstraction*: The disregarding of use-values, the abstraction from use-value, and the disappearance of the useful character of labor give rise to the reduction to abstract labor. I propose to call this (reductive) abstract labor Λ. This abstraction is conveyed by way of a (metaphorical) reference to a transformation in the sense of a transubstantiation (the phrase "transformed in the hand" undoubtedly stresses the connotation of the German term *Verwandlung* when signifying the change of the eucharistic elements at their consecration in the Mass—in the priest's hand).

Anticipating the discussion of the current abstract-labor theory of value below, it may be observed that at this point there is no reference to the market—thus no reference to a real abstraction or an abstraction in practice.[7]

However, from the middle of the second section of Chapter 1 onward, abstract labor is (also) treated as a *simplifying abstraction* (or a simplifying assumption):

> In the interests of simplification, we shall henceforth view every form [*Art*, i.e., kind] of labor-power directly as simple labor-power; by this we shall simply be saving ourselves the trouble of making the reduction. (Marx 1976b, 135)

The extent to which this is important depends not only on how much of a labor embodied theory one wants to read in Marx (see below) but also whether at some stage one would want to apply the theory empirically. I think that within a labor embodied theory this simplification precludes the adding up of labor time before settling the trouble of making the reduction. (However, actually settling the trouble would then take one into Smithian [1933] labor-commanded waters, or the realm of Keynes's [1936] wage unit.) Indeed, I believe that this simplifying abstraction (assumption) makes a quantitative procedure at the empirical level of adding up concrete pre-market hours of labor very dubious.

If *i* and *j* are particular (concrete) kinds of labor, and if we consider that labor only under the aspect of being particulars, then their respective labor hours (L_i and L_j) cannot be added up. (For reasons of simplicity all my equations below are restricted to two kinds of labor, *i* and *j*. Of course they hold for the set of all kinds of labor.)

If α_i and α_j are discounting coefficients and if Λ is (reductive) abstract labor as indicated above, then we may write $\alpha_i L_i + \alpha_j L_j = \Lambda$. Next we may make the simplifying assumption $\alpha_i = \alpha_j$ (= 1), but this does not get us to the concrete empirical level.[8] For that we need a procedure to quantify the discounting coefficients. It is hard to see how this could be done prior to the market.

(Later I show how, because of the dialectical contradiction of particular labor being universal labor at the same time, the labor time *i* and *j* can in principle be added up as labor hours in the abstract (l): $l_i + l_j = l$, even though we cannot add them up as particulars L. This may be done on the basis of a dialectical abstraction rather than on the basis of a [Marxian] reductive abstraction.)

Value

Is value an entity that exists prior to exchange? (This question is discussed again when I examine current Marxist theories of value.) I think that Marx takes it as such, although there are a number of texts that would refute this view. This is how value is introduced for the first time. Abstract labor is further specified as:

> merely congealed quantities of homogeneous human labor, i.e., of human labor-power expended without regard to the form of its expenditure. All these things now tell us that human labor-power has been expended to produce them, human labor is accumulated in them. As crystals of this social substance, which is common to them all, they are values—commodity values [*Warenwerte*]. (Marx 1976b, 128)

And somewhat further on:

> How is the magnitude of this value to be measured? By means of the quantity of the "value-forming [*bildenden*, i.e., constituting] substance," the labor contained in the article. This quantity is measured by its duration, and the labor-time is itself measured on the particular scale of hours, days, etc. (Marx 1976b, 129)

From this and other passages there seems hardly any doubt that there is some kind of labor embodied view of value (see below) and that it is seen to exist prior to exchange. Nevertheless, although value exists prior to exchange, it is always objectified:

> Human labor-power in its fluid state, or human labor, creates value, but is not itself value. It becomes value in its coagulated state, in objective form. (Marx 1976b, 142)

Thus value is identified with the (reduced) abstract labor Λ, insofar as it is objectified or expended. Quite another issue is that exchange-value (the forms of exchange-value) is the only mode of expression or form of appearance of value (which is the subject of section 3, Chapter 1 of *Capital*).

The problem with this concept of value is that it relies on an abstract entity, the reduced abstract labor, but it is also given—already at this level—a fairly concrete meaning, especially because of what is added on measurement. It is not made clear, however, how we can undertake this measurement ("on the particular scale of hours, days, etc.") prior to the market because we are left in doubt about the actual discounting to simple labor.

EMBODIMENT: MORE THAN A METAPHOR?

What do we make of all the natural-physical references that Marx uses in order to explain what he means by abstract labor and value, such as "crystals of this social substance," "congealed quantities of . . . labor," and indeed the notion of "labor embodied" itself? (All these appear for the first time in Marx 1976b, 128, but are used throughout Chapter 1.) Are they merely metaphors? The following quotation seems to point at a "merely" interpretation:

> Not an atom of matter enters into the objectivity of commodities as values; in this it is the direct opposite of the coarsely sensuous objectivity of commodities as physical objects. . . . However, let us remember that commodities possess an objective character as values only insofar as they are all expressions of an identical social substance, human labor, that their objective character as values is therefore purely social. (Marx 1976b, 138–39)

The least we can say is that—apart from in this quotation and a few other places—the metaphors have somewhat taken over the presentation.

In sum, I think we can safely say that Marx presents an abstract-labor *embodied* theory of value. This term may seem confusing with respect to the labor embodied versus abstract-labor debate. My reason for introducing it is not to arrive at a synthesis. The point is that, on the one hand, Marx does not propose to add up concrete labor hours $L_i + L_j$ into an L that is taken for the sum of these concrete labor hours (= concrete-labor embodied). Instead he starts off from abstract entities ("crystals of social substance"):

$$\Lambda_i + \Lambda_j = \Lambda \qquad (1)$$

In objectified form these are values. The abstract entities Λ_i and Λ_j are homogenous. These seem to be equivalent to:

$$\alpha_i L_i + \alpha_j L_j = \Lambda \qquad (2)$$

The L_i and L_j are not homogenous. Thus from (1) and (2) we have:

$$\alpha_i = \Lambda_i / L_i \qquad (3)$$

which is the value productivity of concrete particular labor *i*. (Thus when Marx says value is labor he means presumably that value is simple labor.) By simplifying the assumption, equation (2) reduces to:

$$L_i + L_j = \Lambda \qquad (4)$$

(The simplifying assumption does *not* say $L_i + L_j = L$.) Thus on the one hand we have a reductive abstraction coupled with a simplifying assumption: By way of reductive abstraction we got to abstract entities (Λ); concrete entities (L_i) may actually be discounted to the abstract entities (or the other way around). On the other hand, these entities are taken to be premarket entities, which come into existence in production. As objectified they are values, and this constitutes value as an embodiment. It is a secondary question if the discounting will be seen to be possible prior to exchange. Whatever the answer is, this will not affect the embodied character of the abstract entities.

VALUE-FORM AND VALUE FORM

Marx goes to great lengths to develop the form of appearance of value from the simple form to the money form (section 3 of Chapter 1 of *Capital*). The upshot of this is the demonstration that Ricardian value (L_i, L) does not appear immediately, and that the "whole mystery of the form of value lies hidden in this [the simple] form" (Marx 1976b, 139), not in the money form. (The latter point bears political importance also, in relation to Marx's polemic against Proudhon.) Although I do not wish to dispute the importance of these issues, the stress on these (also in terms of mere length of text) has underrated the importance of the value-form itself. This may sound cryptic. The point is that *value form* has two meanings (which I distinguish by hyphenating one of the meanings as explained below). Let me say first that the two meanings have led to different interpretations of Marx as well as to certain political practices evolving from it. Consider, for example, the following quotations:

IA: Therefore they [commodities] only appear as commodities, or have the form of commodities, insofar as they possess a double form, i.e., natural form and value form. (Marx 1976b, 138)

IB: The price or money-form of commodities is, like their form of value generally, quite distinct from their palpable and real bodily form; it is therefore a purely ideal or notional form. (Marx 1976b, 189)

II: Hence, in the value-relation, in which the coat is the equivalent of the linen, the form of the coat counts as the form of value. (Marx 1976b, 143)

Let us say, for the sake of argument—I do not agree with it—that *value* is a genus and that *exchange value* is its species. In quotations IA and IB it is clear that *value form* refers to the genus value. This is clear from the context, and in IB it says so explicitly: "value generally." Thus we are referred to value as a form itself. In quotation II, "form of value" refers to the species. Although in these quotations the context helps us out, this is often not the case. (The formulations in German do not shed light here; Marx always uses the term *Wertform*.) I am not sure that Marx was aware of this problem with the term *value form*. (But perhaps I say so only because I myself have struggled with it so much.) Anyway, I propose to write *value-form* for meaning I and *value form* for meaning II.[9]

Two final remarks. First, it seems that in much of Marxist writing the problems of the value form have been stressed at the expense of the problems of the value-form. Second, a related issue that I have not been able to analyze properly is Marx's usage of the terms *form*, *expression*, and *appearance*. He just seems to treat them as synonyms.

Labor Embodied versus Abstract-Labor Theory of Value: Some Current Controversies

Interpretations of Marx's Theory of Value

Although the first chapter of *Capital*, discussed in the previous section, is value theoretical, it is not Marx's complete theory of value. The theory extends throughout the three volumes. Much debate has been centered around the consequences of the introduction of the general rate of profit in Volume 3 (the so-called transformation problem). I will not concentrate on this part of the debate[10] but rather proceed to the scope of the transformation alluded to in Chapter 1 of Volume 1 (i.e., the introduction of the concept of abstract labor as identified with value) and the related methodological questions of abstraction. Indeed there are many transformations in

Capital, each located at particular levels of abstraction. All those are important, though not every one of them is equally easy, or difficult, to grasp. In this respect I agree with Tony Smith when he writes:

> Most Marxist and non-Marxist accounts [of *the* Volume 3 transformation] have concentrated exclusively on the problems involved in establishing the quantitative identity of values and prices, surplus value and profits.
>
> It is true enough that Marx himself directed considerable attention to these equations. But there is much in his theory that points away from granting them a place of absolute centrality. Consider, for example, the relationship between "expanded accumulation" and "simple reproduction." No Marxist has ever claimed to prove that the sum total of values accumulated in expanded accumulation equals the sum total reproduced in simple reproduction. No non-Marxist has ever claimed to refute Marx based on a proof of the non-equivalence of these magnitudes. Indeed the question of the mathematical relationship between the two magnitudes hardly makes sense. (Smith 1990c, 171)

There are two main accepted interpretations of Marx's theory of value: a labor embodied theory of value and an abstract-labor theory of value. It is shown below that these may usefully be subdivided. The differences between them are much obscured by the fact that the same terms are attributed different meanings in each of them. After expounding some problems with each of these interpretations in the remainder of this section, I then indicate how a Marxist labor theory of value might be reconstructed along systematic dialectical lines.

CONCRETE-LABOR EMBODIED THEORY

Marx's text in *Capital* opens up the way to a concrete-labor embodied theory of value: $L_i + L_j = \Lambda$. Marx's simplifying assumption, $\alpha_i = \alpha_j$, is then taken for a negligibility assumption and not for a heuristic assumption (in Musgrave's [1981] sense, see note 8). It is then only a small step to get to the immediately empirical observable $L_i + L_j = L$, where L_i and L are taken to be values (so-called labor values, measured in concrete labor time).

Simple as it is, there are three problems related to this theory: (1) It is not clear exactly how this is a theory of capitalism (rather than a transhistorically universal theory); (2) as an interpretation of Marx it is not clear how this theory is different from Ricardo's (it is indeed near to a Sraffian theory, where instead of the force of theoretical abstractions we have the force of just adding up: vectors); and (3) it is not obvious how this theory can be developed so as to be sufficiently explanatory.

ABSTRACT-LABOR EMBODIED THEORY

As I have indicated, an interpretation of *abstract-labor embodied* seems near to what Marx was getting at. But I believe that there are too many problems to stick with it. The problem is not so much that of the reductive abstraction $\Lambda_i + \Lambda_j = \Lambda$ (although I do have methodological objections to it). This need not prevent it from being developed into a consistent and applicable theory. The difficulty, however, is that the Λ is taken to be value, and that value is taken to be a premarket entity. It is not clear how we can ever make this theory operational. If we say, with Marx, that the former equation may be transformed into $\alpha_i L_i + \alpha_j L_j = \Lambda$, where the dimensions are so-called simple labor, then this seems an acceptable link from the abstract to the concrete level. At an abstract level of the development of this theory it is, of course, permissible (within this methodological approach) to assume the discounting coefficients to be one: $L_i + L_j = \Lambda$. That is by way of successive approximation. But one clearly cannot stick to this. If one does stick to it, the theory reduces to the concrete-labor embodied theory. Thus at some stage a procedure has to be developed for getting to the discounting coefficients. It has not been shown how this can be done prior to the market. Indeed, if we need the market to get to the coefficients, then we can no longer hold that value (Λ) is a premarket entity.

SUBSTANCE OF VALUE IN THE LABOR EMBODIED THEORIES

I believe that the labor substance metaphor has much bedeviled the Marxist theory of value, and as I have indicated, the metaphor originates with Marx. (Of course in this respect he was a child of his times.) Apart from anything else, both the concrete- and abstract-labor approaches will have to deal at some point with the transformation problem (i.e., the problem related to the introduction of the general rate of profit). The point is that within the labor embodied approach one has labor embodied at the abstract beginning and at the concrete end (in whatever way the end is the result of "redistribution"). Labor embodied thus seems to be "conserved" within the modifications proposed by the theory—modifications proposed either to capture real processes or to be a stage in, for example, successive approximation. This bears a resemblance to the classical physics conservation principle from which, according to Mirowski (1990), classical political economy borrowed.[11] Thus we seem to have a substance theory of value together with a notion of conservation of this substance that is carried over from the one (analytical) level of abstraction to the next. Thus there is a particular ontology of conservation (of labor embodied "value") behind this theory.

Moving from one level to the other does not involve a transformation in the sense of a "transubstantiation" (cf. Marx 1976b, 128, quoted above). Thus although *the* transformation relates to the move to a specific level of abstraction—the concrete appearances—this does not involve a transformation of substance.

What reason would this labor embodied strand of Marxism have for sticking to the substance metaphor? Clearly the effect of it has been the theory's focus on physical entities rather than the social form of those in capitalism (or rather than a focus on entities having a double form—use-value and value, physical and social—as the dialectical value-form theory would have it). The substance-embodied metaphor seems very much a "negative heuristic" (Lakatos 1974), which should save the priority Marxists give to production. Indeed, the stress on production is in my view one of the strong points of the Marxist paradigm. However, as I will show, it seems possible to theorize production and to give it a central place even if we cut loose the substance-embodied part of the theory. This would open the way for a truly social labor theory of value, which may be said to originate in outline with Marx, but which he did not complete (and which Marxists neglected to complete).

THE ABSTRACT-LABOR THEORY OF VALUE: ABSTRACTION IN PRACTICE

In one variety of the abstract-labor theory of value there is a shift in the status of the abstractions used in the theory. The theoretical abstractions are themselves taken to be a kind of mirror of the abstractions that people make in everyday life. Such a view would of course fit a materialist philosophy, but it is not restricted to it. The theory of value of this approach seems to have certain roots in Marx's theory in *Capital*, though I am inclined to see it more as a development from it. There is some question about the unity of this approach, and it is certainly not a fully developed theory (see, e.g., De Vroey 1982; Gleicher 1983, 1985; Eldred 1984b; and Bellofiore 1989, who expand on this question).[12] I think that with my distinction between concrete- and abstract-labor embodied I have clarified the differences between them. However, the result is that what is called *the* abstract-labor theory of value is now even more obscure and even less of a fully constructed theory.

In this approach, the concept *abstract labor* (also) refers to an "abstraction in practice" (cf. Marx 1971a, 30) or a "real abstraction" (Himmelweit and Mohun 1978, 75) or a "concrete abstraction." Thus it is argued that in the market, concrete labor (the labor of a carpenter or an information worker) actually takes the form of abstract labor expressed in money. Thus the actual abstraction in the market is that concrete labor is reduced to homogenous money; this is so at the input side of the production process (wages) as well as at the output side. The products of concrete labor are homogenized into money when concrete labor is commensurated as or converted into abstract labor.

Abstract-labor *embodied* theoreticians may not disagree with the argument so far, but the point is—further expanded upon below—that this view also entails a shift in the very concept of value. Within the abstraction-in-practice view, value is bound to be established in the market (hence a market concept) rather than having existence prior to it. This does not necessarily imply that this theory underrates the importance of production. Theoreticians within this approach will say that the defect of Sraffian or neo-Ricardian economics is its reduction of production to technical coefficients, that is, to techniques. They say that the production process is of primary importance. It is not clear, however, how this statement fits the importance they allot to exchange and the market.

SUBSTANCE AND THE MEASURE OF TIME

One determination of the concept of the abstraction *labor* and *abstract labor* is the question of whether it is a transhistorical or general abstraction, as opposed to a determinate abstraction particular to capitalism or, more generally, commodity-producing modes of production (cf. Murray 1988b, ch. 10; and Arthur 1986, 11–12 on first-order and second-order mediations). Arthur (1986, 12–19, cf. 47) points out how Marx in the *Economic and Philosophic Manuscripts of 1844*—in contradistinction to *Capital*—uses the term *labor* in a determinate sense. I would prefer to conceptualize labor as a determinate abstraction particular to capitalism, for example.

If we say that labor is needed to produce commodities, this is not very telling. It is more telling if we say that a certain amount of labor is needed to produce a commodity. Labor under the aspect of time is certainly a determinate abstraction. There are numerous cultures in which the aspect of time is of no importance in connection with the activity of labor. Anyway, there are good reasons to believe that labor under the aspect of time is at least determinate to a commodity-producing society if not just a capitalist society. (Cf. Mirowski 1990, 1991, on all kinds of standardization with the emergence of the market—pounds of apples, etc. Mirowski's argument could be extended to argue that labor under the aspect of time is equally a standardization that emerged with the institutionalization of the labor market. If this makes sense, then stories such as Smith's [1933, 1:41–42] on beaver and deer hunters of the "early and rude state of society" for whom "the quantities of labor necessary for acquiring different objects seems to be the only circumstance which can afford any rule for exchanging them for one another" are merely part of a method of theoretical history—as Skinner [1985, 29] suggests.)[13]

It is now tempting to say that labor under the aspect of time, that is, labor time, is a real capitalist abstraction (and perhaps also a real abstraction in other commodity-producing societies). However, there may be a problem of logical order here. Why would labor time be a real social abstraction? Not for its own sake. Pounds of apples (apples are never identical) have become a real social abstraction because apples are sold on the institutional market (i.e., they take the value-form). Similarly, I would argue, labor time is a real social abstraction *because* labor (-power) is sold on the market (i.e., because labor has taken the value-form). Therefore the concept of value is prior to that of labor time.

Thus we have two real social abstractions. First, human activity takes the value-form. (Within the history of capitalism up to now, certain activities have been excluded; increasingly, however, household and leisure-time activities are at least being calculated in terms of value.) Second, because human activity takes the value-form, that activity is considered to be labor under the aspect of time, that is, labor time.[14]

But what does it mean to say that labor time is "embodied" in a commodity? Or that labor is the "substance" of value? Clearly labor time is not some stuff that we find in the commodity (or even "beyond" it: I consider that even within a classical essence-appearance model at least some stuff/substance is not meant to be the essence). Thus *embodiment* and *substance* seem to be metaphors. In general there is nothing wrong with using metaphors to get an idea across. However, the metaphor may be misleading and go on to live a life of its own. In this case I think that within much of Marxism these metaphors have been taken literally. (Of course Marx's language gave rise to this. He took distance from the classical presentation in this respect, but he kept on using the metaphor.)

The point is that the real abstractions referred to are *social* issues.

RECONSTRUCTING ABSTRACT LABOR WITHIN A SYSTEMATIC DIALECTIC VIEW

This section provides some elements of a methodological outline of how a social labor theory of value may be derived from Marx's theory by way of reconstructing that theory. It is not an interpretation of Marx's theory. The reconstruction is one along the lines of a systematic dialectic as briefly introduced earlier. I confine myself to a few stages of such a theory. The systematic context is set out in Reuten and Williams (1989, ch. 1); my remarks expand on the concepts of abstract labor and value set out in that work.

In an earlier section I indicated how Marx derives the concept of abstract labor. He does this on the basis of a reductive abstraction, not a dialectical logical abstraction. Marx arrives at his concept of abstract labor in abstraction from particular and concrete labor: The latter is reduced to elements making up human labor in the abstract, metaphorically referred to as crystals of social substance. As this objectified social substance, they are value(s) (Λ in the notation introduced above).

It was also indicated that the concrete labor L_i and L_j cannot be added up as particulars. However, because of the dialectical contradiction of particular labor being simultaneously universal labor, the labor time *i* and *j* can in principle be added up as labor hours in the abstract (l): $l_i + l_j = l$, even though we cannot add them up as particulars L. Similarly we can add up acres of land even if we know their qualities to be different; the same goes for pieces of fruit. But this is a dialectical logical abstraction and not a simplification. Within an approach of dialectical conceptual development, l_i and l_j may have abstract existence as *l*. But this very approach purports to concretize this abstract existence to the level of concrete and phenomenal existence. At the abstract level it is not impossible to quantify, but any such quantification will have only abstract meaning—and sometimes makes hardly any sense.[15] To take an example: The abstract "animal" has concrete existence as my cat Mitzy or as the fly she is catching; it is not impossible to think of them as two animals and to add them up as such. But we cannot add them up as particulars. Also, many mathematical operations make no sense: Half a cat plus half a fly do not make one animal. The dialectical contradiction is that Mitzy is a cat and an animal at the same time. A fly and a cat cannot be added up as particulars, but only in the abstract.

Thus we have the dialectical contradiction $L_i \cdot\times\cdot l$ (where $\cdot\times\cdot$ indicates dialectical contradiction).[16] At this level, $l_i + l_j = l$ is fairly empty; it is indeed an abstract statement, a statement at the abstract level of theory (though the statement is true and remains true even if we move to concrete levels of the theory: In fact we do speak in practice of U.S. labor expended). In the market, people do not reckon in terms of the abstract *l*. Nor do they reckon in terms of concrete L_i's because these cannot be added up. Because production inputs and outputs diverge (and because in capitalist production such divergence itself is not the aim, it is production for others) they have to be reduced to a common denominator, which is value. Value is thus constituted as universal as opposed to the particularity of the physical inputs and outputs. (Note that in this view, labor, even *l* or *l* objectified, is not value. Here the theory clearly diverges from Marx's.) In the market, value actually gets shape in its expression in terms of money. If we restrict ourselves to the output, and to the value-added component, we may write *m* for the monetary expression of labor, as it is actually realized in the market. Thus *m* is also the value productivity of labor. In the market then, the contradiction $L_i \cdot\times\cdot l$ is transcended at a more concrete level into what I provisionally call mL_i (but should call ml_i as indicated below). mL_i is a sum of money (in terms of dollars, for example, though this belongs to an even more concrete level of the theory). In the market, labor actually takes the value-form. Thus labor is actually converted (transformed) into an abstract entity. It is actual and capitalist abstract labor, which is capitalist value. (This opens up an enormous terminological confusion, because here and in the abstract-labor embodied theory the same words are used to denote different concepts. This is, however, inevitable if one wants to keep in touch with everyday language.)

Perhaps a somewhat subtle differentiation (that is, for the current purposes) is that in the market the $L_i \cdot\times\cdot l$ contradiction is transcended by way of positing it, more concretely, in the abstract moment (*l*) of the contradiction. Thus we should write ml_i.

At a somewhat more concrete level we may have diverging monetary expressions of labor, whence we have $m_i l_i$. (In Reuten and Williams 1989, ch. 2, it is explained how this expression bears on the aggregate income $Y = ml = \Sigma m_i l_i$.)

In comparison with the abstract-labor embodied theory, the upshot of all this is that the simple labor discounting that bedevils the theory pertains to a process that actually takes place in the market (m_i, m_j). Of course the current theory maintains that value has no existence prior to the market. But this is far from saying that it does not affect production. In Reuten and Williams (1989, 66–68)[17] it is explained how the commensuration in the market ($m_i l_i$) is anticipated by capital and so gives rise to what we have called an ideal precommensuration in production (properly written $m_i'L_i$). Thus the labor process is in fact calculated in terms of value (i.e., money).

Let me summarize the different views in terms of the symbols that have been used. The systematic dialectic view states:

$$l_i + l_j = l \qquad (5)$$

This makes sense to the extent labor is considered as universal. The expression is rather empty and in that sense is an abstract statement (of universal labor in the abstract).

$$L_j + L_j = L \qquad (6)$$

This makes no sense: We cannot add up different labor as particular labor.

$$m_i l_i + m_j l_j = ml \qquad (7)$$

This is the expression for real abstract labor. It is also the expression for value (in terms of money).

The concrete-labor embodied view states:

$$L_i + L_j = \Lambda \tag{8}$$

or

$$L_i + L_j = L \tag{9}$$

If there is a concept of abstract labor at all then this is Λ. All the quantities in equations (8) and (9) are in terms of value, measured in hours.

The abstract-labor embodied view states:

$$\Lambda_i + \Lambda_j = \Lambda \tag{10}$$

This is the expression for abstract labor = value (abstract labor is the result of a reductive abstraction). Equation (10) is equivalent to or may be transformed into:

$$\alpha_i L_i + \alpha_j L_j = \Lambda \tag{11}$$

where the dimensions are simple labor = value, measured in hours. Only by simplifying (heuristic) assumption does (11) reduce to (8).

CONCLUSIONS

It is somewhat grandiose to say that *Capital* was an effort at developing systematic dialectics for social science—beginning with political economy—in confrontation with Hegel's work. (But then the qualifications in this respect as set out by Murray [1988b] and Smith [1991] seem plausible.) I have shown that a reconsideration of the first chapter of *Capital* reveals that Marx embarked on a different track from Hegel's logic. Marx felt that this method would have to be developed in the practice of research (cf. Murray 1988b). However, as with all founders of new paradigms, Marx's exact break with the previous paradigm(s) is unclear, and here this applies to both the method and the content. Therefore there is room for several interpretations as well as lines of research developing from *Capital*. And for the time being this does no harm: I sympathize with Feyerabend's anarchistic view even if I myself have rather definite inclinations as to the way in which the paradigm might fruitfully develop.

Systematic dialectical interpretations of Marx have always been in a minority. The majority of the Marxist tradition indeed took the dialectic for Hegelian claptrap. Heuristically the question of how far Marx reached in developing systematic dialectics is not very important—though it is interesting from a historiographic point of view. What is important is that from it a systematic dialectical social science may be (further) developed. If we take this project seriously, then one of its targets should be a critical study of *Capital* from that perspective. The critique of *Capital* in this chapter then has been a critique of Marx with (as far as I am concerned) Marx.

A systematic dialectical study of current society would have to be a four-stage project. These stages are those that I consider the stages of a systematic dialectical methodology.

The first step is a critical phenomenal analysis, which would need to concentrate on phenomena as reported in newspapers and everyday conversations rather than their filtered reports in books and journal articles. It is not obvious, for example, that labor-capital class or exploitation issues are the *phenomena* that require explanation rather than the phenomena, for example, of third-world catastrophes, oppression of women, unemployment, racism, the ecological environment, unequal distribution of income, and authoritarian relations. I am not saying in advance that the latter phenomena cannot be grasped in terms of the capital relation. I am saying that we need to step back regularly in order to think over our theory.

The second step is to reanalyze the analyses of those phenomena, as well as the existing systematic outlines in books and journal articles. This includes a critical study of philosophy and social science in perspective of the analysis carried out in the first step. The abstract determination should result from this.

Third is the reproduction of the concrete from the abstract determination in the second step.

And the fourth step is the critique of the analyses done in the second step.

All this may sound familiar, but it has to be carried out as an ongoing project. We cannot—ever—just take for granted what has been accomplished yesterday.

In this chapter I have picked out some value theoretical issues of the second step mentioned. I have suggested that although Marx provided the rudiments of a theory of social value (which nobody after him took any further), he was enmeshed in the physical substance-embodiment metaphor inherited from Hegel (substance) and classical political economy (embodiment). The Marxist tradition, rather than taking off from Marx in this respect, seems to have "fetishized" the metaphor (which is remarkable in the face of the antinaturalism that is one of the main characteristics of the Marxist tradition). This seems related to the priority Marxists give to the theorization of production. Indeed this is the strong point of the Marxist paradigm in comparison with any other. However, with it Marxism has tended to theorize the economy in one-sided physical terms. I believe that the metaphor has prohibited the breakthrough to a true theory of social value. It may be added that no other paradigm in economics has been able to undertake this breakthrough. I have indicated how the ground may be cleared for developing a social labor theory of value. Within such an approach it seems possible to dispense with the metaphor and the related concept of value without, however, cutting loose from the theorization of production.

Notes

I am grateful to Chris Arthur, Martha Campbell, Mino Carchedi, Paul Mattick, Jr., Patrick Murray, Fred Moseley, and Tony Smith for the intensive and enjoyable discussion of an earlier version of this paper, which has also benefited from comments by Michael Williams and Alexander van Altena, and especially from a second-round comment by Fred Moseley.

1. Paolucci (1974, 108) indicates how Francis Bacon was inspired by Machiavelli, who had taken the laws of statecraft as statecraft really is, rather than as it ought to be. Cf. Mattick, Jr. 1986, 113, on the natural law metaphor taken from "the medieval Christian picture of God as lawgiving sovereign of creation."
2. The remainder of this section draws on a section on method in Reuten 1988. An extensive discussion is in Reuten and Williams 1989, pt. 1.
3. If we are primarily interested in historiographic questions with respect to Marx's *Capital*, then the relevant phenomena are those of 1850.
4. Note, however, that Reuten and Williams (1989) is not an interpretation of Marx, although it owes a lot to Marx.
5. In Murray's (1988b) work, "contradiction" and its developmental powers are far less prominent than in either Smith (1990c) or Reuten and Williams (1989). In both Murray and Smith the concept of *form* is treated differently than in Reuten and Williams. Form is at the very basis of Reuten and Williams; it is developed as expressions of form, whereas both Murray and Smith allow for forms of form. As an interpretation of Marx, forms of form is correct, though I think it is a confusing concept.
6. Two examples that spring to mind are Hegel's view on the male-female functions, divisions, and roles and the role of the monarch. Even if Hegel's views on these issues can be explained in terms of the culture of his time, and even if in his time (around 1800) his views were far from conservative, they are still inadmissible if we take his own logic seriously: The systemic necessity of the roles referred to is not developed in Hegel 1967.
7. Later on there is such a reference: "But the act of equating tailoring with weaving reduces the former in fact to what is really equal in the two kinds of labor, to the characteristic they have in common of being human labor" (Marx 1976b, 142). However, if one wishes to read an abstract-labor theory of value in the first chapter of *Capital*, it might then be argued that a real abstraction is implicit in the transformation referred to in Marx 1976b, 128. Indeed the

concept of commodity is clearly connected to the market and exchange: "In order to produce the latter [commodities], he must not only produce use-values, but use-values for others, social use-values" (Marx 1976b, 131).

8. Musgrave (1981) distinguishes three kinds of assumptions: negligibility, domain, and heuristic. The simplification at hand does not say that the theory applies only to cases where $\alpha_i = \alpha_j$ (domain assumption). I assume that it also does not say that we can neglect the differences between the concrete labors because they have a negligible effect with respect to the problematic the theory addresses (negligibility assumption). Thus the simplification at hand might be a heuristic assumption, one that plays a role in one stage of a theory but must then be dropped in a later stage (as in the method of successive approximation).
9. In order to emphasize the possible confusions, I give a few more examples:
   A. "Human activity takes on the form of value" = "Human activity takes on the value-form." An abstract category (activity) takes on a particular—historically specific—form (the value-form).
   B. Were value assumed to be a transhistorical category (which I do not so assume), only then might one speak of "the form of value" = "the value form," as in: "The capitalist form of value is money" = "The capitalist value form is money."
   C. "The money-form and the capital-form are [particular] value forms," or, "The form of money is a [particular] form of value."
   D. "Money is a form of value" is very confusing, because it can be read as in (B) or (C). The same goes for: "The money form of value" (i.e., "the money-form of value," or, "the money form-of-value").
10. See Chapters 8 and 9 in this volume.
11. On redistribution, see Fine and Harris (1979), as well as the critique (on the manuscript) by Himmelweit and Mohun (1978). Note that within the usual algorithms the concrete-labor embodied theory is formally equivalent to a technical coefficients framework (see Gerstein 1976). This is also the point of the Steedman (1977) "Marx after Sraffa" critique.
12. References to the germinal literature of this approach are given by these authors as well as by Reuten and Williams 1989, 64. Although most adherents of a Hegelian-Marxist dialectic incorporate elements of this theory in theirs (e.g., Arthur, Backhaus, Eldred, Hanlon, Kleiber, Roth, Reuten and Williams), it is surely not the case that most abstract-labor theoreticians adhere to a Hegelian-Marxist dialectic. Conversely, not all of the later seem to take the nonembodied abstract-labor view.
13. Cf. also Marx (1976b, 164): "In all situations, the labor-time it costs to produce the means of subsistence must necessarily concern mankind, although not to the same degree at different stages of development." In a footnote he adds that among the ancient Germans the size of a piece of land was measured according to the labor of a day. However, such were accidental personal not standardized measures; cf. Mirowski 1991.
14. Therefore we can, as a representation of these real abstractions, formally write *ml* (where *m* is the monetary expression of labor, and *l* is labor). This is further explained later. (The argument in Reuten and Williams 1989, ch. 2, §16, for writing *ml* is somewhat obscure. I thank Alexander van Altena for pointing this out to me.)
15. Reuten and Williams (1989) aim to show how the abstract category *l* develops,

via the existence of the market and the complex of market relations, into the more concrete category of *ml.*

16. We can look at this contradiction both as particular labor L_i under the aspect of universal labor l: $l(L_i)$, and as universal labor under the aspect of particular labor: $L_i(l)$. Using this notation we may write: $l(L_i) + l(L_j) = l$. However, $L_i(l) + L_j(l) = L$ makes no sense.
17. See also Reuten 1988, 53–55.

5

Marx's Dialectic

Paul Mattick, Jr.

Replying, in the Postface to the second edition of *Capital*, to the accusation of Hegelianism leveled at him by critics of his publication, Marx insisted that his "dialectical method is, in its foundations, not only different from the Hegelian, but the exact opposite of it." At the same time he avowed himself "the pupil of that mighty thinker," acknowledging that he had "even, here and there in the chapter on the theory of value, coquetted with the mode of expression peculiar to him" (Marx 1976a, 102–3). It is evident that this verbal coquetry cannot be the measure of Marx's pupilship. To begin with, his initial writings are largely dominated by a determined struggle with Hegelian idealism. And, more to our point, his engagement in the project of a critique of political economy in 1857 involved a second phase of attention to Hegel, with a new appreciation of the "mighty thinker."

The remarks in a letter to Engels of 16 January 1858 are well known:

> In the *method* of treatment the fact that by mere accident I again glanced through Hegel's *Logic* has been of great service to me. . . . If there should ever be time for such work again, I would greatly like to make accessible to the ordinary human intelligence, in two or three printer's sheets, what is *rational* in the method which Hegel discovered but at the same time enveloped in mysticism. (Marx and Engels 1975b, 121)

The service rendered by Marx's reading of the *Logic* is evident in the rough draft of his critique of political economy now generally referred to as the *Grundrisse*, notably in the chapter on money.[1] That this influence lasted, at least on some level, to the writing of *Capital* can be seen in the corresponding section of that book, the analysis of money as the form of value in the first chapter of Volume 1, where the verbal flirtation with Hegelian categories is, as Marx said, apparent. In addition, his recourse to Hegel for inspiration in the treatment of the transformation of money into capital is both obvious in the *Grundrisse* and to be inferred from the existence of notes made on Hegel's "Doctrine of Being" between 1860 and 1863, that is, in the period between the publication of *A Contribution to the Critique of Political Economy* and that of the first volume of *Capital.*[2]

The question remains, however, what significance is to be attached to this. The rediscovery of the *Grundrisse* has led to a flood of interpretations of Marx's work as a materialist use of Hegel's dialectical logic, exemplified by Hans-Jurgen Krahl's declaration: "The basic concept of the Marxian critique of political economy, the commodity form of the product in its general validity for the capitalist social formation, can not be explained without Hegel's dialectic of Essence and Appearance" (Krahl 1970, 113–45). Roman Rosdolsky's book, *The Making of Marx's "Capital,"* similarly claimed that the *Grundrisse*, a key to the understanding of *Capital*, was a "massive reference" to Hegel's *Logic*, so that "academic critics of Marx will no longer be able to write without having first studied his method and its relation to Hegel" (Rosdolsky 1977, xiii).

The thought that mastery of Hegel's *Logic* is, as Lenin was one of the first to declare, a sine qua non for the comprehension of *Capital* is an alarming one, given the obscurities of the former work. It may even be seen as at loggerheads with Hegel's own conception of dialectic as "not an external form, but the soul and concept of the content," for "it can only be the nature of the content itself which spontaneously develops itself in a scientific manner of knowing" (Hegel 1892, 378; 1969b, 27)—an opinion certainly shared by Marx, though with a somewhat different meaning. Even if Marx's analysis of capital has, as he suggests, the form of an inversion of the Hegelian dialectic, its means and method should be discoverable in that analysis itself. Nonetheless, it is of interest to examine Marx's conception of the dialectic in *Capital*, with an eye both to the *ideegeschichtliche* question of Marx's use of the Hegelian logic and to a clarification of Marx's methodological procedure for its own sake.

Commenting in the Postface on the criticism of his book as overly "German-dialectical," Marx distinguished the "method of presentation" of theoretical material from the "method of inquiry." "The latter has to appropriate the material in detail, to analyze its different forms of development and to track down their inner connection. Only after this work has been done can the real movement be appropriately presented." It is the success of this presentation, he explains, that has given readers the impression of "an a priori construction" in the Hegelian fashion, while in fact the method employed is "exactly opposite" to such a procedure (Marx 1976a, 102).[3] In the *Grundrisse* Marx had already shown himself aware of this problem, noting (in the chapter on money) that "It will be necessary later . . . to correct the idealist manner of the presentation, which makes it seem as if it were merely a matter of conceptual determinations and of the dialectic of these concepts" (Marx 1973, 151).[4] We may ask both what was at stake for Marx in the differentiation of his method from Hegel's, and whether it might not have turned out, as the proponents of a neo-Hegelian Marx would have it, that the confusion of the two was not so easy to avoid, because of the logical structure proper to the value categories.

In the Postface Marx singled out the review of *Capital* by I. I. Kaufmann for its accurate depiction of the dialectical method. This depiction has two main aspects. First, Marx has sought to construct a social theory on the model of the natural sciences, understood as the attempt to discover the laws governing some domain of phenomena on the basis of empirical investigation. In social as in natural science, the facts that are to serve as material for theoretical generalization are to be determined by the researcher, independently (in the former domain) of the conceptions that the people studied have about their social circumstances. Whatever people imagine the character of their social life to be, "The only things of importance for this inquiry are that the facts be investigated as accurately as possible, and that they actually form different aspects of development vis-à-vis each other." Second, objects in the particular domain of knowledge investigated—society—are unlike those studied by physics and chemistry, but are like the objects investigated by biology in being characterized by laws of their evolution "from one form into another, from one series of connections into a different one." That is, there are no general laws of social life; "on the contrary, in [Marx's] opinion, every historical period possesses its own laws" (Marx 1976a, 100–101).

It is this second aspect of his theory that Marx identifies as its specifically dialectical one. The first constitutes the core of the "inversion" necessary to transform the dialectic from what he calls the "mystified form" it has in Hegel's hands to the "rational form" in which "it regards every historically developed form [of society] as being in a fluid state, in motion, and therefore grasps its transient aspect as well" (Marx 1976a, 103). The dialectic, that is, is identified not with a logic of theory construction, but with the idea of the essentially historical character of social formations, and so (in its "rational form") with the principle of the nonexistence of transhistorical laws of social reality.

Marx restated this principle in November 1877 in correspondence with another Russian student of his work, Mikhailovski, who had questioned what he took to be a general theory of history requiring passage of all social systems through a series of necessary stages. On the contrary, Marx replied, it was only his critic who

> must absolutely transform my sketch of the genesis of capitalism in Western Europe into an historico-philosophical theory of the general march, fatally imposed on all peoples, . . . [towards socialism]. But I beg his pardon. This is to do me at once too great honor and too great shame. (Marx 1968a, 1555)

One can of course come to more or less general conclusions, wrote Marx, by comparing the results of detailed studies of different areas and times. But a scientific understanding of social phenomena will never be achieved "with the master-key of a historico-philosophical theory whose supreme virtue consists in being supra-historical" (Ibid.).[5]

The rejection of such a "historico-philosophical theory" was at the heart of the youthful critique of Hegelianism—as represented by the work of the master himself and by the (in Marx's eyes) inadequate criticism of that work by the Young Hegelians—which culminated in Marx's collaboration with Engels on the writing of *The German Ideology*. "Where speculation ends," Marx wrote here,

> where real life starts, there consequently begins real, positive science, the expounding of the practical activity, of the practical process of development of people. Phrases about consciousness end, and real knowledge has to take their place. When reality is described philosophy as an independent pursuit loses its medium of existence. At the best its place can only be taken by a summing-up of the most general results, abstractions which are derived from the observations of the historical development of people. These abstractions in themselves, divorced from real history, have no value whatever. They can only serve to facilitate the arrangement of historical material. (Marx and Engels 1976, 37)[6]

This, of course, gives the choice of abstractions fundamental importance; in a passage prefiguring the remarks on the two methods (of inquiry and presentation) in the Postface, Marx describes the difficulty of comprehending history as beginning "when one sets about the examination and arrangement of the material—whether of a past epoch or the present—and its actual presentation" (Ibid.).

It is this difficulty that we find Marx confronting directly when in 1857–58 he began work on the critique of political economy. Summarizing his critique of the economists' assumption of the existence of general laws of production, Marx insists that although "there are characteristics which all stages of production have in common, and which are established as general ones by the mind . . . the so-called *general preconditions* of all production are nothing more than these abstract moments with which no historical stage of production can be grasped" (Marx 1973, 88). In the absence of a general theory of social life, how is the scientific study of a particular social formation to formulate its basic conceptual apparatus? Such "premises," Marx had explained in *The German Ideology*, are to be discovered through "the study of the actual life-process and the activity of the individuals of each epoch" (Marx and Engels 1976, 36).

The "study of the actual life-process," writes Marx in the Introduction to the *Grundrisse*, may seem to begin necessarily with consideration of a given population, the subject of economic activity. But this is wrong, because "population is an abstraction if I leave out, for example, the classes of which it is composed. These classes in turn are an empty phrase if I am not familiar with the elements on which they rest, e.g., wage labor, capital, etc. These latter in turn presuppose exchange, division of labor, prices, etc." That is, the concept *population*, insofar as it applies indifferently to all identifiable populations, does not serve to identify the particular character of a specific population. In order to do so it is necessary to add specifications (in Marx's terminology, "further determinations") to this high-level abstraction, until the analysis disengages the "simplest determinations" of this population's existence, that is, those on the basis of which an explanatory theory of the specific characteristics of its social order can be constructed (Marx 1973, 100).

These specifications are themselves abstractions, of course. "For example, the simplest economic category, say e.g., exchange value, presupposes population, moreover a population producing in specific relations. . . . It can never exist other than as an abstract, one-sided relation within an already given, concrete whole" (Marx 1973, 101). Its simplicity is not ontological but theoretical: That is, it is simple in relation to the particular explanatory project in which it plays a part, in that it is used to identify the system of social relations under investigation. Thus Marx commends Hegel for beginning his *The Philosophy of Right* with the concept of *possession*, for, although "there is no possession preceding the family or master-servant relations," this concept names the simplest juridical relation (Marx 1973, 102).

We may isolate two aspects of this conception of theory construction that correspond to the methods of inquiry and presentation discussed in the Postface to *Capital*. First the "simple" or elementary abstractions are discovered through analysis, on the basis of observation of the domain under study. "Observation," of course, itself denotes a complex operation, which makes use of the concepts made available by an existing discourse (in this case, that of political economy)—concepts that, in Marx's view, must themselves be critically rethought in terms of their relation, as products of it, to the specific historical period to whose description they are to be applied.[7] To the second method corresponds the subsequent construction of a theoretical system from the elementary concepts. The basis for this construction is the systematic relation between the elementary concepts discovered in the process of analysis ("For example, capital is nothing without wage labor, without value, money, price, etc.") (Marx 1973, 100).

Is there in this methodological conception an echo of the Doctrine of Being in Hegel's *Logic*? Population, though it may seem to designate a concrete object of economic analysis, is, says Marx, in reality a very abstract term, since it applies to all populations in all territories under all social-historical conditions. If it is to be used for explanatory purposes, it must be related to more specific determinations. Similarly, "Being," according to Hegel, seems the most "immediate" and simple concept for the description of reality because it applies to everything; but for this very reason it is inadequate for such description. It is an empty abstraction: "being, the indeterminate, is in fact *nothing*, and neither more nor less than *nothing*" (Hegel 1969b, 82). To acquire conceptual content, things described as being must be distinguished from other things by some features, thus becoming "determinate beings." Similarly, Hegel's conception that the further progress of logic involves the demonstration of the systematic interconnection of the elementary categories of thought is paralleled by Marx's "return journey" from the "simplest determinations" to a synthesized "rich totality of many determinations and relations" (Marx 1973, 100).

However striking this parallel may be, however, what Hegel and Marx have in common here is only the idea that the most abstract concept employed in an area of investigation, to be usefully applied in the analysis of specific objects, requires analytic specification. Although the *Logic* was undoubtedly in Marx's mind when he wrote his Introduction (which at any rate he omitted as inessential when he came to publish the results of his work), his text employs not a logic of being or even a logic of concepts, but an image of the theoretical analysis and synthesis of empirical data.

Marx demonstrates that a knowledge of Hegel is not required for this theoretical practice by observing that the correct method of inquiry was in fact "the path originally followed by economics at the time of its origins." The seventeenth-century founders of political economy "always begin with the living whole, with population, nation, state, several states, etc.; but they always conclude by discovering through analysis a small number of determinant, abstract general relations such as division of labor, money, value, etc." (Marx 1973, 100).[8] Unlike population, these abstractions identify fundamental traits of the particular social system—early capitalism—that the economists were concerned to analyze (though they mistakenly believed that they were discovering sociohistorical universals). Subsequently, the principle of synthesis was exemplified by "the economic systems" that followed these beginnings and "which ascended from the simple relations . . . to the level of the state, exchange between nations, and the world market" (Marx 1973, 100–101).

Moreover, Marx is at pains to emphasize that at every point in the process of empirical analysis and subsequent synthesis we are dealing with "a product of the working-up of observation and conception into concepts," that is, with "a product of a thinking head, which appropriates the world in the only way it can." A philosopher like Hegel, for whom (as a result of his place in the division of labor) "the conceptual world as such is the only reality," and to whom "the movement of the categories appears as the real act of production," may fall into the illusion of mistaking the resulting system of categories "as a product of the concept which thinks and generates itself" (Marx 1973, 101).[9] It was this illusion that Marx wished to ward off by correcting "the idealist manner of the presentation."

Though Marx speaks of "the concrete" reality that is the object of analysis as "the concentration of many determinations," these determinations are themselves categories, any of which "can never exist other than as an abstract, one-sided relation within an already given, concrete, living whole." The "concrete totality" achieved through theoretical synthesis following the process of analysis "is a totality of thoughts, concrete in thought, in fact a product of thinking and comprehending" (Ibid.).[10] Here the employment of a Hegelian mode of speech makes for confusion. The use of "abstract" and "concrete" as terms for the analysis of theories is unambiguous only for a system like Hegel's, in which both terms refer to cognitive elements, since the synthesis of a cognitive "concrete" from (relatively) "abstract" concepts is treated as ultimately identical with the really evolving structure of the natural and social world. It is because as "conceptions" abstractions are not aspects of reality but aspects of the conceptual appropriation of reality that concepts cannot, according to Marx, be said to have a life of their own, to be exhibited at work either in the process of history or in the arrangement of categories in a theoretical construction. The presentation of categories cannot, that is, be said to follow an "immanent logic," but must be understood as governed by the effort to account for the fundamental features of the social system under investigation.

We must then ask, however, what principles, if not those of a putative dialectical derivation, guide the sequence of categories in the construction of the Marxian theory. In attempting to answer this question, we may at the same time cast light on why Marx found the categories of the *Logic* so suitable a mode of speech for the unriddling of the nature of money by the working out of the value-form. There are two central issues to be discussed. The first is that of the choice of elementary concepts as a starting point; the second is that of the method by which the conceptual structure of commodity value is revealed.

The starting point is determined by the character of the enterprise: as Marx explained it in a letter to Lassalle of 22 February 1858, a "*critique of the economic categories* or, if you like, the system of bourgeois economy critically presented. It is a presentation of the system and simultaneously, through this presentation, a criticism of it" (Marx and Engels 1975b, 125). *Capital* is thus at once an attempt "to reveal the economic law of motion of modern society" (Marx 1976a, 92) and, as the subtitle reminds us, a "critique of political economy." As Marx conceived it, his enterprise constituted a response to a specific historical condition. The founders of political economy, as we saw, first worked out the elementary categories; these were then employed in the construction of theoretical systems. But economics "can only remain a science while the class struggle remains latent or manifests itself only in isolated and sporadic phenomena." The development of that struggle after 1830 "sounded the death knell of scientific bourgeois economics"; henceforth scientific progress could only take the form of the *critique* of that science (Marx 1976a, 96–97).

By designating his writings on economics with the word *Kritik*, Marx continued Kant's use of the word to denote an inquiry into the limits of application of a set of concepts in certain spheres of inquiry. The question of limits arises when the application of a system of concepts in some area leads to problems unsolvable by means of this system.[11] A critique in this sense corresponds to what Hegel called *Aufhebung* (translated hopelessly, but traditionally, as "supercession" or "sublation"). *Aufheben* has a double meaning, as Hegel explains it: "(1) to clear away, or annul . . . ; (2) to keep or preserve" (Hegel 1892, 180, §96). With respect to the critique of a conceptual system (or theory), the idea of *Aufhebung* involves a new system that replaces the prior one but "preserves" it at the same time, in the sense that it explains both the phenomena that formed the subject matter of the prior theory and its limitations.

But more is at stake in Marx's work than a relation between two theories, even when it is of the sort now commonly described as a scientific revolution. Since in Marx's conception theories are to be understood as representations of socially regulated experience, theoretical critique here echoes

Hegel's remark that dialectical consciousness is not "peculiarly confined to the philosopher," so that it "would be truer to say that dialectic gives expression to a law which is felt in all other grades of consciousness, and in general experience" (Hegel 1892, 149–50, §81). In this, Hegel's formulation of dialectic goes well beyond Kant's. Marx's represents a further, and distinct, development of the idea, since he regards his theoretical *Aufhebung*, the critique of political economy, as a response not to some inherent necessity located in the inadequacy of the conceptual structure of classical economics but as called for and rendered possible by the experienced crisis tendency of capitalism and the workers' movement responding to it. It was experience of the limits of capital that suggested the limits of political economy.

Marx's theory of capitalist society is not meant to be a replacement for political economy. It aims not just to demonstrate the analytic limits of economic theory but also to explain the hold of that theory over the inhabitants of the system. Thus the opening chapter of *Capital* ends with a discussion, under the heading of the "fetishism of commodities," of the way in which the money form obscures the working of the system by concealing "the social character of private labor and the social relations between the individual laborers" (Marx 1976a, 168–69). The discussion of the "Trinity Formula" at the conclusion of Volume 3 aims to demonstrate how not only "vulgar economics" but even the "best representatives" of classical theory, by accepting as fundamental categories for social analysis the representations of social relations developed within the system itself, inevitably "fell more or less into inconsistencies, half-truths and unresolved contradictions" (Marx 1982, 969).

In his *Contribution to the Critique of Political Economy* of 1859, the first published fruits of the labors undertaken in the *Grundrisse*, Marx described the crisis in economic theory at the time as follows:

> Since the determination of exchange-value by labor-time has been formulated and expounded in the clearest manner by Ricardo, who gave to classical political economy its final shape, it is quite natural that the arguments raised by economists should be primarily directed against him.

There follows a list of the four points to which the disagreements of the post-Ricardian economists can be reduced:

> *One*. . . . given labor-time as the intrinsic measure of value, how are wages to be determined on this basis? . . .
>
> *Two*. . . . how does production on the basis of exchange-value solely determined by labor-time lead to the result that the exchange-value of labor is less than the exchange-value of its product? . . .

> *Three*. . . . The exchange-value of commodities is . . . determined not by the labor-time contained in them, but by the relation of demand and supply. In fact, this strange conclusion only raises the question how on the basis of exchange-value a market-price differing from this exchange-value comes into being. . . .
>
> *Four*. . . how does the exchange-value of natural forces arise? (Marx 1970a, 61–63)

A striking fact about this list of problems is that it contains a summary of *the main questions to which classical political economy had addressed itself*: an explanation of the distribution of the social product among the three great classes of workers, capitalists, and landlords, to be made possible by an explanation of the market-price system as a regulator of social production.

Thus the theoretical difficulties that produced the "disintegration of the Ricardian school" and called for a "scientific revolution" (Marx 1972, 8; Marx and Engels 1975b, 196–97) lay at the heart of the classical theory itself, and indeed (as Marx was to show) in the very concept of *labor* used to define the basic concept of *value*. Marx's critique—his "scientific revolution"—therefore involved not merely a reworking of economic categories but the construction of another set of concepts, explicitly social and historical ones. As Engels explained the break effected in the theory of capitalist society by the critique of political economy, that field

> begins with *commodities*, begins from the moment when products are exchanged for one another. . . . The product . . . is, however, a commodity solely because a relation between two persons or communities attaches to the *thing*, the product. (Engels 1970, 226)

The starting point of Marx's critique, accordingly, must be the category that is most elementary with respect to capitalist society *as theorized by classical theory*: the commodity. Its conclusion will be the replacement of this category as fundamental by that of the class relation between laborers and capitalists.

Hence the opening sentences of *Capital*: "The wealth of societies in which the capitalist mode of production prevails appears as an 'immense collection of commodities'; the individual commodity appears as its elementary form" (Marx 1976a, 125). The word "appears" (*erscheint*) is the first point at which we may, if we wish, detect the influence of Hegel's *Logic* on Marx's book, for in Hegel's usage it indicates a distinction between visible phenomenon and underlying essence (see Hegel 1892, 239ff., §131ff.). Here it points to the place at which Marx's critique will transform classical theory, by demonstrating the inadequacy of the concept of "commodity" for the analysis of capitalism as a mode of accumulation of wealth.

Marx begins, therefore, with the analysis of the commodity. He makes it clear that what is being analyzed is the commodity as theorized by the classical tradition, with footnotes relating basic statements in his text to classical writings. The result of this analysis is the description of the commodity as an object with both use-value and exchange-value, "the quantitative relation . . . in which use-values of one kind exchange for use-values of another kind" (Marx 1976a, 126). The form of use-value, the shape in which it is to be recognized, is the same as that of the commodity as a kind of thing itself; for exchange-value to be knowable it must also have some "form of appearance." As always, "appearance" indicates that exchange-value represents some more fundamental property of a commodity, its value. In section 3 of this first chapter Marx considers exchange-value as the form of value in great detail. It is here that his coquetry with the Hegelian vocabulary is the most visible, where Marx wishes "to trace the development of the expression of value contained in the value-relation of commodities from its simplest, almost imperceptible outline to the dazzling money-form" (Marx 1976a, 139). Here if anywhere we will find a dialectical logic. Let us look, therefore, at the mode of this development.

The dialectic that Hegel aims to follow in the argument of the *Logic* may be described (with all the distortions of concision) as follows: a category, originally found at play in ordinary language, is shown to be necessary for the description or reality but is also found to lead to an incoherent, or "contradictory," characterization of reality. This provides the demonstration of the indispensability of a further category, which makes possible the resolution of the contradiction discovered in the application of the earlier one. The chain of categories constructed in this manner is to demonstrate (to quote Charles Taylor's lucid commentary) "that our categorial concepts as we ordinarily understand them, unrelated by radical necessity, are in some way contradictory; and that this contradiction can only be resolved (or, in fact, reconciled) by seeing them as linked in a rational structure" (Taylor 1975, 227). In fact, as Taylor among other students of Hegel has pointed out, the actual sequence of concepts in Hegel's *Logic* does not strictly follow this scheme, nor are the transitions from one category to the next often convincingly shown to be necessary. Even in the best cases, it must be said, the *necessity*, as opposed to the plausibility or illuminating character, of the transition between categories in the Hegelian dialectic—and hence of its being a *logic*—has not been convincingly made. Hegel, at any rate, simply asserts it. Nevertheless, the pattern of this "dialectical logic" does seem the model for Marx's analysis of the value-form in *Capital*.

Thus he begins section 3 of the first chapter with the results as demonstrated (in section 1) that commodities have a dual nature, as both use-values and exchange-values, so that they can "only appear as commodities . . . insofar as they possess a double form, i.e., natural form and value form." The value form required is known to all in money, which represents the values of commodities in contrast to "the motley natural forms of their use-values." Value, a property of all commodities, is represented only in the form of a particular commodity, the money commodity.[12] But how can this be? How does money represent the value of commodities? Section 2 has demonstrated that as values commodities are expressions of a "social substance," abstract labor, so that their character as values "is therefore purely social. From this it follows self-evidently that it can only appear in the social relation between commodity and commodity," that is, in exchange-value. This produces the following apparent contradiction: Value, a property of commodities, is visible only in the relation between commodities. Value, that is, seems to be at once an individual and a relational property. It is by resolving this contradiction that Marx attempts to explain the form of value, money, on the basis of the category of exchange-value (Marx 1976a, 138–39).

How is the value of a commodity represented? In line with his methodological prescription, Marx begins with "the simplest value-relation," that of one commodity to another of a different kind. Basic to this relation as "the simplest expression of the value of a single commodity" is the difference between the roles played by the two commodities involved. If y amount of commodity B is the exchange-value of x amount of commodity A, then A's natural form represents its use-value, and B's represents A's value: y is what, in B terms, x amount of A is worth. The equation of A and B as exchangeable represents their character as values as opposed to their character as use-values, with respect to which they are different and not exchangeable. But the value character of each is therefore visible only in the use-value body of the other.

The classical economists' analysis of value as labor explains why commodities have value, but it does not explain why we should find out what that value is in the act of exchange. But once we realize that this act, as an equation of two commodities, is thereby an equation of the kinds of labor that produced them, we can understand why the general character of being products of labor finds representation in exchangeability. "It is only the expression of equivalence between different sorts of commodities which brings to view the special character of value-creating labor, by actually reducing the different kinds of labor embedded in the different kinds of commodity to their common quality of being human labor in general" (Marx 1976a, 139–42). (This follows from Marx's conclusion in section 2 that "only the products of mutually independent acts of labor, performed in isolation, can confront each other as commodities" [Marx 1976a, 132]. Under such conditions of production there is no representation of social labor in abstraction from the particular kinds that make it up outside of exchange.)

That is: Value can be expressed only in the relation between two different things equated by the act of exchange; in its value-relation to B, A "signifies more than it does without it, just as some men count for more when inside a gold-braided uniform than they do otherwise" (Marx 1976a, 143). The analogy is not just a stroke of wit. Like the use of gold braid to signify authority, the use of commodity exchange to signify the social character of labor is a social-historical institution, not a fact of nature. This is shown, according to Marx, by the fact that commodity exchange could not be fully understood, even by as brilliant a theorist as Aristotle, until the advent of a form of society in which a generally accepted conception of human equality had rendered possible the idea of equating all forms of labor—a conception that became "possible only in a society where the commodity-form is the universal form of the product of labor, hence the dominant social relation is the relation between men as possessors of commodities." Thus "it is only a historically specific epoch of [social] development which presents the labor expended in the production of a useful article as an 'objective' property of that article, i.e., as its value" (Marx 1976a, 152–54).

So far, what Marx claims to have shown is that under certain historical conditions—those of capitalism, in fact—the labor expended in individual units of production is made into social labor (only) when the products of those units are exchanged, so that the social character of the labor expended in the production of any commodity is represented (only) by its exchangeability and the quantity of that social labor is represented (only) by the quantity of goods for which it can be exchanged. In the vocabulary of economics, value is represented (only) by exchange-value. Marx claims further that to have explained this is already to have in principle explained the riddle of money. He introduces his justification of this claim by a most Hegelian set of phrases:

> We perceive straight away the insufficiency of the simple form of value: it is an embryonic form which must undergo a series of metamorphoses before it can ripen into the price-form [in which value is represented by a quantity of money]. (Marx 1976a, 154)

Here we have one of Hegel's favorite metaphors for conceptual development, that of organic growth, and more fundamentally the suggestion that it is the "insufficiency" of the simple form that requires the appearance of the price form—of money. But the appearance of "dialectical logic" here is misleading. The insufficiency of the simple form is not logical but practical and material: It would not suffice as a mode of representation of value in a system in which all goods are conceived as products of homogeneous (social) labor. For this to be accomplished, value must be represented in the form of a commodity to which all other commodities can be simultaneously equated by exchange.

As Marx says a few paragraphs later, "the simple form of value automatically passes over into a more complete form" (Marx 1976a, 154). Although this rhetoric ("passes over") also derives from Hegel, Marx again has something very straightforward in mind. Given that the value of a commodity is represented in the form of another, the natural form of that other commodity does not matter. What does matter is that some one commodity should play this role in relation to all others, because only in this way can value as such, as opposed to the value of one or another particular commodity, be represented. The value-form is not, that is, a form that "value takes" (like the appearance of essence in Hegel) but a form in which people represent something, the social character of their labor. The argument depends not on a purported logic of contradiction and resolution but on the gradual exposition of the (practical) requirements of a social practice.

To put it in the terms of Marx's two methods, the analysis of money begins by conceptual isolation of the elementary form of the relationship between a commodity and a sum of money, namely, that of a relation of exchange between commodities. In combination with the further basic conception that exchange functions in a capitalist economy as a means for the socialization of private labor, the necessity of a form, based in the exchange-relation, for the representation of value as a property shared by all commodities (as contributions to the social product) is demonstrated. In this way Marx explains the fact that commodity value is representable (in Hegelian terms, "appears") only in the form of the money equivalent.

It is true that the vocabulary of the *Logic* is present throughout this argument in forms that I have not discussed here; thus, much of the discussion in section 3 recalls the dialectic of quantity and measure, which links the Doctrine of Being to the Doctrine of Essence. But here too the appearance of "an a priori construction" due to the mode of expression is belied by the actual matter of the argument. Thus, for example, the important contention that "the magnitudes of different things only become comparable in quantitative terms when they have been reduced to the same unit" (Marx 1976a, 141) is not in its origins a "materialist inversion" of Hegel's treatment of quantity but derives directly from Sismondi's discussion of value in the *Etudes sur l'economie politique* studied and excerpted by

Marx in his preparatory studies for the *Grundrisse* (Schrader 1980, 128ff.). In short, there is no reason why we should not, as Fred Schrader suggests, accept Marx's own explanation of the place of Hegel's logic in his work from the *Grundrisse* on: "There is no portentous reception of Hegel, no World Spirit unmasked as Capital, and no need to decode an identity between the movements of Being and Value." There is rather the pragmatic utilization of Hegel's mode of expressing the systematic interconnection of categories "to bring propositions of the theory of money, already worked out for all essentials" on the basis of the ideas of Storch and Sismondi, "into a systematic interrelation" (Schrader 1980, 136).

This still leaves us with the questions why Marx found the Hegelian mode of expression so congenial, and what, finally, it might mean to speak of a Marxian dialectic.

The *Grundrisse*, as Schrader has demonstrated, provides a key to the answer to the first of these questions. It is important to remember that Marx undertook his critical investigation of political economy not with the aim of working out a logic of economic categories but out of a desire to understand the nature of the crisis tendency of the capitalist economy (its "law of motion"). This brought him, through the literature on money and banking, into a confrontation at once with bourgeois economic theorizing and with Proudhonian (and English utopian socialist) attempts to elaborate a socialist currency policy, which would revolutionize the relations of production and distribution "by a change in the instrument of circulation, in the organization of circulation." In opposition to such views, Marx argued that no form of money "is capable of overcoming the contradictions inherent in the money relation," and that such projects can "only hope to reproduce these contradictions in one or another form" (Marx 1973, 122–23). Thus it was in the first place a concrete political issue that led Marx to concentrate on the questions: "Does not the bourgeois system of exchange itself necessitate a specific instrument of exchange? Does it not necessarily create a specific equivalent for all values?" (Marx 1973, 127).

This Marx argues by demonstrating that in a commodity-market system, social labor time cannot be represented directly, but only in the form of exchange-value, specifically in the price form, so that any attempt to represent abstract labor, say by "time-chits," would only result in the creation of a new form of money. In the course of working out this demonstration, Marx comes suddenly to the realization that provides the key to his theory of money: "Because labor time as the measure of value exists only ideally, it cannot serve as the material for price comparisons. (Here at the same time it becomes clear how and why the value relation obtains a separate material existence in money. This to be developed further)" (Marx 1973, 140).[13] The understanding of value as an abstract idea Marx had discovered in Sismondi, and that of money as a "common term of comparison" between all commodities he found in Storch's *Cours d'economie politique* (Schrader 1980, 126ff.). Marx's own insight was the idea that the abstract relation between commodities as products of social labor had to be represented by something distinct from the commodities themselves. Money as value-form thus provides a means for the representation of abstract labor time. It is the material incarnation of an idea: "Such a symbol presupposes general recognition; it can only be a social symbol; it expresses, indeed, nothing more than a social relation" (Marx 1973, 142).

This idea has arisen, in fact, as a representation of the social relations that constitute capitalism as a system. Although "individuals are now ruled by *abstractions*," these abstractions, or ideas, are "nothing more than the theoretical expression[s] of those material relations which are their lord and master" (Marx 1973, 164). Those relations are ultimately—in the progress of theory in *Capital* (as before it in the *Grundrisse*)—to be described in terms of the relation between the controllers of the means of production and those who have nothing but their ability to work. To put it crudely, labor can be socialized as commodity-producing labor only when the ability to labor has itself become a commodity. In order for the product of labor to have the character of value represented by its exchangeability against money, that labor must be wage labor. Alternatively put, wage labor and capital are not only types of commodity but the fundamental types, whose existence alone makes the existence of a social system governed by value relations possible (see Marx 1973, 224–25).

The revelation of this truth is the ultimate outcome of Marx's critique of political economy. That critique aims to demonstrate how the categories of economic theory represent a systematization of the representations of the social relations definitive of capitalist society in everyday language and thinking. These representations are taken for logically ultimate descriptions of structures and forces—"the economy"—regulating social experience just because, in capitalism, the social relations of production have no other form of representation than those of commodity-value and money. As Marx explained this in the concluding section of the first chapter of *Capital*:

> The private producer's brain reflects [the] twofold social character of his labor [as concrete and abstract] only in the forms which appear in practical intercourse, in the exchange of products. . . . The value character of the products of labor becomes firmly established only when they act as magnitudes of value. These magnitudes vary continually, independently of the will, foreknowledge and actions of the exchangers.

Hence, though only forms of thought, the categories of bourgeois economics are "socially valid and therefore objective" (Marx 1976a, 166–69). They have, that is, the character of an autonomous system, even though "the characteristic which objects of utility have of being values is as much men's social product as is their language" (Marx 1976a, 167).

For this reason, one can understand how Hegel's dialectical logic provided Marx with an irresistibly attractive rhetoric for the depiction of the system of economic categories that structure social action in capitalist society. Hegel's illusion that his concepts themselves generated the movement of his systematic treatment of cognition mirrors the illusion of humankind under capitalism that the social relations that are their own historical product have an ineluctable life of their own.[14] At the same time, although not strictly speaking a logic, the Hegelian system included a highly sophisticated account of theory construction, in particular in the social sciences, stressing the interconnectedness of theoretical categories.

But the fundamental feature of the Hegelian viewpoint for which Marx honored him as a "mighty thinker" was the idea of the dialectic as realized in social history, as the principle (as Marx put it in the Postface to *Capital*) according to which "every historically developed form" is to be conceived as being in a fluid state, in motion, and therefore as "transient." Hegel's expression of this idea indeed represented a "mystification," due, as Marx explained it in *The German Ideology*, to the tendency of intellectuals (he is thinking of the tradition that began with the Enlightenment and took on new forms in the German philosophers of the first half of the nineteenth century) to see ideas, the stuff of their profession, as the determinants of history. It is only too easy then for someone like Hegel to "bring an order into this rule of ideas, prove a mystical connection among the successive ruling ideas [in different historical periods], which is managed by regarding them as 'forms of self-determination of the concept' (this is possible because by virtue of their empirical basis these ideas are really connected with one another and because, conceived as *mere* ideas they become self-distinctions, distinctions made by thought)" (Marx and Engels 1976, 62).

In contrast, the Marxian dialectic is neither a theory of history nor a special "method" of theory construction, but the principle of the critique of ideology. This critique is not primarily logical but anthropological and historical, in that it aims to demonstrate that the insufficiencies of economic theory for the comprehension of capitalist reality are due to its practice of taking the forms of social interactions—in reality the product of human history—for ineluctable structures. As a result, "something which is only valid for this particular form of production, . . . namely the fact that the specific social character of private labors carried on independently of each other consists in their equality as human labor, and, in the product, assumes the form of the existence of value, appears to those caught up in the relations of commodity production . . . to be just as ultimately valid as the fact that the scientific dissection of the air into its component parts left the atmosphere itself unaltered in its physical configuration" (Marx 1976a, 167).[15] The critique of this view is an attempt, therefore, not to display the "self-development of concepts" but to explain the development of concepts by the "real individuals" (as Marx puts it in *The German Ideology*) whose activity constitutes the history of society.

Notes

1. For a detailed discussion of Hegelian categories in the *Grundrisse*, see Schrader 1980, 113–45.
2. See O'Malley and Schrader 1977.
3. Cf. Marx's criticism of Lassalle's attempt at a Hegelianization of political economy: "He will learn to his cost that to bring a science by criticism to the point where it can be dialectically presented is an altogether different thing from applying an abstract ready-made system of logic to mere inklings of such a system." Marx to Engels, 1 February 1858, in Marx and Engels 1975b, 123.
4. As John Mepham has observed, the treatment of money in *Capital* is quite different from that in the *Grundrisse*, in which Marx indeed undertakes "a thoroughly Hegelian discussion of 'the transition from value to money'"—a discussion replaced in the later work by the analysis of what Marx called "real relations" of society (see Mepham 1979, 161).
5. For further discussion of Marx's denial that he had a theory of history, in the context of his rejection of the possibility of a general theory of society altogether, see Mattick, Jr. 1986a, ch. 6.
6. The translation has been amended. Cf. Marx and Engels 1962, 27.
7. Hence he wrote in the 1880 "Notes on Wagner" that in *Capital* "I do not start out from 'concepts,' hence I do not start out from 'the concept of value'" but from "the simplest social form in which the labor-product is presented in contemporary society," the commodity. Accordingly he insists that his "*analytic* method . . . has nothing in common with the academic German method of connecting concepts" (Marx 1975b, 198, 201).
8. A few pages earlier we find production, distribution, exchange, and consumption described as forming "a regular syllogism" as exemplars of the triad of generality, particularity, and singularity from the Doctrine of Essence in the *Logic*. "This is admittedly a coherence," Marx says—"but a shallow one" (Marx 1973, 89). The same model is followed in the arrangement of material in one of the plans for the analysis of capital sketched out in the *Grundrisse* (Marx 1973, 275), only to be dropped from further discussion.
9. Marx did not, of course, deny that the phenomena conceptualized by the simpler categories may "have an independent historical or natural existence predating" the more complex ones. Thus money, basic to the capitalist system

of production, existed before capital came into being. But it is not in general the case that "the path of abstract thought, rising from the simple to the combined, [corresponds] to the real historical process." Thus the explanatory priority of concepts relative to the analysis of one or another specific social system neither reflects nor explains the historical sequence of social institutions but is entirely a function of the nature of the specific system under investigation (see Marx 1973, 102).

10. Compare Hegel's description of the progress of the notion's dialectical advance as "determined as beginning from simple determinednesses, the succeeding ones becoming ever *richer and more concrete*" (Hegel 1969b, 840).
11. See the interesting discussion in Witt-Hansen 1960, 9ff.
12. Cf. Marx's letter to Engels of 2 April 1858: "From the contradiction between the general character of value and its material existence in a particular commodity, etc. . . . arises the category of money" (Marx and Engels 1975b, 127).
13. Translation amended. See the discussion in Schrader 1980, 113ff.
14. Indeed it has been suggested by Herbert Schnädelbach, in a very stimulating essay, that "the Hegelian form of logic itself is not as a system independent of the world view in which the bourgeoisie imagines its own social relationships" (Schnädelbach 1970, 59).
15. Further discussion of this principle would lead to Marx's conception of the relation between what he called the "material foundation" and the "ideological superstructure" of social reality; see Mattick, Jr. 1986b, especially ch. 5.

6

Marx's Concept of Economic Relations and the Method of *Capital*

Martha Campbell

Marx describes economic relations both as relations of production and as property relations, asserting that the two "express the same thing"(Marx 1970a, 21).[1] For the classicals, by contrast, production and property relations are distinct. This follows from the thesis, stated most explicitly by J. S. Mill (1965), that production is determined by natural laws, independently of the distribution of wealth—in other words, of property ownership. Utility theory makes the corresponding division by abstracting from property relations to present need as a relation between human beings and things. This figures as prominently in Adolph Wagner's (1879) theory as the dichotomy between production and distribution does in Mill's.

In his critique of Mill in the *Grundrisse* Introduction and in the "Notes on Wagner," then, Marx is confronting essentially the same division in two different forms. In the earlier critique, Marx focuses on the historical character of capitalism, charging Mill with eternalization. In the later one, he shifts attention to the social character of economic relations. Here, the division appears as I have just portrayed it—as the dichotomy between property relations as social and economic relations as purely material.

I begin with this second version of Marx's critique to show that he opposes the division itself. I then turn to *Capital* to show that Marx does, in fact, present the relations that constitute the capitalist system as property relations. By his account these are social, not only because they presuppose social recognition, but also because they establish a framework for the collective use of the elements and results of production. This notion underlies Marx's redefinition of economic as property relations. In brief, each collective way of producing and satisfying needs has its own goal; in the capitalist case, this is to expand value. Because satisfying needs is the means for expanding value, this goal determines the character of need in capitalist society. Against Wagner's division between need and property relations, therefore, Marx contends that the goal realized by economic activity within capitalist property relations determines the character of need. The analogous case applies against Mill's division between property relations and production. Moreover, it is Marx's true case against Mill, replacing the eternalization critique.

Last, linking Marx's redefinition of economic relations to his method in *Capital*, I argue that Marx eliminates the division of need and production from property relations by beginning *Capital* with the commodity. By Marx's account, commodities are values because social production is private and independent. Since, for Marx, production and property relations are synonymous, private and independent production is another name for production carried out under conditions of private ownership. According to his explanation of value then, the commodity as the bearer of value expresses the property relations under which it is produced.

MARX'S CRITIQUE OF WAGNER

GENERAL ECONOMIC CATEGORIES: NATURAL VERSUS SOCIAL

Making sense of Marx's comments on Wagner requires some sense of Wagner's theory itself. The relevant features of Wagner's economic doctrine are fairly straightforward and are implicit in his opening sentence:

> Man stands as a needy being in continuous contact with the external world around him and discovers that in the external world lie many conditions of his life and well being.[2]

Wagner makes need the topic of his first sentence because he defines the economic as that aspect of life that "results from the existence of human needs" (Wagner 1879, 11). It is also clear that Wagner regards need as a relation between human beings and things, the things being "the conditions of life . . . in the external world." Because Wagner derives all other economic categories from this initial concept of need, they too refer to human being–thing relations. This reflects and gives precise meaning to Wagner's thesis that the "purely economic" is "purely natural."[3] Finally, because Wagner conceives all economic characteristics to be natural, he necessarily also conceives them to be transhistorical or general. For Wagner, then, economic characteristics as natural are common to all societies but are not characteristics of society.

Marx insists, by contrast, that economic characteristics are characteristics of society. He makes this point in his response to Wagner's category, "individual use value." The counterpart of need as defined in Wagner's opening sentence is use value that "stands opposed to the individual and to his needs, apart from considerations of social organization" (Marx 1975a, 204).

Dismissing this as "sheer nonsense," Marx illustrates the proper conception of general categories by his definition of the labor process in *Capital*:

> The *labor-process* as purposeful activity for the manufacture of use-values etc. "*is equally common*" "to all its" (human life's) "*social forms*" and "*is independent of any of them.*" (Marx 1975a, 204; emphasis Marx's)

Each taken by itself, "apart from considerations of social organization" and "independent of any . . . social form" are both ambiguous phrases. The contrast between them shows that Marx and Wagner are making two different abstractions: Wagner means apart from society altogether; Marx means apart from the features that distinguish one kind of society from another. This clarifies Marx's own account of general characteristics in *Capital*. In describing labor in general as the "universal condition for the metabolism between man and nature," Marx is tacitly assuming that labor activity presupposes some kind of relation "between man and man" (Marx 1977b, 290, 173).[4]

In objecting to Wagner's abstraction, Marx is opposing the isolation of human being–thing relations from relations among human beings. Indicating the grounds for this objection, Marx suggests that need as Wagner defines it is need as "physiological concept" (Marx 1975a, 207). The implication is that by abstracting from society altogether, Wagner has eliminated the economic characteristics of need. Since in Marx's view economic relations are social, need in the economic sense is need insofar as it is determined by social relations. Hence Marx maintains "need . . . is only possible in some quite definite social organization" (Marx 1975a, 205). Since Marx illustrates this point by referring to the labor process, he evidently means it to apply to all economic relations rather than to need specifically. He is claiming, in other words, that human being–thing, or material, relations in isolation from social relations are not economic. As I argue below, Marx's rejection of Wagner's concept of need as physiological implies an analogous critique of the classical theory of production.

In the next section, I show both that Wagner's "considerations of social organization" are property relations and why he defines economic relations apart from them.

PROPERTY RELATIONS

Wagner recognizes that in reality, or at least in contemporary reality, most needs are satisfied by goods acquired from others, hence by means of social interaction. He recognizes further that free trade is a historically specific way of distributing goods. He maintains, however, that the "individual economic system," meaning the free market system, is "not a purely economic phenomenon but is at the same time dependent on the form of law" (Marx 1975a, 209). This expresses Wagner's view that the actual economic system is a combination of two mutually independent elements: characteristics that arise from the existence of human needs and characteristics that arise from law.

On one side of this division, Wagner classifies all "social categories" as "historico-legal" (Marx 1975a, 180). These "social categories" refer to property relations and all elements of the actual economy that Wagner takes to be their effects.[5] The term *historico-legal* expresses Wagner's view that property relations are established by law, the historical part indicating that property law changes historically (see Marx 1975a, 182). Thus Wagner recognizes that property relations are social. Since he maintains that they are established by law, he takes them to be completely defined by law. Finally, because property relations result from law, they are "non-economic"—they do not result from the existence of human needs.

To take one example, Wagner maintains that exchange value is historico-legal. As evidence that it presupposes definite property relations—namely, the property relations underlying free trade—Wagner notes that exchange value is "not applicable to many of the most important economic goods . . . [for example] to the state and its services" (Marx 1975a, 201).[6] Establishing that exchange value is historico-legal, in turn, gives Wagner a way of eliminating the distinction between value in use and value in exchange. Value, for Wagner, is an economic category. That exchange value is historico-legal means that "there is only one kind of value," namely, use value (Marx 1975a, 204). Instead of being a different kind of value, exchange value is the "historical covering" of the economic relation, use value "in a determinate historical period" (Marx 1975a, 204, 205).[7]

On the other side of Wagner's division, the "considerations of social organization" Wagner sets aside to define need are property relations. Thus his historico-legal/economic division amounts to the claim that property relations have no effect on need. With this clarification, Wagner's definitions of use value and need can be made more precise. Wagner subscribes to the view, common to all utility theory, that the quantities of use value of various goods are determined by laws of choice. He defines need as a human being–thing relation because he regards these laws as natural laws of human psychology.[8] The idea that need is always determined by laws of choice is perfectly consistent with the position that what people want is determined by society; hence Wagner maintains that "human needs are very different according to individuals and peoples, land and time periods" (Wagner 1879, 9).[9] Since in this sense Wagner regards need as socially determined, his thesis that "the economic is natural" is more accurately expressed by the claim that property relations satisfy given needs, meaning needs determined independently of property relations.

Marx's objections also need to be modified somewhat. Marx, of course, knows that Wagner's "considerations of social organization" are property relations. By the claim that "need is only possible in some quite definite social organization," he means that need is always satisfied within the framework of some kind of property relations and its character determined by them. Further, as I argue below, the characteristics of need that are determined by property relations are, for Marx, the economic characteristics of need. According to his account in *Capital*, these include the determination of need by individual choice. Restated, then, Marx's case against the "economic" side of Wagner's theory is that Wagner has not really abstracted from property relations; he has simply failed to recognize the effect of private property on need. If Wagner had really abstracted from property relations, he would be speaking of physiological needs.

On the "non-economic" side, Marx rejects Wagner's account of the source of property relations. As noted earlier, Wagner never says explicitly that property relations are established by law. One of Wagner's many ways of implying this, however, is by saying that the

> *acquisition* (of goods through commerce) "necessarily presupposes a determinate *legal order* on the *basis of which*" (!) "commerce is carried out." (Marx 1975a, 210; emphasis Marx's)

Evidently, Wagner does not mean simply that commerce presupposes the relation among private proprietors but that it presupposes the legal system in which property is defined as private property.

Marx disputes this on historical grounds. Wagner's statement implies that "there is, first, the law, and then commerce." Marx maintains that "in reality, it's the other way around": the "practical relation" in which exchangers "offer their goods to one another . . . only later attains a *legal form* in contracts" (Ibid.).[10] If the relation of persons exists without its legal form, as it does in commerce before the development of contract law, then, clearly, it cannot have been established by law. This, rather than the matter of historical sequence, is Marx's point. Making the same point in *Capital*, Marx argues that the exchange process presupposes the "juridical relation" of persons whether this relation is "part of a developed legal system or not" (Marx 1977b, 178).[11] This means that the law makes this relation explicit and gives it an institutional form only apart from the "practical relation" in which it already exists. It is not, as Wagner maintains, the source of property relations independent of the process of satisfying needs.

As I argue next based on Marx's account in *Capital*, at least one of Marx's reasons for rejecting Wagner's thesis that property relations are established by law is that it identifies property relations with their legal form. In Marx's view, modern property law—contract law—does not express all the characteristics of capitalist property relations. Further, Marx contends that the extra characteristics of capitalist property relations—those that are not expressed in law—show these relations to be means for the expansion of value. In opposition to Wagner's division between need and property relations, Marx argues that the character of need in capitalist society is determined by this goal.

Economic Relations as Property Relations

Commerce or the Exchange Process

Marx introduces private property in *Capital* as a logical consequence of the commodity. Private ownership, he argues, is a necessary condition for the commodity form because the exchange value relation among commodities presupposes the relation among private owners of commodities (see Marx 1977b, 178). Marx does consider the relation of owners by itself to show that it is a relation of mutually recognized self-determination (or, as he says later, a relation of "reciprocal isolation and foreignness") (Marx 1977b, 178). Here Marx speaks of participants in the exchange process simply as owners, and of commodities simply as privately owned objects.

Marx's derivation of private property from the commodity, however, makes the relation of persons inseparable from the commodity's other characteristics, use value and value. Anticipating the argument he is about to present, Marx indicates that the three are inseparable because the goal of the relation of persons is given by the commodity's other characteristics. As he puts it: "the content of this juridical relation . . . is itself determined by the economic relation" (Marx 1977b, 178).[12]

To summarize Marx's case for this claim: First, because exchange value is the relation of all commodities to money, exchange is a transaction between an owner of an ordinary commodity and an owner of the money commodity. Hence the exchange value character of the commodity implies not only that economic agents are private owners but also that they confront each other as sellers and buyers, in Marx's terms, as "representatives" of opposing features of the commodity (Marx 1977b, 179). Second, since commodity owners are self-determining, they enter into an exchange only if it realizes their individual goals. This means that the outcomes of an exchange for the seller and buyer reveal their respective goals. That a sale begins with an ordinary commodity and ends with money shows that the ordinary commodity is not useful to its owner and that the seller's goal is to realize its value. That a purchase begins with money and ends with an ordinary commodity shows that the buyer has chosen that particular commodity from all others offered for sale, thus that the buyer judges it to be useful and has entered into exchange in order to satisfy a need (in other words, to realize the commodity's use value). Thus one meaning of Marx's claim that the goal of the relation of persons is given by the "economic relation" is that sellers and buyers engage in exchange to realize the commodity's value and use value, respectively. Finally, since an exchange realizes the goals of both parties, it realizes the commodity's use value and value simultaneously. This means that exchange satisfies individually determined needs, but only if they are expressed in money purchases.

In this account, the commodity's exchange value appears as the source of social relations, which include but are not limited to property relations. That the commodity implies these relations shows its character as a social product. In other words, the commodity's exchange value shows that commodities must be distributed in order for their use value to be realized (they are not useful to their original owners, the sellers). Social interaction in exchange, then, is the precondition for satisfying needs; it is also the precondition for the seller's goal, realizing the commodity's value. In addition, exchange value identifies the particular relations involved in commodity distribution as relations among owners and further specifies these as relations between sellers and buyers. The use value of the commodity is realized only by means of these relations, and they determine its character. In other words, they determine that commodities satisfy needs of buyers or, in the language of Smith and Keynes, individually determined "effective demands." In the "Notes on Wagner," Marx calls this kind of use value "use value for others"—referring presumably to the character of buyers as individuals or "foreigners" in relation to sellers—and states that it is the "determinate social form of use value . . . where commodity production is dominating" (Marx 1975a, 205). Supplying another possible meaning of Marx's claim that the content is given by the economic relation, the goal realized by the exchange process as a whole, as it appears from Marx's argument up to this point, is the satisfaction of a definite kind of need.

In his account of the exchange process, Marx presents these conclusions as logical consequences of the commodity and takes the dominance of the commodity as given.[13] This replaces Wagner's claim that "commerce presupposes a determinate legal order" with the not entirely satisfactory alternative that commerce presupposes a social product composed of commodities, products whose distinguishing feature is value. The addition of Marx's explanation for the dominance of the commodity supplies his alternative to Wagner's claim in its complete form. This is that commerce—as the way of distributing the total social product—presupposes capitalist production.

CAPITALIST PRODUCTION

Marx's argument, as I interpret it, connects the dominance of the commodity to capitalist production by a series of sufficient conditions for the commodity's presence. These conditions are simply listed here with the sole objective of establishing what Marx's position is.[14]

First, since commodities are products of a definite kind, the commodity's dominance is the manifestation of a process that produces products only of the commodity form. For commodities to be its necessary result, this process must be aimed at the distinguishing feature of the commodity—value—and, since value is purely quantitative, at value expansion. Stated in other words, the dominance of the commodity presupposes capital or money spent with the objective of obtaining more money.

Second, as Marx argues in Chapter 5 of *Capital*, circulation can only redistribute rather than increase the quantity of value in the economy as a whole. The commodity's dominance, however, presupposes the possibility of value expansion in the latter sense; that the total social product is composed of commodities is evidence that economic activity is directed exclusively by capital or, in other words, that needs are satisfied and production undertaken for the sake of expanding value. Because circulation, although required for value expansion, cannot increase the total quantity of value, Marx argues that specifically capitalist surplus value must arise from a different source, namely, the production process itself.

Third, for the production process to be both the source of surplus value and consistent with the relation among economic agents as private owners—another implication of the commodity's dominance—production must involve the use of wage labor. Completing the sequence, this means that the dominance of the commodity presupposes the particular way of owning the necessary elements of production that guarantees the availability of labor power in the form of wage labor. Because products, including produced means of production, are commodities, money, as the means of acquiring them, is one of the necessary elements of production. The others are the nonproduced elements, land and labor power. To assure the presence of wage labor, these elements must be not only private property but unequally distributed. Specifically, the division of society as a whole into owners and nonowners of land and money makes the latter wage laborers and the former potential capitalist producers.

This sequence of logical conditions is meant to establish that there is only one kind of ownership of the elements of production that corresponds to the dominance of the commodity. By Marx's account, this kind of ownership is established by the original accumulation, and once established it is perpetuated by capitalist production.[15] As I argue below, in Chapter 1 of *Capital*, Marx explains that commodities are values because the means of production are private property. Thus, although private ownership does not appear explicitly until Marx considers the exchange process, it is tacit in his explanation of value. Incorporating this point into the logical sequence presented here, Marx's argument is that universal private property presupposes the unequal distribution of money and land that divides society into wage laborers and capitalists.

THE EXCHANGE PROCESS RECONSIDERED

Reconsidered as the result of capitalist production, the exchange process involves not just private property but an unequal distribution of property parallel to and resulting from the unequal distribution of the elements of production. After production, all members of society are money owners or buyers. Only capitalists, however, are sellers or own ordinary commodities as well as money. The division of all participants in production into owners and nonowners of money and land is reproduced in the division of all participants in the exchange process into owners and nonowners of ordinary commodities. With the additional specification that sellers are capitalists, the characteristics of the exchange process over and above private property appear as means for value expansion. That is, the buyer-seller relation, which transforms a particular commodity into money, is the means for the final phase of value expansion in which value "asserts its identity with itself" (Marx 1977b, 255). Alternatively, seller-capitalists satisfy only "effective demands" because this is the only kind of need whose satisfaction is a means for value expansion, the goal of capital. In its final and most inclusive meaning, then, Marx's claim that the "content" of the relation of persons is given by the "economic relation" refers to the goal, value expansion.

Since value is expanded only by capitalist production and the exchange process taken together, the "economic relation" must refer to both.[16] In calling economic relations "relations of production," therefore, Marx does not mean what economists—neither utility theorists, such as Wagner, nor, as I show shortly, classical theorists, such as Mill—normally mean by the same term. To begin with, Marx regards the exchange process as a relation of production because it is the form of product distribution corresponding to capitalist production. Further, capitalist production and the exchange process, as Marx presents them, are an interdependent set of property relations. The relation between wage laborers and capitalists is defined by the private and unequal ownership of the necessary elements of production. The relation between capitalists as sellers and all members of society as buyers in the exchange process is defined by the private and unequal ownership of products that results from capitalist production.

It is because Marx conceives economic relations as property relations that he regards them as social and historically variable. It also follows that, for Marx, the economic characteristics of need and production are those that are determined by property relations. In the case of need, for example, these include individually determined effective demand as well as the "needs" of capital. These include money's use value as the adequate appearance form of social labor, which provides the form in which social labor is accumulated, and labor power's use value as the source of surplus value.[17]

WHY MARX REDEFINES ECONOMIC RELATIONS AS PROPERTY RELATIONS

Marx is evidently well aware that he is defining economic relations in an unusual way, and he does so quite intentionally. His claim that the content is given by the economic relation is intended, as he indicates in his note, as a refutation of Proudhon. This comment on Proudhon, together with the critique of Wagner, shows Marx's reasons for defining economic relations as property relations.

Proudhon conceives the goal of property relations to be *justice eternelle* rather than value expansion. By Marx's account, this is an ideal of justice Proudhon has created from private property, "the juridical relations that correspond to the production of commodities" (Marx 1977b, 178 n. 2). Having formulated his ideal in terms of the legal form of property, Proudhon considers the essence of property to be private property. Wagner does the same thing for the more mundane reason that he conceives property relations to be established by law. Marx emphasizes one consequence of identifying capitalist property with private property in his comment on Proudhon and another in his critique of Wagner.

Marx's comment on Proudhon challenges Proudhon's attempt to sever private property from the goal of expanding value. Proudhon notices the two unequal distributions of property and the goal realized by means of them—the use of money as capital. Because they contradict the ideal of justice he has formulated from the character of property as private property, he "seeks to reform the actual production of commodities" to eliminate them (Ibid.). Since Proudhon's reforms are supposed to preserve private property and eliminate capital, they show that he conceives the relation between the two to be accidental. Similarly, Wagner recognizes that there are "external conditions . . . wholly or primarily independent of the economic subject"—meaning conditions not attributable to the individual actions of private owners (Marx 1975a, 213). Because Wagner defines the free market system by private property, he regards all such external conditions as accidental. Giving them a name rather than an explanation, Wagner classifies the symptoms of value expansion, such as "speculative gains," along with acts of God, such as the "influence of the weather" on crops, under the heading of "conjuncture" (Marx 1975a, 213, 214).[18]

Marx's critique of Wagner challenges the idea that property relations satisfy given needs. Relative to Marx's account, this idea can also be seen as a consequence of reducing capitalist property to private property. With the addition of Marx's unequal distribution of private property, capitalist property relations appear as a particular way of producing and satisfying needs collectively that achieves the expansion of value. Thus social interaction appears as a precondition for satisfying needs and for producing; by its specific form, it determines the character of need. That is, wage laborers and buyers can satisfy their needs only by interacting with capitalists. Accordingly, needs must have the characteristics that make their satisfaction a means for value expansion. On the other side, capitalists can expand value only by interacting with wage laborers and buyers.

Severed from its capitalist distribution, however, private property by itself does not appear as a collective way of satisfying needs. This being the case, the process of satisfying needs could scarcely seem to realize a social goal. Hence it seems to have no other purpose than to satisfy given needs. It is reasonable to conclude, then, that Wagner's notion that need is determined independently of property relations results from his identification of capitalist property with its legal form, private property. In turn, as a result of this notion, he eliminates the effective demand character of need entirely and conceives the individual determination of need as a natural principle of human psychology rather than as the consequence of private property.[19]

To bring these two objections together, Marx defines economic relations as property relations in opposition to the division made by both idealist philosophy of law and economics between property and the "material conditions of life" (Marx 1970a, 20).[20] The connection Marx sees between them follows from his perception that property relations are relations for the collective use of both the elements and results of production. This collective use assumes different forms, each with its own goal. To state the point in other words, each way of life established through property relations is a way of satisfying needs and itself realizes some goal comparable to the expansion of value in capitalism. As I will explain more fully in a moment, Marx's case against idealist philosophy of law is that the goal of each particular way of life is realized through the process of satisfying needs; against economics, it is that satisfying needs is the means for realizing the goal of a particular way of life.

From Marx's standpoint, idealist philosophy of law misrepresents the goal of capitalist property relations. Taking private property as a model, it conceives property relations as individual "power over things" rather than as a collective way of satisfying needs.[21] As a result, it fails to see both that there is a goal realized through the process of satisfying needs and that this goal contradicts the principles of justice derived from private property alone. On the other side, Marx contends that economic theory misrepresents the character of need and production. In failing to see the collective character of capitalist production, it also fails to see the goal realized by it. Hence it presents need and production simply as material relations, independent of any social goal.

In Marx's view these are complementary misconceptions arising from the character of capitalist property as private property and its counterpart, as I argue below, the value character of the commodity. The legal concept of property as individual power over things corresponds to the economic concept of value as a material relation. The two are linked by both Wagner and Proudhon: Proudhon because he combines Hegel's philosophy of law with Ricardo's labor theory of value, and Wagner because he maintains that property is established by law and that value is use value.[22]

J. S. MILL AND MARX'S "ETERNALIZATION" CRITIQUE

Wagner's distinction between economic and socio-legal categories is a utility theory version of the division between economic relations as material and property relations as legal. J. S. Mill's distinction between production and distribution is the most explicit classical version of the same division. Mill describes production as a purely material relation, maintaining that "the laws and conditions of production partake of the character of physical truths" (Mill 1965, 199). By distribution, Mill means the distribution of wealth—of both the elements and the results of production. Distribution in this sense encompasses property relations, and Mill's dichotomy between production and distribution severs production from property relations. Distribution, Mill reasons, "depends on the laws and customs of society," since property cannot be held except by the protection, hence "by the permission of society" (Ibid.). By the argument that property is dependent on law enforcement, Mill arrives at the same result as Wagner and Proudhon: The necessary characteristics of property are those expressed in law; property distribution is accidental.[23]

Since Marx's critique of Wagner focuses on the division between material and property relations rather than on need per se, it suggests an analogous critique of Mill. Adapted to production, Marx's claim that "need is only possible in some quite definite social organization" would be that labor power and technology cannot be isolated from property relations. To put it another way, if need apart from property relations is need in the "physiological sense" and is, as such, irrelevant to economics, labor power and technology subject to the same abstraction would seem to be similarly irrelevant. Indeed the example of the labor process, by which Marx illustrates the proper conception of general economic categories in his critique of Wagner, applies more directly to Mill.

This only suggests a possible parallel critique, which is not developed here.[24] Instead I argue that Marx's mature critique in the "Notes on Wagner" shows his early eternalization critique to be misguided. The implication is that if Marx had reconsidered Mill's theory after completing *Capital*, his critique of Mill would have taken the same form as his critique of Wagner.

Although "Notes on Wagner" emphasizes the social character of economic relations, the eternalization critique emphasizes their historical character. Of course, economic relations cannot vary historically unless they are social. In focusing on their historical character, however, Marx is addressing the symptom rather than the source of his disagreements with the classicals. Because it is misguided, the eternalization critique presents both an ambiguous and a limited view of Marx's disagreements with the classicals.

To begin with, eternalization either refers to two different mistakes or is an inaccurate description of one. For example, as already noted, Mill maintains that property, with rare and minor exceptions, has always been private property. He does not maintain, however, that it is the only possible form of property, a position he could not entertain unless he recognized that it is an "institution," in other words, that it is determined by society. Is the transformation of a specifically modern institution into an eternal, albeit potentially mutable, institution a case of eternalization? If so—and Marx suggests that it is—then eternalization encompasses two different mistakes (see Marx 1973, 87–88). The second mistake is the transformation of social into material relations, as exemplified by the identification of capital—means of production within definite property relations—with means of production as physical objects. If eternalization refers only to the second mistake, then the term *eternalization* does not express the real problem. It is because social, and therefore historically variable, characteristics are misconceived as material that they are held to be immutable or eternal.

Second, eternalization identifies only one of two mistakes that arise from isolating need and production from property relations. The point can be illustrated by an example from Wagner's theory: Wagner eternalizes the individual determination need in capitalism, but he omits the effective demand character of need entirely. Eternalization refers to the first kind of mistake but not the second. Worse yet, Cohen argues that the charge of eternalization does not even apply to Mill. Capital, in Mill's usage, refers to the means of production in the physical sense. According to Cohen, Mill restricts his discussion of capital to physical characteristics (Cohen 1978, 108–11). To the extent that this is true, however, Mill omits Marx's socially determined characteristics of production. This is the mistake the eternalization critique does not recognize.

Finally, Marx's own statements in the *Grundrisse* include at least one element of classical theory that is ultimately inconsistent with his own position. This is the idea that general characteristics, in particular use value, are material. In his response to Wagner's individual use value in the "Notes on Wagner," Marx flatly rejects the concept of use value as a material relation. Further, this concept is inconsistent with Marx's presentation of economic relations as property relations in *Capital*. The eternalization critique does imply that economic relations, and therefore the general characteristics of such relations, are social. Because it focuses on the historical character of economic relations, however, it does not make the social character of general characteristics explicit. It seems likely, therefore, that Marx's failure to recognize the inconsistency between his concept of economic relations as property relations and the concept of use value as a material relation corresponds to his inadequate formulation of his differences with the classicals.

To cite one particularly telling example, in the last fragment on value, Marx sets up a dichotomy between use value as the "material side" of the commodity and exchange value as the "specific economic relation" in which this material is presented (Marx 1973, 881). Not only does Marx equate use value with the material side, but he also identifies it as the general characteristic of the commodity, the characteristic that "the most disparate epochs of production may have in common." On the other side, Marx identifies the social character of the commodity with the historically specific characteristic, exchange value. In addition, he identifies exchange value as the "simplest, most abstract expression" of a definite kind of property relation, "appropriation through sale" (Marx 1973, 882, 881).

Marx's dichotomy between use value and exchange value in this passage is, like Wagner's historico-legal/economic and Mill's production/distribution distinctions, the division between common as material and historically specific as social—in particular, property—relations. Employing the same conceptual division as Wagner, Marx defines political economy in exactly the opposite way. Whereas for Wagner the economic is the material side, for Marx political economy includes only "the *specific* social forms . . . of the production of wealth. . . . The material of wealth . . . lies beyond political economy" (Marx 1973, 852, 881; emphasis added). Marx will continue to subscribe to the second half of this statement.

At this point, however, he is missing two concepts that inform his thinking in *Capital*. One is the concept of general economic—meaning social—characteristics. His announcement in the Preface to the *Contribution to the Critique of Political Economy* that these are "results" presumably signals the end of his confusion over whether they are social or material (Marx 1970a, 19). The other is the concept of the commodity—as opposed to exchange value, the distinguishing feature of the commodity—as a specific form.

As I argue next, in *Capital* Marx attributes political economy's division of production and need from property relations to its misunderstanding of the commodity form. This explanation, the commodity fetishism, replaces the eternalization critique. With this, Marx poses his critique of political economy in the form it assumes in the "Notes on Wagner," directly confronting political economy's conception of economic relations as purely material.

The Commodity as a Concrete or Specific Form of Product

By Marx's account, the commodity is the particular kind (or as Marx calls it, form) of social product that results from productive activity within the framework of capitalist property relations. Accordingly, the commodity is the manifestation of the effect of property relations on production. By beginning with the commodity, therefore, Marx overcomes classical theory's division between property relations and production and, indirectly, utility theory's analogous division between property relations and need.

Marx expresses this in the "Notes on Wagner" by describing the commodity as a "concretum" (Marx 1975a, 189). The most straightforward meaning of this description is that the commodity is the unity of value and use value.[25] But it also means that the commodity does not involve abstraction from property relations. Thus Marx differentiates his method from

Wagner's by the contrast between the concrete character of the commodity and the abstract character of Wagner's starting definition of need.[26] On Wagner's side of this contrast, the particular abstraction that produces Wagner's concept of need is the abstraction from property relations. On Marx's side, the commodity overcomes this abstraction. Its distinguishing feature—value—according to Marx's explanation, results from the private ownership of the means of production.

Marx argues that the exchange-value relation among commodities, by which he means the relation of all commodities to money, establishes the relation among the various labor activities that make up the total labor of society.[27] The correlate to this is that there is no direct association among labor activities themselves but, in its place, the relation of all products to money. By value, Marx means the determinant of the commodity's relation to money. By his argument, value expresses the character of each individual commodity as a component of the total social product and, indirectly, the labor devoted to the production of each commodity as a component of the total labor of society. Putting the elements of this argument together, the social character of labor appears as an objective property of its products—the basis of the relation of all commodities to money—because the collective relation among various activities that make up the total labor of society is established only by the relation among the products of labor.

Marx expresses the absence of any direct association among commodity-producing labor activities by saying that commodities "are products of the labor of private individuals who work independently of each other" (Marx 1977b, 165).[28] Another way of expressing the same thing is to say that commodities are the results of producing under conditions of universal private property. That is, production or labor activity is carried out privately and independently because all the elements of production are private property and all participants in production are owners or individuals. By Marx's argument, therefore, value, the distinctive feature of the commodity, is the counterpart of the character of capitalist property as private property.[29]

From the standpoint of Marx's theory of value, economic theory's abstraction from property relations can be attributed to the failure of both classical and utility theory to recognize value as the counterpart of universal private property. By the theory of commodity fetishism, Marx attributes this failure, in turn, to the objective character of value, "objective" meaning that value is a characteristic that "pertains to [the commodity] as a thing" because it is the basis of the commodity's relation to money (Marx 1975a, 207).[30] Because value is objective, economic theory takes it to be a characteristic that commodities have apart from their relation to money; hence it attributes value to the commodity's physical characteristics. This is most obvious in utility theory, which attributes value to the material relation between the commodity's physical properties and given needs. According to Marx, it is equally true of the classical theory of value. As he says: "Ricardo has not grasped or explored the substance of value, e.g., the collective character of the labor process in primitive community life," of which value is "another form" (Ibid.). As this remark indicates, classical theory, unlike Marx, attributes value to the material relation between labor activity and physical objects. This transformation of value—the manifestation of the collective character of commodity production—into a material relation is responsible for the concept of production as a purely material process. From this it follows that production satisfies given needs.

In opposition to both classical and utility theory, Marx's theory of value is meant to establish that capitalist production is collective. This renders capitalism comparable to other kinds of appropriation. As Marx illustrates by a variety of examples—feudal society, the peasant family, and his "association of free men"—other kinds of appropriation involve various structures of direct social relations through which "the means of production are held in common" (Marx 1977b, 171). Since these kinds of appropriation are directly collective, they show that appropriation relations are relations for the collective use of means of production and products. Marx's point is that capitalism is another form of the same thing, the difference between it and the others being that capitalism is indirectly rather than directly collective. It is only when Marx has established that capitalist production is collective that he can proceed to identify the goal realized by the particular form of collectivity that constitutes capitalist society.

Marx's comparison between capitalism and other kinds of appropriation makes another point: As the only system of universal private property, capitalism is the only kind of appropriation that does not appear as what it is, a process of collective production. Private property appears directly as individual control over objects. The unequal distribution of property, which reveals the collective character of production, is not and does not need to be expressed in law.[31] By Marx's account, once the collective character of production is established by the original accumulation, it perpetuates itself through capitalist production. Finally, the other manifestation of the collective character of production, value, does not appear as the means for a collective relation because it is an objective characteristic of products. Whereas other kinds of appropriation show the characteristics of production in general, capitalism does not. In the capitalist case, general characteristics are "results," according to Marx, of the correct understanding of value (Marx 1970a, 19).[32]

CONCLUSION

Taking Mill as a representative of classical and Wagner as a representative of utility theory, I have argued that Marx's concept of economic relations as property relations distinguishes his theory from both of the major traditions of economic thought. This gives precise meaning to Marx's claim that economic relations are social and establishes the sense in which they are nonsocial in these other traditions. I have argued further that Marx's redefinition of economic relations is not simply a matter of terminology.

Wagner and Mill recognize that property relations are social, but only in the sense that each individual's power over things rests on the consent of society as a whole. Understood in this way, property relations have no effect on the character of need and production. Marx contends that property relations are social in an additional sense: that they are relations for the collective use of means of production and products. This additional sense of the social character of property means that each particular kind of collectivity itself has some goal that is realized through the process of producing and satisfying needs. Because needs are satisfied and production undertaken as a means for realizing the goal of some particular kind of collective relation, this goal determines the character of need and production. On these grounds Marx contends that need and production are not relations between human beings and things, as they are portrayed by political economy, but are instead property relations.

This difference means that there are no counterparts to Marx's economic concepts in either classical or utility theory. I have already dealt with the difference in the concept of value. In addition, the objects within economic relations—means of production and products—are, for Marx, not simply material objects but objects within some kind of appropriation relation. This gives rise to Marx's concept of kinds or forms of products and means of production, as exemplified by commodities and capital. These concepts do not exist for the other theories because they abstract from property relations.

Last, although Marx rejects political economy's dichotomy between property relations and the economic relations, need and production, he does not simply dismiss it. He attributes the notion that need and production are determined independently of property relations to the way capitalism appears. It arises specifically from the twin characteristics of universal private property and the objective character of value. By this explanation, Marx presents political economy as a reasonable reconstruction of capitalism at the same time that he contends that it is a false one.

Notes

1. Marx's equation of production and property relations is also noted by Moore (1980, 221) and Sayer (1987, 69), who cites additional evidence from Marx's early writings. Marx's attention to property relations is also noted by Pejovich (1982).
2. Quoted in Marx 1975a, 193.
3. See the translator's note 3 in Marx 1975a, 180.
4. See also Marx 1977b, 133.
5. Marx does not cite any statement in which Wagner explicitly identifies social with property relations. All examples of historico-legal characteristics, however, are consequences of property relations. The clearest example is productive credit, which Wagner classifies as historico-legal because "it is connected with the possession of assets, not with the asset as a purely economic category" (Marx 1975a, 211).
6. Wagner identifies the property relations underlying free trade as "private property in real estate and movable capital" (Marx 1975a, 211).
7. In a somewhat clearer version of the passage Marx quotes (1975a, 205), Wagner states that "exchange value is . . . not a kind of value coordinated with use value . . . but it is a historical concept, which corresponds to the determinate historical period of free trade and there is alongside it another historical value concept in tax value" (Wagner 1879, 48).
8. Wagner describes the laws of choice as "psychological facts" (Wagner 1879, 47). His theory is premarginal but contains the essential elements of all utility theory: the elimination of the distinction between use value and exchange value, the ordering of preferences—in Wagner's terms, the rank ordering of needs—and substitution (see Marx 1975a, 195, 202).
9. Unlike most utility theorists, Wagner states, in his rather unclear way, that he is abstracting from property relations. As his account illustrates, no utility theorist would regard the cultural determination of need, including Veblenesque effects, as proof against the theory. See, for example, Hayek's argument against Galbraith (Hayek 1961).
10. The term *practical relations* is one of Marx's synonyms for economic relations (see Marx 1977b, 173).
11. Wagner's "legal order" is evidently the same as Marx's "developed legal system."
12. By "content," Marx means goal. (See, for example, Marx 1977b, 250.)
13. Marx indicates that his account of the exchange process describes actual exchange to the extent that exchange is the distribution of the total social product (see Marx 1977b, 181–83). He presents the dominance of the commodity as a fact in the opening sentence of *Capital* and as the reason for analyzing the commodity. It is the first macroeconomic feature of capitalism to be identified in *Capital*.
14. The series of conditions is presented in Chapters 4 through 7 of *Capital*. For a more detailed version of this interpretation, see Campbell (forthcoming). Banaji (1979) gives the same interpretation, arguing that Marx intends to establish that simple circulation presupposes capitalist production.

15. Marx's sequence of logical conditions, therefore, is not meant to imply that the other elements of the capitalist system come into being because they are logically entailed by the dominance of the commodity. Marx attributes this way of thinking to Hegel and rejects it (see Marx 1973, 101; 1977b, 102).
16. See also Marx 1977b, 203, where Marx describes as an "economic relation between men" the "relation between owners of commodities in which they appropriate the produce of the labor of others by alienating the produce of their own labor." Because Marx has not yet shown that commodities are products of capital, "the produce of their own labor" takes the place of capitalist production. Otherwise this definition is the same as the one I have given.
17. Marx lists these in the "Notes on Wagner" as characteristics of use value he has identified in *Capital* (see Marx 1975a, 200). Since he is presenting *Capital* as a model of the proper conception of use value in economics, these are, in his view, the economic characteristics of use value and need.
18. Showing the extent to which other economists share Wagner's views, Marshall maintains that the concept of conjuncture "meets a need which is much felt in English economics" (Marshall 1979, 103 n. 1).
19. There are indications that Wagner, like Smith, attributes the need for social interaction—for participation in the exchange process—to the division of labor. He states, for example, that "social use value"—meaning use value realized through exchange—"presupposes the division of labor and private property in the material means of production and therefore the necessity of an organization for the distribution of goods acquired by the division of labor" (Wagner 1879, 48). By an "organization for the distribution of goods," Wagner means the exchange process. As this passage shows, the necessity for distribution does not follow from private property by itself but only from private property plus the division of labor. The division of labor, however, only increases productivity. It does not determine the character of need.
20. Sayer makes the same point by the argument that the concept of base and superstructure is meant to overcome the division between material conditions on one side and law and property relations on the other. Against the historical materialist interpretation that base determines superstructure, Sayer argues that Marx is simply linking the superstructure to the base, in his words, denying that they are "substantially separable orders of reality" (Sayer 1987, 84). Making the same point by a different route, Mattick emphasizes that the base-superstructure metaphor is directed against Hegel's explanation of the evolution of legal and political relations in terms of an independent logic of concepts. One of the points of the metaphor, therefore, is that legal and political relations are of a piece with the base. (See Mattick, Jr. 1986, 75, 102–4).
21. For the concept of property as power over things, see Hegel 1967, 42, 45.
22. For a more detailed account of this linkage in Proudhon, see Murray 1988b, ch. 7.
23. For Mill, as for Proudhon, the unequal distribution of private property "is not of the essence of the institution but a mere incidental consequence which . . . conflicts with the ends which render private property legitimate" (Mill 1965, 208).
24. This critique would involve a case against the historical materialist thesis, clearly stated by Cohen (1978), that the forces of production are independent and determinative of economic relations.
25. A concrete is a "unity of the diverse" (Marx 1973, 101) or, as Banaji puts it citing Hegel, "'differentiated within itself' hence something analyzable"

(Banaji 1979, 30). In the "Notes on Wagner," Marx stresses that the distinction between exchange value and use value is inherent in the commodity, that he notices rather than makes it (see Marx 1975a, 198).

26. Describing Wagner's method as "the methodology of man," Marx states that it consists of arranging the world "under abstract rubrics," these rubrics being Wagner's historico-legal and economic categories (Marx 1975a, 193). The same contrast appears in Marx 1975a, 201, 206.
27. Marx indicates that he is assuming that the total labor of society is producing commodities (see, e.g., Marx 1977b, 129, 165). This corresponds to the dominance of the commodity.
28. See also Marx 1977b, 132.
29. Hodgson (1988) remarks on the connection between private property and value in Marx's work, noting that value, like private property, "is seen as a relationship between persons as well as between things" (293).
30. See also Marx 1977b, 176–77.
31. If Marx is correct in maintaining that capitalism is the only system of universal private property, then the incomplete specification of property relations in law is unique to capitalism. That is, if all other kinds of appropriation involve various kinds of direct relations, if a legal system exists at all, the law would have to specify these relations completely. See Sayer's discussion of E. P. Thompson's objections to the historical materialist division between economic and legal relations (Sayer 1987, 50–53).
32. Marx's oft quoted description of general characteristics as "flat tautologies," it should be noted, refers to production in general as presented by Mill and Smith (Marx 1973, 86). It is not entirely clear that Marx would say the same of general characteristics as he defines them. Moreover, for the reasons given in the text, Marx's general characteristics are so far from obvious that it is not clear that he himself recognizes what they are at the time he makes this statement.

7

Marx's Logical Method and the "Transformation Problem"

Fred Moseley

The long and continuing controversy over Marx's analysis of the "transformation problem" has not paid sufficient attention to the logical method employed by Marx in the three volumes of *Capital*. The most common interpretation of the transformation problem is based on the work of Bortkiewicz (1952), Sweezy (1968), Seton (1957), Morishima (1973), Medio (1972), Steedman (1977), and others. This interpretation of Marx's theory is referred to in this chapter as the "neo-Ricardian" interpretation. The logical method attributed to Marx's theory by this interpretation is essentially the same as the method of linear production theory (e.g., Sraffa's theory). This chapter argues that the logical method of linear production theory differs in fundamental respects from Marx's own method and thus that the conclusions reached by the neo-Ricardian interpretation of Marx's theory do not apply to Marx's theory, but instead apply only to linear production theory.

The first section of this chapter briefly reviews the well-known neo-Ricardian interpretation of the transformation problem. The next four sections discuss important aspects of Marx's logical method and contrast these aspects with the neo-Ricardian interpretation of Marx's method, that is, with the method of linear production theory. The next section responds to the widely accepted neo-Ricardian criticism that Marx "failed to transform the inputs of constant capital and variable capital" in his determination of prices of production. The last section briefly contrasts the interpretation presented here with the "new solution" to the transformation problem presented in recent years by Foley, Dumenil, and Lipietz.

NEO-RICARDIAN INTERPRETATION

As stated above, the neo-Ricardian interpretation assumes that the method of Marx's theory is essentially the method of linear production theory. The fundamental givens in linear production theory, and assumed to be in Marx's theory, are the physical quantities of the technical conditions of production and the real wage. These technical conditions and real wage provide a system of simultaneous equations that determines the unknown variables of the exchange-values (labor-values or prices) of the commodities produced and the rate of surplus-value or the rate of profit (depending on the equilibrium condition assumed).

According to the neo-Ricardian interpretation, Volume 1 of *Capital* is concerned with the "value system" in which the primary variables determined are the labor-values of individual commodities. These individual labor-values are derived from the technical conditions of production and the real wage, which are taken as given. The rate of surplus-value in value terms is also determined along with the values of individual commodities. The logic of this method is shown by the following "value equation":

$$a_{ij}\lambda_j + (l_i b_j \lambda_j)\,(1 + s) = \lambda_i \qquad (1)$$

in which a_{ij} refers to the material inputs required to produce each commodity, l_i refers to the current labor inputs required to produce each commodity, b_j to the goods included in the real wage, s to the rate of surplus-value, and λ_i to the value of each commodity. The matrices a and l constitute the "technical conditions of production," which together with the real wage determine the individual values and the rate of surplus-value.

The quantities of constant capital, variable capital, and surplus-value (either for individual industries or for the economy as a whole) can then be derived from these individual labor-values in the following way: Constant capital is assumed to be equal to the labor-value of producer goods, variable capital is assumed to be equal to the labor-value of wage goods, and surplus-value is assumed to be equal to the labor-value of surplus goods. Finally, the rate of profit is defined as the ratio of surplus-value to the sum of constant and variable capital, with the absolute magnitudes in both these ratios defined in labor-value terms as above.

Volume 3, according to this interpretation, is concerned with the "price system," in which Marx attempts to transform the labor-value variables determined in Volume 1 into the corresponding price variables. In the Volume 3 analysis, the technical conditions and the real wage are again taken as given, as in Volume 1. In addition, the value magnitudes derived in Volume 1 are also taken as given. From these givens, a set of "transformation multipliers" is derived that then can be used to convert the labor-value of each commodity (or each department) into its corresponding price. The rate of profit in price terms is also determined along with the prices of individual commodities. This logic is shown by the following "price equation":

$$(a_{ij}\lambda_j x_j + l_i b_j \lambda_j x_j)\ (1 + r) = \lambda_i x_i = p_i \qquad (2)$$

in which *x* stands for the set of transformation multipliers (price per unit of value for each commodity) and *r* for the rate of profit. Here we can see that the individual prices are determined by the technical conditions of production, the real wage, and the individual values. The quantities of constant capital, variable capital, and surplus value are "revalued" in price terms as the price of producer goods, wage goods, and surplus goods, respectively.

The neo-Ricardian interpretation concludes that the above is a logically satisfactory solution to the transformation problem. However, three important implications follow from this method of solving the transformation problem that significantly reduce or even eliminate the usefulness of Marx's value theory. First, only one of the two important aggregate equalities emphasized by Marx (see below) can hold at the same time: *either* aggregate price equals aggregate value (or price proportional to labor-value) *or* aggregate profit equals aggregate surplus-value, but *not both* at the same time. Second, the "price" rate of profit derived in the price system is different from the "value" rate of profit derived in the value system, and these two rates of profit may have divergent trends. Finally, the ultimate criticism made by many neo-Ricardians is that the Volume 1 analysis of the value system is "redundant" or an "unnecessary detour" (e.g., Steedman 1977). The same prices and rate of profit can be derived directly from the given technical conditions of production and real wage without first deriving values and then transforming these values into prices.

I argue below that the logical method of linear production theory assumed in this neo-Ricardian interpretation of Marx's theory differs in fundamental respects from Marx's own logical method. In the following sections, I discuss the most important differences between Marx's method and the neo-Ricardian interpretation.

Capital in General and Many Capitals

The first important difference between the neo-Ricardian interpretation and Marx's theory has to do with the order of determination between aggregate economic magnitudes (such as total price or total profit) and the corresponding individual magnitudes. The neo-Ricardian interpretation generally ignores aggregate magnitudes, but it implicitly assumes that these aggregate magnitudes are determined subsequent to individual magnitudes as the sum of these individual magnitudes. I argue, to the contrary, that in Marx's theory, aggregate magnitudes are determined prior to and independent of individual magnitudes. Individual magnitudes are then determined at a later stage of the analysis, with the predetermined aggregate magnitudes taken as given.

Marx expressed this assumed order of determination between aggregate magnitudes and individual magnitudes in terms of the distinction between "capital in general" (or "total social capital") and "many capitals" (or "competition").[1] The analysis of capital in general is concerned with the properties that all capitals have in common. Since these common properties are shared by *all* capitals, the analysis of capital in general is necessarily an analysis of the all capitals taken together, that is, of the total social capital:

> We are concerned here with *capital as such*, (let us) say the capital of the whole society. The differentiation, etc. of capitals does not concern us yet. (Marx 1973, 346)
>
> If I regard the total capital of e.g., a nation as distinct from total wage labor, . . . then I regard it in general. (Marx 1973, 852; see also Marx 1963, 416; Rosdolsky 1977, 46)

The most fundamental and essential common property of all capitals is their capacity for self-expansion. Thus the main aim of the analysis of capital in general in Volume 1 is to show how the total social capital increases its magnitude, that is, how the total amount of surplus-value in the economy as a whole is determined.

Marx introduced the general framework for his analysis of capital in general in Chapter 4 of Volume 1 ("The General Formula for Capital"). This general analytical framework is expressed symbolically as M-C-M′, where $M' = M + \Delta M$. In this formula, M represents the aggregate money-capital invested in the capitalist economy as a whole and M′ represents the aggregate money-capital recovered after some period of time (not specified at this early stage of the analysis). ΔM represents the aggregate amount of surplus-value produced during this period in the capitalist economy as a whole, which includes not only industrial profit, but also merchant profit interest, and rent. The remainder of Volume 1 is devoted primarily to an analysis of the determinants of the magnitude of this ΔM.

> The fact that the purpose of the process is that x should be transformed into $x + \Delta x$ also points to the path our own investigation should take. (Marx 1977a, 977)
>
> The investigation of the origin of surplus-value has therefore formed the most important problem of political economy from the Physiocrats to the present day. (Marx and Engels 1988, 28)

Marx often illustrated the analysis of capital in general with an individual capital, usually a capital in the cotton industry. However, this individual capital is not the real subject of Marx's analysis. An individual capital is considered in Volume 1 only as a typical representative of the total social capital for the purpose of illustration (Rosdolsky 1977, 48; Foley 1986, 6). Since the analysis is about the common properties shared by all capitals, any capital may serve as the representative of the total capital.

> In capitalist production [i.e., in Volume 1], each capital is assumed to be a unit, an aliquot part of the total capital. (Marx 1963, 416)

Volume 3 is then concerned primarily with the level of abstraction of many capitals.[2] The main subject of the analysis of many capitals in Volume 3 is the division of surplus-value among individual capitalists and into individual component parts. In other words, the analysis of many capitals is concerned with the distribution of surplus-value, as distinct from the production of surplus-value. Since individual magnitudes are determined subsequent to aggregate magnitudes, the distribution of surplus value is determined subsequent to the production of surplus-value.

> The profit of the capitalists as a class, or the profit of capital as such, *has to exist before it can be distributed*, and it is extremely absurd to try to explain its origin by its distribution. (Marx 1973, 684; emphasis added)

Part 2 of Volume 3 analyzes the distribution of surplus-value among the individual branches of production, and Parts 4–6 analyze the further division of surplus-value into industrial profit, merchant profit, interest, and rent. This chapter is concerned with the first of these two issues: the distribution of surplus-value among branches of production. Since the distribution of surplus-value is accomplished primarily by means of the prices of individual commodities, the analysis of many capitals also necessarily involves the determination of these individual prices. In this analysis of individual prices and individual components of surplus-value, the total price of all commodities together and the total surplus-value for the economy as a whole are *taken as given*, as determined in Volume 1 (see below for a further discussion of this last point).[3]

Marx considered his analysis of the total amount of surplus-value prior to its division into individual parts one of the three "fundamentally new" aspects of *Capital*.

> In contrast to all former political economy, which from the very outset treats the different fragments of surplus-value with their fixed forms of rent, profit, and interest as already given, *I first deal with the general form of surplus-value in which all these fragments are still undifferentiated*—in solution as it were. (Marx and Engels 1975b, 186; emphasis added; see also Marx and Engels 1975b, 180; Marx 1963, 40, 92)

In Marx's analysis of capital in general, the individual parts of surplus-value and other phenomena related to individual capitals are intentionally disregarded altogether; that is, these individual phenomena are abstracted from.

> The introduction of *many* capitals must not interfere with the investigation here. The relation of the *many* will, rather, be explained after what they all have in common, the quality of being capital, has been examined. (Marx 1973, 517)

This method of abstraction is important to keep in mind because individual phenomena often seem prima facie to contradict the assumptions made and conclusions reached in the analysis of capital in general. In the later analysis of many capitals, the division of surplus-value into individual parts and other individual magnitudes is explained on the basis of the assumptions made and the conclusions reached in the prior analysis of capital in general. In the process, the apparent contradictions are resolved and shown to be consistent with the earlier assumptions and conclusions. In this way, the analysis of capital in general provides what Marx called "intermediate links," which are necessary before an explanation of the phenomena related to many capitals can be given (see the passages quoted below and Rosdolsky 1977, 374–75, 565–68).

Marx called attention to his method of abstraction in two important passages in Volume 1 of *Capital*. In Chapter 5, Marx argues that the origin of surplus-value cannot be explained as long as the analysis is restricted solely to the sphere of circulation, in which the only activities considered are buying and selling. By Marx's assumption, buying and selling involve the exchange of equivalent values. No surplus-value can be created through this exchange of equivalents. Marx points out that this conclusion seems to be contradicted by the existence of merchants' profit and bankers' interest. Merchants and bankers are engaged (more or less) exclusively in activities of circulation, yet merchants obtain a profit and bankers obtain interest as a result of their activities.

Marx remarks that in order to explain these apparently contradictory phenomena, "a long series of intermediate steps" is necessary, which is "entirely absent" in the analysis thus far. In other words, before Marx analyzes the individual components of surplus-value, he first analyzes the determination of the total amount of surplus-value at the level of capital in general. In this prior analysis, the individual parts of surplus-value are ignored altogether. Marx promises to explain this apparent contradiction at a later stage in the analysis:

> In the course of our investigation, we shall find that both merchants' capital and interest-bearing capital are *derivative forms* [of industrial capital]. (Marx 1977a, 267; emphasis added)

The second passage relates specifically to the "transformation problem." In Chapter 11, Marx discusses three laws that follow from his theory of surplus-value. The third law is that the amount of surplus-value produced during a given period of time is proportional to the amount of variable capital invested (with the rate of surplus-value as the factor of proportionality). Marx notes that if this law is applied directly to individual industries, then it seems to be contradicted by the observable phenomenon that individual capitals with unequal proportions of variable capital and constant capital tend to make equal rates of profit (i.e., that profit is proportional to the total capital, not just to the variable capital). Marx then notes that "for the solution of this apparent contradiction, many intermediate terms are still needed" (Marx 1977a, 421). In other words, this apparent contradiction cannot be resolved at the level of analysis of capital in general, but can only be resolved in the later analysis of many capitals. Marx's resolution of this apparent contradiction is of course his solution to the transformation problem.[4]

Marx argued that Ricardo and his followers were not able to provide a satisfactory explanation of the phenomenon of equal rates of profit precisely because they failed to follow the method of abstraction described above. Rather than first abstracting from equal rates of profit in the analysis of capital in general and then explaining this phenomenon in the subsequent analysis of many capitals on the basis of prior conclusions, Ricardo assumed equal rates of profit along with the law of value in the very first chapter of his *Principles* and then examined the extent to which these different assumptions were mutually contradictory. Thus Ricardo omitted the essential "intermediate links" and sought to prove the direct conformity of the law of value with equal rates of profit. This is an impossible task, as Malthus and many others have pointed out.

In Chapter 10 of *Theories of Surplus-Value*, Marx discussed at length this fatal methodological weakness in Ricardo's theory. Because of the importance of this point, it is worthwhile to quote a few passages at length from this chapter:

> Ricardo's method is as follows: He begins with the determination of the magnitude of the value of the commodity by labor-time and then examines whether the other economic relations and categories contradict this determination of value or to what extent they modify it. The historical justification of this method of procedure, its scientific necessity in the history of economics, are evident at first sight, but so too is, at the same time, its scientific inadequacy. This inadequacy not only shows itself in the method of presentation (in a formal sense) but leads to erroneous results because it *omits some essential links* and directly seeks to prove the congruity of the economic categories with one another. (Marx 1968b, 164; emphasis added)

> Instead of postulating this general rate of profit, Ricardo should have examined how far its existence is consistent with the determination of value by labor-time and he would have found that instead of being consistent with it, prima facie, it contradicts it, and that its existence would therefore *have to be explained through a number of intermediary stages, a procedure very different from merely including it under the law of value.* (Marx 1968b, 174; emphasis added)
>
> One can see that though Ricardo is accused of being too abstract, one would be justified in accusing him of the opposite: *lack of power of abstraction, inability, when dealing with the values of commodities, to forget profits, a factor which confronts him as a result of competition.* (Marx 1968b, 191; emphasis added)

In a letter to his friend Dr. Kugelmann, Marx commented again on this crucial difference between his method and Ricardo's:

> Science consists precisely in demonstrating how the law of value asserts itself. So that if one wanted at the very beginning to "explain" all the phenomena which seemingly contradict that law, one would have to present the science before science. It is precisely Ricardo's mistake that in his first chapter on value he takes as given a variety of categories that have not yet been explained in order to prove their conformity with the law of value. (Marx and Engels 1975b, 196)[5]

Thus we conclude that, according to Marx's method, aggregate economic magnitudes are determined in the analysis of capital in general in Volume 1, prior to and independent of the determination of individual magnitudes in the analysis of many capitals in Volume 3, and that the previously determined aggregate magnitudes are taken as given in the subsequent analysis of individual magnitudes. Most important, the total amount of surplus-value is determined prior to the individual parts into which this surplus-value is divided and is taken as given in the subsequent analysis of the individual parts. The following sections discuss further the nature of the givens in Marx's theory at these two levels of abstraction.

Givens in Terms of Money

A second important difference between the neo-Ricardian interpretation and Marx's method has to do with precisely what is taken as given, first of all in Marx's theory of surplus-value in Volume 1 and then in his theory of prices of production in Volume 3. The neo-Ricardian interpretation assumes that the fundamental givens in both of these stages of Marx's theory are the same as those in linear production theory: the physical quantities of the *technical conditions of production and the real wage*. I argue, to the contrary, that the fundamental givens in Marx's theory are *quantities of money, quantities of abstract labor, and the quantity of money that represents one hour of abstract labor.* This section focuses on the sums of money that Marx takes as given.

The analytical framework for Marx's theory is the circulation of capital. As discussed above, Marx first introduced the circulation of capital in Chapter 4 of Volume 1 in the abbreviated form in which it appears in circulation: M-C-M′. As is well known, the complete form of the circulation of capital, which includes the production process, is M-C . . . P . . . C′-M′. The important point for our purposes is that the *starting point* in these formulas is M—a sum of money invested as capital to purchase the means of production and labor-power.

> [A]ll new capital, in the first instance, steps onto the stage—i.e., the market . . .—in the shape of money, money which has to be transformed into capital by definite processes. (Marx 1977a, 247)

I argue that the magnitude of this M that initiates the circulation of capital is *taken as given* in Marx's theory of the emergence of surplus-value in the later stages of the circulation of capital. Indeed, Marx's theory of surplus-value explains how this given amount of money increases its magnitude, that is, how money is transformed into capital. The givens in the Volume 1 theory of surplus-value are aggregate sums of money invested as capital in the capitalist economy as a whole. This interpretation is supported first of all by the very structure of Marx's formulation of the circulation of capital, which begins with a sum of money.

The neo-Ricardian interpretation, to the contrary, ignores Marx's formulation of the circulation of capital in terms of money and seems to imply that the analytical framework for Marx's theory is something like C . . . P . . . C, which may be described as "the production of commodities by means of commodities," in which the fundamental givens are physical quantities of inputs into production. This analytical framework is fundamentally different from the transformation of money into capital.

My interpretation that the initial money-capital in the circulation of capital is taken as given is further supported by the the logical development of Marx's key concepts in Parts 1, 2, and 3 of *Capital.* In Part 1, Marx derives the necessity of money from an analysis of commodities (see Murray, Chapter 2, this volume). In Part 2, as we have seen, Marx defines capital in terms of this previously derived concept of money: as money that becomes more money. The title of Part 2, it should be recalled, is "The Transformation of Money into Capital." Marx clearly expresses this logical relation between money and capital in the following passage:

> [T]he development of capital already *presupposes* the full development of the exchange-value of commodities and consequently its independent existence as money. The *point of departure* in the process of the production and circulation of capital, is the independent form of value which maintains itself, increases, measures the increase against the original amount. . . . The relation between the value antecedent to production and the value which results from it—capital as antecedent value in contrast to profit—constitutes the all-embracing and decisive factor in the whole process of capitalist production. (Marx 1971b, 131; second emphasis added)

Part 3 then analyzes the origin of the increment of money that is characteristic of capital, with the initial money-capital taken as given. Marx does not suddenly in Part 3 ignore the prior logical development of money and capital and surplus-value in Parts 1 and 2 and introduce out of nowhere the technical conditions of production and the real wage as the givens in his theory of surplus-value. Instead, Parts 1 and 2 provide the logical presuppositions for his analysis of surplus-value in Part 3 and beyond. The arguments presented in other chapters in this volume by Smith (Chapter 1), Murray (Chapter 2), and Arthur (Chapter 3), which demonstrate the necessary connections between Marx's concepts of commodities, money, and capital, also support the interpretation presented here that the givens in Marx's theory of surplus-value are sums of money invested as capital. The neo-Ricardian interpretation, on the other hand, has no explanation for Marx's analysis in Parts 1 and 2 or for the logical relation between these two parts and the theory of surplus-value in Part 3.

Finally, my interpretation is also supported textually by the numerous passages throughout the various drafts of *Capital* that refer to the money-capital, which initiates the circulation of capital as the "*presupposed* capital" or the "*postulated* capital" or the "*starting point*" or the "*point of departure*" for the circulation of capital (see, for example, Chapter 4 of Volume 1 of *Capital* and the several earlier drafts of this chapter in Marx 1973, 250–64; Marx and Engels 1987, 501–7; and Marx and Engels 1988, 9–20). One especially clear passage is the following from the manuscript entitled "Results of the Immediate Process of Production":

> Here, where we are concerned with money only as the *point of departure* for the *immediate process of production*, we can confine ourselves to the observation: capital exists here as yet only as a *given quantum of value* = M (money), in which all use-value is extinguished, so that nothing but the monetary form remains. . . . If the original capital is a quantum of value = x, it becomes capital and fulfills its purpose by changing into x + dx, i.e., into a quantum of money or value = the original sum + a

> balance over the original sum. In other words, it is transformed into the given amount of money + additional money, into the *given value* + *surplus-value*. . . . As a *given sum of money*, x is a constant from the outset and hence its increment = 0. In the course of the process, therefore, it must be changed into another amount which contains a variable element. Our task is to discover this component and at the same time to identify the mediations by means of which a constant magnitude becomes a variable one. (Marx 1977a, 976–77; emphases in the original)

As this passage indicates, Marx's methodological procedure is to take a sum of money as given and to analyze how this given sum of money increases its magnitude—that is, how it is transformed into capital.

The initial money-capital that Marx takes as given in his theory of surplus-value is assumed to be the objective "form of appearance" of abstract social labor. This function of money as the form of appearance of abstract labor is the main conclusion of Marx's prior analysis of commodities in Part 1 of Volume 1.

> Money as a measure of value is the necessary form of appearance of the measure of value which is immanent in commodities, namely labor-time. (Marx 1977a, 188)
>
> Money is now objectified labor, irrespective of whether it possesses the form of money or a particular commodity. (Marx and Engels 1987, 502)
>
> The starting point [of capital] is money . . . the converted form of the commodity, in which . . . the labor contained in it has the form of general social labor. (Marx and Engels 1988, 11)
>
> Capital is money, the independent existence of exchange-value, objectified general social labor. (Marx and Engels 1988, 134)

This important conclusion is then presupposed in the remainder of *Capital* and in his theory of surplus-value in particular. Thus the aggregate money-capital taken as given beginning in Part 2 of Volume 1, like any other quantity of money, is assumed to represent a definite quantity of abstract social labor. The precise quantity of abstract social labor represented by a given quantity of money depends on the value of money (more on this below), which Marx also takes as given (Marx 1977a, 214).

Theory of Aggregate Price and Surplus-Value

This section examines in greater detail Marx's theory of aggregate price and surplus-value presented in Part 3 of Volume 1. We have seen above that

Marx takes as given the initial money-capital invested in the first phase of the circulation of capital. Marx divided this given initial money-capital (M) into two component parts: constant capital (C), invested in means of production; and variable capital (V), invested in labor-power. Algebraically: M = C + V (all defined in terms of money). According to Marx's theory of value and surplus-value, these two given quantities of aggregate money-capital play entirely different roles in the determination of the aggregate price of commodities and thus in the determination of the aggregate amount of surplus-value.

The quantity of constant capital, which is equal to the price of the means of production, becomes one component of the aggregate price of the final product. In other words, the price of the means of production is "transferred" to the price of the final product.

> Since, with the exception of the additional labor, the elements of capitalist production already enter the process of production as commodities, i.e., with specific prices, it follows that the *value added by the constant capital is already given in terms of a price.* For example, in the present case it is the $80 for flax, machinery, etc. (Marx 1977a, 957; emphasis added except for the last word, "price")
>
> If we take society at any one moment, there exists simultaneously in all spheres of production . . . a definite constant capital—presupposed as a necessary condition of production. . . . The value of this constant capital . . . is a *postulated value which must reappear in the value of the product.* (Marx 1963, 109; emphasis added; see also Marx 1973, 762; Marx and Engels 1988, 20)

The constant capital that is taken as given and transferred to the price of the final product is the *current replacement costs* of the existing means of production, not the actual historical costs of these means of production (Marx 1977a, 317–18, 677; 1982, 112, 139–41, 206–7; 1963, 109; 1968b, 415–16, 473; 1971b, 178). The current replacement costs may differ from the actual historical costs for two reasons: technological change in the production of means of production and/or changes in the value of money. Carchedi discusses at length the case of technological change in Chapter 8 of this volume and in Carchedi 1984 and 1988.[6]

The variable capital, which is equal to the price of labor-power, does not become a component of the price of the final product. Instead, the variable capital is replaced by current labor, and this labor produces new-value, which becomes the second component of the aggregate price of commodities. This new-value component of the price of commodities produced by current labor both reproduces the variable capital invested in labor-power and provides the surplus-value of capitalists (see below).

> The characteristic feature of variable capital is that a definite, *given* (and as such constant) part of capital . . . is exchanged for a self-expanding, value-creating power, viz. labor-power, which not only reproduces its value, paid by the capitalist, but simultaneously produes a surplus-value, a value not existing previously and not paid for by any equivalent. This characteristic property of the part of capital laid out for wages . . . distinguishes it *toto coleo* as variable capital from constant capital. (Marx 1981, 217–18; first emphasis added)

The different roles played by constant capital and variable capital in the determination of the price of commodities are emphasized by Marx in his discussion of the category of "cost price" in Chapter 1 of Volume 3 of *Capital*. Marx's main point in this discussion is that the category of cost price obliterates the crucial distinction between constant capital and variable capital and makes it appear as if *both* constant capital and variable capital transfer their value to the price of the product. Marx emphasizes that, according to his theory, only the value of the constant capital is transferred to the price of the product.

> We know from Volume 1 that the value of the product newly formed, in this case $600, is composed of (1) the reappearing value of the constant capital of $400 spent on the means of production, and (2) a newly produced value of $200. . . .
>
> By the purposive character of the labor . . . the value of the means of production consumed, a total of $400, is transferred from these means of production to the product. This old value reappears therefore as a component of the product's value, though it does not originate in the production process of *this* commodity. It exists only as a component of the commodity's value because it existed previously as a component of the capital advanced. The constant capital that was spent is thus replaced by the portion of commodity value that it itself adds to this commodity value. This element of the cost price . . . forms a component of this commodity value because it is the value of capital that has been used up, or because the means of production cost such and such an amount.
>
> It is quite the reverse with the other component of cost price. . . . This advance of capital value does not go in any way into the formation of the new value. (Marx 1982, 119–20)

In addition to these sums of money-capital, Marx also takes as given in his theory of the aggregate price of commodities two additional variables: (1) the aggregate amount of current abstract labor that is required to produce commodities (L_c), and (2) the quantity of money that represents one hour of abstract labor, or the rate at which abstract labor produces new-value per hour (m). Abstract labor is defined by Marx to be homogeneous labor in which concrete labors of different skills and different intensities are reduced to equivalent quantities of skilled labor of average intensity. Marx's concept of current abstract labor thus differs from the current labor requirements taken as given in linear production theory because the latter treats all kinds of labor as equal and does not take into account labor of different skills and different intensities.[7] The quantity of money that represents one hour of abstract labor is equal to the inverse of the labor value of a unit of money.[8] These two variables together determine the aggregate amount of new-value (N) produced during the current period ($N = mL_c$).

Marx's theory of the determination of the aggregate price of commodities can thus be represented algebraically by the following equations:

$$P = C + N \qquad (3a)$$

$$P = C + mL_c \qquad (3b)$$

where P represents the price of commodities and C represents constant capital.

Thus, according to Marx's theory, the constant capital and the money-value transferred from the means of production to the price of the final product are not derived from, nor are they necessarily proportional to, the labor required to produce the means of production. Instead this transferred value is assumed to be equal to the constant capital invested in the means of production, which as we have seen above is taken as given. This constant capital, like every other quantity of money, represents a definite quantity of abstract social labor.

> The value of the means of production is presupposed, since the labor-time contained in the means of production was expressed in their prices in its general form, as social labor. (Marx and Engels 1988, 73)

The precise quantity of "past" abstract labor (L_p) represented by constant capital depends on the value of money (1/m) and is determined by the equation:

$$L_p = C/m \qquad (4)$$

This quantity of past abstract labor represented by the constant capital will be equal to the labor required to produce the means of production, or the labor "embodied" in the means of production, *if and only if* the price of the means of production is proportional to their labor value (i.e., $P_{mp} = mL_{mp}$):

$$L_p = \frac{C}{m} = \frac{P_{mp}}{m} = \frac{mL_{mp}}{m} = L_{mp} \qquad (5)$$

In Volume 1, Marx provisionally assumes that the price of the means of production is proportional to the labor "embodied" in them. Strictly speaking, the exact proportionality between price and labor-time applies only to the aggregate product; but since the prices of individual commodities are not analyzed in Volume 1, there is no basis for making any other assumption about these individual prices or about the price of any subset of the aggregate product, such as the means of production. In Volume 3, of course, it is determined that the prices of individual commodities will in general not be proportional to the labor embodied in them. In this case, the past abstract labor represented by the constant capital will not be equal to the labor embodied in the means of production. However, this inequality makes no difference in the quantity of money-value transferred from the means of production to the price of the final product. In either case, the value transferred is equal to the constant capital, which is taken as given. Other authors who have argued that the value transferred from the means of production to the price of the final product is equal to the *price* of the means of production, regardless of whether this price is proportional to the labor embodied in the means of production, include Carchedi (1984), Mattick, Jr. (1981), Wolff et al. (1983), and Mage (1963, appendix A).

From this theory of aggregate price, Marx derives the aggregate amount of surplus-value (S) produced in a given period of time. This derivation may be briefly summarized algebraically as follows:[9]

$$S = P - K \tag{6}$$

$$P = C + N \tag{7}$$

$$K = C + V \tag{8}$$

$$\begin{aligned} S &= (C + N) - (C + V) \qquad (9) \\ &= N - V \\ &= mL_c - mL_n \\ &= m(L_c - L_n) \\ S &= mL_s \end{aligned}$$

where K stands for total costs of production, L_n for necessary labor-time or the time required for current labor to reproduce the equivalent of variable capital (= V/m), and L_s for surplus labor-time.[10] The main points about this derivation for our purposes are: (1) the givens in this theory are C, V, L_c, and m, as discussed above; (2) the aggregate amount of surplus-value is derived as a function of the aggregate amount of surplus labor; (3) the aggregate amount of surplus-value that is determined in this way is then *taken as given* in Marx's subsequent analysis of the distribution of surplus-value and of prices of production in Volume 3, which is discussed in further detail in the next section.

Theory of Prices of Production

I first specify the quantities that are taken as given in Marx's theory of prices of production. To begin with, as just discussed, the total quantity of surplus-value is taken as given, as determined by the prior analysis of capital in general, in keeping with Marx's method of abstraction in which the conclusions of one level of abstraction are presupposed at later stages of the analysis. In this way, the analysis of the determinants of the aggregate surplus-value at the level of capital in general is a necessary "intermediate link" in the analysis of the distribution of surplus-value at the level of many capitals.

> *In considering profit, surplus-value is assumed as given.* (Marx 1971b, 369; emphasis added)
>
> Profit (profit of enterprise plus interest) and rent are nothing more than characteristic forms assumed by particular portions of the surplus-value in commodities. *The size of the surplus-value sets a quantitative limit for the parts it can be broken down into.* (Marx 1982, 971; emphasis added)
>
> *We have thus an absolute limit for the value component that forms surplus-value and can be broken down into profit and ground-rent*; this is determined by the excess of the unpaid portion of the working day over its paid portion, i.e., by the value component of the total product in which this surplus labor is realized. If we call the surplus-value whose limits are thus determined profit, when it is calculated on the total capital advanced, as we have already done, then this profit, considered in its absolute amount, is equal to the surplus-value, i.e., it is just as regularly determined in its limits as this is. (Marx 1982, 999; emphasis added)

These latter two quotations concern the division of surplus-value into industrial profit, interest, and rent, but the same methodological principle that the aggregate amount of profit is determined prior to the individual parts and sets the limit for the latter also applies to the division of surplus-value among individual branches of production.

Also taken as given in this analysis of prices of production is the general or average rate of profit, again as determined by the prior analysis of capital in general in Volume 1. The general rate of profit is equal to the ratio of the aggregate surplus value to the aggregate capital.

> The *general rate of profit* is formed through the total surplus-value being calculated on the total capital of society (of the class of capitalists). (Marx 1968b, 433)

> This rate of profit, expressed in absolute terms, can be nothing else than the *surplus-value* produced (annually) by the *capitalist class* in relation to the total capital advanced by *society* as a whole. (Marx and Engels 1975b, 193)
>
> The prerequisite [of prices of production] is the existence of a general rate of profit. (Marx 1982, 257)

Finally, the individual quantities of constant capital and variable capital invested in each industry are also taken as given, as quantities of money, in this analysis of prices of production.[11]

> The variable and constant capital consumed in the production of the commodities in each particular investment *would be given*. (Marx 1982, 259; emphasis added)

The two sums of these individual quantities of constant capital and variable capital obviously equal the aggregate quantities of constant capital and variable capital that are taken as given in the Volume 1 analysis of capital in general.

We now turn to Marx's method of determining prices of production, based on these given quantities. According to Marx's method, the determination of the prices of individual commodities is a simple and straightforward matter.

> If the limits of value and surplus-value are given, it is easy to grasp how the competition of capitals transforms values into prices of production. (Marx 1982, 429)

According to Marx's theory, individual commodities do not in general exchange at prices that are proportional to the labor-time contained in them. In other words, individual commodities do not exchange at prices that enable the capitalists in each industry to collect the exact amount of surplus-value produced in that industry. Instead, individual commodities tend to exchange at prices that enable capitalists in each branch to recover the capital consumed in production and to collect the average rate of profit on their total advanced capital. The average rate of profit is itself equal to the general rate of profit for the total capital, which, as stated above, is determined in the Volume 1 analysis of capital in general and presupposed in this analysis of the distribution of surplus-value. Marx calls the prices of individual commodities that provide such a proportional distribution of surplus-value among the individual industries the *prices of production* of commodities.

The determination of the price of production of each commodity is given by the equation:

$$P_i = (C_i + V_i) + R\,M_i \qquad (10)$$

where P_i stands for price of production of each commodity, C_i for the periodic flow of constant capital consumed in each industry, V_i for the periodic flow of variable capital expended in each industry, R for the general rate of profit, and M_i for the total stock of money-capital advanced in each industry.

The amount of profit included in the price of each commodity (= RM_i) will in general not be equal to the amount of surplus-value actually contained in that commodity, and hence the price of production of each commodity will in general not be proportional to the labor-time required to produce it. However, the total amount of surplus-value is not altered by this redistribution of surplus-value among the individual industries according to the total amount of capital invested. Taken together, the divergences of individual profits from individual surplus-values balance out so that the sum of individual profits is equal to the total amount of surplus-value (S), as determined in the Volume 1 analysis of capital in general. This can be trivially shown as follows:

$$E(RM_i) = R\,E(M_i) = RM = (S/M)\,M = S \qquad (11)$$

where E stands for summation.

Similarly, the sum of the prices of production of individual commodities is equal to the aggregate price of commodities, as determined in the Volume 1 analysis of capital in general:

$$\begin{aligned} E(P_i) &= E[(C_i + V_i) + RM_i] \qquad (12) \\ &= E(C_i + E(V_i) + RE(M_i) \\ &= C + V + S \\ &= C + N \\ &= P \end{aligned}$$

Finally, in contrast to the neo-Ricardian interpretation, the general rate of profit obviously does not change in Marx's determination of prices of production, since it is taken as given in this analysis and *not* determined simultaneously along with the prices of production, as in the neo-Ricardian interpretation. According to Marx's method, there are not two rates of profit; there is only one rate of profit, the "price rate of profit," which is determined in the Volume 1 analysis of capital in general and is taken as given in the Volume 3 analysis of many capitals.

RESPONSE TO NEO-RICARDIAN CRITICISM

According to the neo-Ricardian interpretation, Marx's analysis of the determination of prices of production summarized above is logically incomplete and contradictory because Marx failed to transform the amounts of constant capital and variable capital invested in each industry from value magnitudes to price magnitudes. This criticism began with Bortkiewicz:

> [Marx] made the mistake of carrying over certain magnitudes without alteration from the table of values into that of prices. In transforming values into prices, it is inadmissible to exclude from the recalculation the constant and variable capital invested in the various spheres of production. (Bortkiewicz 1952, 9)

Sweezy repeated this criticism in his influential *Theory of Capitalist Development*:

> The source of Marx's error is not difficult to discover. In his price scheme, the capitalists' outlays on constant and variable capital are left exactly as they were in the value scheme; in other words, the constant capital and variable capital used in production are still expressed in value terms. Now it is obvious that in a system in which price calculation is universal, both the capital used in production and the product itself must be expressed in price terms. The trouble is that Marx went only halfway in transforming values into prices. It need occasion no surprise that this procedure leads to contradictory results. (Sweezy 1968, 115)

In the subsequent debate, it was concluded that it is possible to correct Marx's "error" and to complete the transformation of the inputs of constant capital and variable capital from value magnitudes to price magnitudes. However, as discussed in the first section above, three important implications follow from this neo-Ricardian "solution": (1) only one of Marx's two aggregate equalities can in general hold at the same time; (2) the "price" rate of profit will not be equal to the "value" rate of profit; and (3) the Volume 1 analysis of the value system is "redundant" or an "unnecessary detour" because the same prices and rate of profit can be derived directly from the given technical conditions of production and real wage.

I argue that these criticisms are based on the neo-Ricardian interpretation of Marx's theory, which assumes a different logical method from Marx's own method, as discussed above. In particular, this criticism assumes a different method of determination of the individual quantities of constant capital and variable capital invested in each industry. According to the neo-Ricardian interpretation, the fundamental givens in Marx's theory (as in linear production theory) are the physical quantities of the technical conditions of production and the real wage. According to this method, the quantities of constant capital and variable capital invested in each industry are *derived from these given technical conditions and real wage*. In Volume 1, the quantities of constant capital are determined as the labor-values of the given means of production employed in each industry. In Volume 3, these quantities of constant capital in value terms are taken as given and then transformed into the corresponding prices of these same means of production. Thus, in the transition from Volume 1 to Volume 3, the quantity of the means of production remains the same (taken as given), but the quantity of constant capital derived from these given means of production changes. A similar method is followed for variable capital. Variable capital in each industry is first determined as the labor-values of the given wage goods and then transformed into the prices of these same wage goods. It is precisely these transformations of constant capital and variable capital from value magnitudes to price magnitudes that Marx is accused of having failed to make.

However, it has been argued above that, according to Marx's method, the individual quantities of constant capital and variable capital invested in each industry are *not* derived from the technical conditions of production and the real wage, but are instead *taken as given in money terms.* In the Volume 1 analysis of capital in general, these quantities of constant capital and variable capital invested in each industry are not considered at all; more precisely, they are not determined as the labor-values of given quantities of means of production and wage goods in each industry. Only the aggregate quantities of constant capital and variable capital are considered in the Volume 1 analysis, and these aggregate quantities are taken as given. Thus the individual quantities of constant capital and variable capital in value terms cannot be taken as given in Volume 3, as determined in Volume 1, since they are not even analyzed in Volume 1. Instead, the individual quantities of constant capital and variable capital are taken as given in the subsequent Volume 3 analysis in *price* terms (i.e, as quantities of money). According to Marx's method, these quantities of constant capital and variable capital do not need to be transformed from value terms into price terms; instead, *they are already in price terms because they are taken as given in price terms.* The transition from Volume 1 to Volume 3 is not a transition from labor-values to prices; it is a transition from aggregate prices to individual prices. Thus Marx did not "fail to transform the inputs" from values to prices. According to Marx's method, *there is no such transformation to be made.* Carchedi (1984) and Mattick, Jr. (1981) also emphasize that the inputs of constant capital and variable capital are taken as given in price terms in the determination of prices of production and thus do not have to be transformed from value magnitudes to price magnitudes.

On the other hand, the quantities of means of production and wage goods that the given quantities of constant and variable capital will purchase will be different depending on whether or not the prices of the means of production and wage goods are proportional to their labor-values. For example, if the price of the means of production is greater than their price proportional to labor, then the given amount of money-constant capital will purchase a smaller quantity of means of production than if these two prices were equal. Similarly, if the price of wage goods is less than their price proportional to labor, then the given amount of variable capital will purchase a greater quantity of wage goods than if these two prices were equal (Marx 1973, 436–38).

Thus, Marx's method is essentially the *opposite* of the neo-Ricardian interpretation: In moving from Volume 1 to Volume 3, Marx holds the money quantities of constant and variable capital invariant, and this transition results in changes in the physical quantities of means of production and wage goods that the given constant and variable capital will purchase. (This change does not refer to an *actual* change, but rather to a change from the *hypothetical* quantity of means of production and wage goods that the given constant and variable capital *would* purchase, *if* prices were proportional to their labor-values, to the *actual* quantity of means of production and wage goods that the given constant and variable capital actually purchase with prices not proportional to their labor-values.) The neo-Ricardian method, on the other hand, holds the quantities of means of production and wage goods invariant, and the transition to Volume 3 results in changes in the quantities of constant capital and variable capital (again, not an actual change). Thus the failure to transform the quantities of constant capital and variable capital can be a problem only within neo-Ricardian theory, but cannot be a problem for Marx's theory.

It is often argued that although Marx failed to transform constant capital and variable capital from value terms to price terms, he explicitly acknowledged in a few passages that such a transformation should be made, but did not recognize the full implications of completing the transformation (e.g., Steedman 1977, 31–33). The passages most often cited in this regard are Marx 1982, 261, 265, 309. However, a reexamination of these passages from the perspective of Marx's method as outlined above suggests an entirely different interpretation. As discussed above, the "value transferred" from the means of production to the price of the final product is equal to the given constant capital, or to the price of the means of production, whether or not this price is proportional to the labor-time embodied in the means of production. In these passages in Volume 3, Marx is simply calling attention to the fact that in Volume 1 he made the provisional assumption that the price of the means of production is proportional to the labor-time embodied in the means of production, but now that provisional assumption is dropped. However, this further determination of the price of the means of production does not imply that the constant capital needs to be further transformed, because constant capital is not derived from the labor-time required to produce the means of production, but is instead taken as given. Nor does this further determination of the price of the means of production affect the value transferred from the means of production, which is equal to the given constant capital in either case. It simply means that the given constant capital and thus the value transferred is no longer assumed to be proportional to the labor-time embodied in the means of production.

Finally, the three important implications of the neo-Ricardian "solution" to the transformation problem discussed above do not follow from Marx's own logical method. As shown in the previous section, both of Marx's aggregate equalities are true simultaneously, and the determination of individual prices does not alter the rate of profit; instead the rate of profit is taken as given in the determination of individual prices. With respect to the third implication, the "redundancy" criticism of the neo-Ricardians, it follows from the characteristics of Marx's logical method discussed above that the *values of commodities, as defined by Marx, cannot be derived from the technical conditions of production*, for two main reasons: First, Marx's concept of abstract labor differs from the current labor requirements included in the technical conditions of production because the latter do not take into account different skills and different intensities of labor. Second, the "past labor" represented by constant capital is in general not equal to the labor "embodied" in the means of production. Therefore, the values of commodities, as defined by Marx, are not an "unnecessary detour" from the technical conditions of production to the prices of commodities, but are instead an indispensable assumption in Marx's theory of profit.[12]

Comparison with the "New Solution" to the Transformation Problem

In recent years, a "new solution" to the transformation problem has emerged that occupies a sort of middle ground between the neo-Ricardian interpretation and the interpretation presented here. This new solution was originally presented independently by Foley (1982), Dumenil (1980, 1983), and Lipietz (1982) and has gained increasing attention and acceptance among Marxian and radical economists (although no doubt it is still a minority view). This section briefly reviews a few important points of this new solution and contrasts it with the interpretation presented here.

The main similarity between the new solution and the interpretation presented here is that the new solution also takes variable capital as given in money terms, rather than deriving variable capital from a given quantity of wage goods, as in the neo-Ricardian interpretation. This given quantity of variable capital in money terms remains invariant in the transition from Volume 1 to Volume 3. The justification for this interpretation is not made in terms of Marx's logical method; instead it is argued that this assumption provides a more accurate representation of the actual exchange relation between capitalists and workers in capitalist society.

> Workers in capitalist society do not bargain for, or receive, a bundle of commodities as payment for the labor power, they receive a sum of money, the money wage, which they are then free to spend as they wish. (Foley 1982, 43)

Foley also argues that this interpretation also provides a better understanding of the specific nature of exploitation in capitalism and of the nature of the class struggle between capitalists and workers. He believes that this interpretation enables one to perceive that capitalist exploitation is not identical with the existence of a surplus product and that the goal of workers' struggles should not be the elimination of the surplus product per se, but should instead be the elimination of the social relations of capitalism in which the surplus product is appropriated in the form of surplus-value by capitalists.

This new solution also redefines the aggregate price equality to refer to the *net* price of the total product rather than the *gross* price. It follows from this interpretation (and the assumption of a given money wage) that this redefined aggregate price equality and the aggregate profit equality can both hold at the same time.

However, this new solution treats constant capital differently from variable capital. It does not take constant capital as given in money terms, but instead derives constant capital from a given quantity of means of production, as in the neo-Ricardian interpretation. Thus the magnitude of constant capital will change in the transformation from values to prices, as in the neo-Ricardian interpretation. Since the magnitude of constant capital changes, the total price of commodities will not be proportional to the total labor value of commodities, and the "price" rate of profit will not be equal to the "value" rate of profit, again as in the neo-Ricardian interpretation.

Thus there is a methodological inconsistency in this new solution in its treatment of constant capital and variable capital. Variable capital is taken as given in money terms, but constant capital is derived from given physical quantities. Proponents of this view do not provide a rationale for this inconsistent treatment. I argue that since both constant capital and variable capital are components of the total capital invested by capitalists, these two components should be treated in parallel fashion. Either they both should be taken as given in money terms, as in Marx's theory, or they both should be derived from given physical quantities, as in linear production theory.

At one point, Foley seems to present a general argument for taking as given all the money-capital invested in capitalist firms (both constant capital and variable capital), rather than taking as given "the production and distribution of use-values":

> One striking difference between Marx's treatment of the problem and later treatments is that Marx describes the two economies solely in terms of the accounts of the capitalist firms; he does not specify the actual production and distribution of use-values. Later treatments, perhaps in the name of theoretical rigor, describe both economies in terms of the production and distribution of particular use-values, and *derive* the accounts of the capitalist firms from this assumed data on production and distribution. When one holds constant the production and distribution of use-values, it turns out that . . . aggregate value added and aggregate profit cannot both be the same in the two [economies].
>
> I want to suggest that Marx had good theoretical reasons for describing the two economies in terms of the accounts of the capitalist firms rather than in terms of the production and distribution of use-values. The social facts relevant to struggle and change in a capitalist society concern the production and distribution of value itself, and the actual production, distribution, and consumption of use-values that follow from these struggles take a secondary place. (Foley 1982, 44–45)

It seems to me that Foley's argument could be applied to constant capital as well as to variable capital. However, Foley applies it only to variable capital, that is, only to the distribution of use-values. He does not apply it to constant capital or the production of use-values.

I have argued above that, according to Marx's method, *both* constant capital and variable capital are taken as given in terms of money. This argument is based on (1) Marx's formula for the circulation of capital, M–C–M′, which is the general analytical framework for Marx's theory and which begins with a given sum of money; (2) the logical relation between Parts 1, 2, and 3 of Volume 1 of *Capital*, according to which the development of the concepts of money and capital in Parts 1 and 2 provide the logical presuppositions for the analysis of surplus-value in Part 3 and beyond; and (3) the numerous passages in which Marx states that the quantity of the initial money-capital is presupposed in his theory of surplus-value. Those who accept this new solution should provide an explanation for their different treatments of constant capital and variable capital and should either refute the above three points or show how they are consistent with their interpretation.

CONCLUSION

This chapter has argued that the prevailing neo-Ricardian interpretation attributes to Marx's theory a logical method (the method of linear production theory) that is fundamentally different from Marx's own method. The two main differences discussed were the order of determination between aggregate magnitudes and individual magnitudes and the nature of the givens or presuppositions in Marx's theory. This chapter has argued further that, if Marx's method is followed, then his determination of prices of production in Volume 3 of *Capital* is not logically flawed as the neo-Ricardians claim. *Both* of Marx's two aggregate equalities (aggregate price equals aggregate value, and aggregate profit equals aggregate surplus-value) follow as necessary conclusions of this method. And, finally, the rate of profit does not change as a result of this determination of prices of production. Thus the long line of neo-Ricardian literature on Marx's "transformation problem," from Bortkiewicz on, does not in fact apply to Marx's theory, but instead applies only to linear production theory, or to the misguided attempt to interpret Marx's theory in terms of linear production theory.

I have not argued that Marx's theory is necessarily superior to linear production theory. The relative explanatory power of these two theories is beyond the scope of this chapter, but this is obviously the next question that should be addressed. However, a meaningful evaluation of the relative merits of these two theories is not possible without first gaining a clear understanding of the uniqueness of Marx's theory and its differences from linear production theory. The purpose of this chapter has been to contribute to such an understanding of Marx's theory.

Notes

I benefited greatly from the discussion of my paper at the conference on Marx's method in *Capital* (Mount Holyoke College, 3–7 June 1991). I have also benefited very much from ongoing discussions over the past several years with Paul Mattick, Mino Carchedi, and Geert Reuten, although they do not agree with all the views expressed here and are certainly not responsible for any remaining errors.

1. My interpretation of Marx's distinction between capital in general and many capitals draws heavily from the work of Mattick, Sr. 1959, 1969, and Rosdolsky 1977.
2. Parts 1 and 3 of Volume 3 remain at the level of abstraction of capital in general. Volume 2 is also at the level of abstraction of capital in general. Volume 2 analyzes the various characteristics that are shared by all capitals that grow out of the process of circulation, as distinct from the process of production.

3. We can see from Marx's methodological distinction between capital in general and many capitals that the "successive approximations" interpretation of Marx's method, adopted by Sweezy and many others, is erroneous. According to the successive approximations interpretation, Volume 1 of *Capital* makes the simplifying assumptions that the prices of individual commodities are equal (or proportional) to their values, and the composition of capital in all industries is equal. Then in Volume 3, unequal compositions of capital are introduced, and a more realistic theory of prices is developed. The rate of profit is also determined simultaneously with prices in this Volume 3 analysis, similar to the linear production interpretation of Marx's method.

   However, according to Marx's distinction between capital in general and many capitals, the Volume 1 analysis of capital in general disregards altogether the prices of individual commodities and the compositions of individual capitals. *No assumption is made* about the equality of individual compositions of capital, because individual capitals do not yet enter into the analysis. Further, the logical transition to Volume 3 is not marked by a change of assumption with regard to the composition of individual capitals, but is instead marked by a shift in the level of abstraction from capital in general to many capitals, in which individual phenomena, such as the composition of individual capitals, are considered for the first time. Finally, the total amount of profit and the general rate of profit are taken as given in the Volume 3 analysis of the distribution of surplus-value and the determination of individual prices, as will be discussed in the following section.

   For a further discussion of the successive approximations interpretation of Marx's method, see Moseley 1982, ch. 1.
4. Note that Marx does not suggest here (or anywhere else) the simplifying assumption of equal compositions for all capitals. Instead, in his analysis of capital in general, Marx abstracts from individual capitals and their compositions altogether and promises to take them into account at a later stage of the analysis.
5. Ricardo's followers (James Mill, James McCulloch, Thomas DeQuincey, and others) continued to attempt to deduce the particular phenomena of capitalism directly from the law of value, without success. Marx discusses these "pitiful" attempts in detail in Chapter 20 of Volume 3 of *Theories of Surplus-Value* ("The Disintergration of the Ricardian School"). See especially pp. 71, 86–89, and 190.
6. Carchedi was one of the first, along with Mattick, Jr. (1981), to emphasize that, contrary to the prevailing neo-Ricardian interpretation, constant capital and variable capital in Marx's theory are taken as given in terms of money. To my knowledge, no neo-Ricardian author has answered Carchedi's arguments.
7. See Moseley 1992, 44–53; 1991, 30–31, for a further discussion of Marx's concept of abstract labor.
8. Marx usually assumed for purposes of illustration that $m = 0.5$ shillings per hour.
9. Marx himself illustrated his theory of surplus-value with numerical examples and did not present a general algebraic formulation.
10. For Marx's definitions of necessary labor-time and surplus labor-time, see Marx 1977a, 324–27.
11. Like the aggregate constant capital discussed above, these individual quantities of constant capital are taken as given in terms of the current replacement costs, not the actual historical costs, of the existing means of production.
12. Other neo-Ricardian criticisms of Marx's theory of value—e.g., that in the case

of joint production, values can be indeterminate or even negative, and that with a choice of technique, the determination of the rate of profit is logically *prior* to the determination of values—also assume the logical method of linear production theory (in particular, they assume that the fundamental givens in Marx's theory are the physical quantities of the technical conditions of production). Thus, these criticisms, like the criticisms discussed in the text, do not apply to Marx's theory, but apply only to the mistaken interpretation of Marx's theory in terms of linear production theory.

8

Marx's Logic of Inquiry and Price Formation

Guglielmo Carchedi

As is well known, Marx transforms individual values into prices of production by adding to constant capital and variable capital in percentage terms the average rate of profit. This procedure has been the object of much misunderstanding and debate since Boehm-Bawerk's critique of the third volume of *Capital* in 1896 (1973). This chapter first reviews and shows the fallacy of the two most influential lines of critique, the circularity and the infinite regression critiques, both of neo-Ricardian matrix. It then proceeds to theorize the complete notion of production prices, one in which technical change affects the production price not only of the output of a production process but also of its inputs. Throughout, the basic argument is that value, and thus the transformation of individual into social values, can be properly understood only from the point of view of the collective laborer and thus only by employing a dialectical class analysis.

In itself, the neo-Ricardian critique is worthless. It stems from imaginary economics, from an economic theory in which dynamic categories have been replaced by static convolutions and dialectical class analysis has been replaced by formal logic. Since the critique is faulty, the debate that has followed from it is largely irrelevant. However, a review of this critique is warranted both because of its impact on recent economic debates and because its assessment provides the opportunity to clarify the dialectical and class nature of Marx's transformation procedure. Consequently, this chapter is divided into two parts. The first part[1] deals with some questions of method regarding social research that are necessary in order to follow the argument in the second part, which deals with the "transformation problem" and the discussion around it.

The Method of Social Research

Let us begin with an example of how Marx applies the dialectical method and then extract from this application the basic features of that method. We meet Marx's concept of dialectics as early as in the first chapter of the first volume of *Capital*, where he deals with the relative and the equivalent forms of value. In the expression "20 yards of linen are worth 1 coat," the two commodities play different roles. "The value of the linen is represented as relative value, or appears in relative form. The coat officiates as equivalent, or appears in equivalent form" (Marx 1967a, 1:48). From the analysis developed by Marx, the following five points can be extracted.

First, "the relative form and the equivalent form are two intimately connected, mutually dependent and inseparable elements of the expression of value" (Ibid.). Second, "the opposition, or contrast existing internally in each commodity between use-value and value, is . . . made evident externally by two commodities being placed in such relation to each other, that the commodity whose value it is sought to express, figures directly as a mere use-value, while the commodity in which that value is to be expressed, figures directly as mere exchange-value" (Marx 1967a, 1:61). Or, "the antagonism between the relative form of value and the equivalent form, the two poles of the value form, is developed concurrently with that form itself" (Marx 1967a, 1:68). Third, "the former [the relative form] plays an active, the latter [the equivalent form] a passive, part" (Marx 1967a, 1:48). Fourth, "whether a commodity assumes the relative form, or the opposite equivalent form, depends entirely upon its accidental position in the expression of value" (Marx 1967a, 1:49). Fifth, these forms "are mutually exclusive, antagonistic extremes—i.e., poles of the same expression" (Marx 1967a, 1:48). What is the relevance of these five points for a theory of dialectics?

1. Point one stresses the mutual existential relationship between the two forms. Each form cannot exist without the other, that is, they are each other's conditions of existence. More generally, all parts of reality are tied by mutual existential interdependence.
2. Point two stresses that both the relative form (which figures merely as a use value) and the equivalent form (which figures merely as exchange value) are potentially contained in both the linen and the coat. In fact, both commodities are already both a use value and an exchange value before officiating as either just the former or just the latter. It is only in the value relation, in the expression of value, that the linen counts exclusively as a use value and the coat exclusively as an exchange value. In more general terms, reality is both what has realized itself and what is potentially present.

3. Point three stresses that one form is more important than the other, that one is "active" and the other is "passive." Since Marx, throughout his work, repeatedly uses the terms *determinant* and *determined*, a more general way to put this is that some parts of reality are determinant and other parts are determined. This relationship of determination can be expressed by conceptualizing the determined form as being the condition of existence of the determinant form. In the expression of value the linen, which counts only as a use value, determines the coat, which counts only as an exchange value. (But in the creation of value it is the exchange value of a commodity that determines its use value.)
4. Point four stresses the possibility of the relative (more generally, the determinant) form becoming the equivalent (or determined) form and vice versa, according to the position they take in the value relation.
5. Finally, point five stresses that these two forms are antagonistic, that is, mutually exclusive. Although the former points are generally applicable, this last point refers only to the specific nature of this particular relationship. Here, the determinant and the determined instance are conditions of each other's existence. However, a determined instance can also be a condition of supersession of the determinant instance. Let us now cast these concepts in a general framework.

DETERMINATION IN THE LAST INSTANCE

I begin by defining three important terms. The first is *instance*. This is a general term that indicates an event that is a part, or element, of a process. The elements of a process are processes themselves. For example, the process of production and distribution is the combination of the process of production and the process of distribution. Thus, we can also say that instances are processes that are part of a wider process. The second is *unity*. This term indicates that in reality instances are tied to each other by a relation of existential interdependence, that they exist only as part of the same process. The third term is to *supersede*. This verb means both to preserve and to cause to cease to exist. This statement is only apparently paradoxical. If an instance is superseded, it ceases to exist in the sense that it is its nature, or essence, that ceases to exist. At the same time, that instance is preserved because, having entered into unity with its opposite, it is preserved as something essentially different from what it was before (this is the sense in which capitalism is superseded by socialism).[2] Therefore, to be superseded does not mean to be annihilated; it means to be preserved as something essentially different.

We can now turn to the notion of determination in the last instance. This is based on three postulates.[3]

The first postulate is that of the *unity of all instances*. Unity means, as said above, a tie of existential interdependence. This is the basic difference between a dialectical and a metaphysical view. The latter considers the objects of analysis taken out of their context and viewed in isolation. The former considers the objects of analysis in their mutual and existential interrelation. An example taken from this work is that of the mutual interrelation of all prices.

The second postulate is the *unity of potential and realized instances.* This means that reality encompasses in a unity both instances that have already realized themselves and instances that are only potentially present. The relation between the individual and the social value of a commodity in the process of price formation is a case in point.[4]

The third postulate is the *unity of determinant and determined instances.* This means that some realized instances are determinant and some others are determined in the sense that the latter are called into existence as conditions of the former's reproduction or supersession. It is in this sense that the determinant instance is "primary," in the sense that it calls into existence, rather than being called into existence. For example, the determinant instance is the structure of production and the determined instance is the structure of individual values. These, however, are only potentially conditions of reproduction of the economic structure. To become actual conditions of reproduction, they must realize themselves as social values (prices).

If the determinant instance is indicated as A, the determined instance as B, and the determination of B by A as =>, the determination of B by A is depicted as A => B.

The question now arises as to where the determined instances come from. The answer is that they are already potentially present in the determinant one. This is why the latter can express the former. The determined instances are contained *in nuce* in the determinant one. As such they are formless potentials, possibilities, which realize themselves in their concrete characteristics only in the process of interrelation with both already realized instances and other newly emerging instances (see below). These possibilities are not (in a structuralist fashion) different combinations of the same, already realized, elements. They can be truly new and yet be contained in the determinant instance only in a potential state in the sense that they are inscribed in the actual composition, structure, and nature of the determinant instance. It is in this sense that they are *real possibilities.*

These three postulates allow us to define *determination in the last instance.* This is a relation between the elements of a process (determinant and determined instances) that are tied by a relation of mutual and existential interdependence in the specific sense that some realized instances (the determined ones) are the actual conditions of reproduction or of supersession of some other instances (the determinant ones) because they were already contained in a potential state in these latter, the determinant, ones. As a short-cut, to be determined in the last instance means to be called into existence as a condition for the reproduction or supersession of the determining instance, irrespective of the concrete form taken by both types of instances.[5]

Notice that a determinant instance can, and usually does, determine more than one determined instance, that is, more than one condition of its own reproduction or supersession. But it would be a mistake to think that each determinant instance has its own "exclusive" determined instances. A determined instance can be, and usually is, determined by more than one determinant instance so that it can be at the same time a condition of reproduction of one or more determinant instances and a condition of supersession of one or more other determinant instances. To give just one example, labor mobility determines wage equalization. But wage levels are determined also by other factors, say, capital mobility. Capitals move from high wage areas or branches to where lower wages are paid. In short, wage equalization is determined by many determinant factors (in this example, labor and capital mobility) all acting conjointly.

CONCRETE REALIZATION

In order to be an actual condition either of reproduction or of supersession, an instance must leave the realm of the potential and realize itself, take concrete, specific features. But determination in the last instance does not explain the concrete aspects in which the different instances are realized, their concrete realization. In the example above, the structure of production determines the structure of individual values. But this does not explain the values actually realized that alone can be a condition of reproduction of the economic structure.

In general, if all instances are related to one another, they must realize themselves in a process of mutual interrelation, through their reciprocal interaction. This holds for both the determinant and the determined instances. Thus, to realize what they potentially are, the determined instances (e.g., individual values) must interact with one another and, in this process, modify one another: They realize themselves (as social values, as prices) in their process of mutual interrelation. At the same time, the social values react upon and modify their determinant instance (the structure of production) in its specific, concrete form. Realization is at the same time modification. This is the *general principle of realization*. Each category of instances, in its turn, also has its own principles of realization.

If, at any given time, all instances realize themselves in the process of mutual interaction and thus mutual modification, they realize themselves simultaneously. Thus, in terms of concrete realization, to determine means to contribute to shaping the form of. In terms of concrete realization, no instance is primary. In these terms, A determines B because it acts upon B's form of realization, but B determines A because it reacts upon A, thus determining A's form of realization.

DIALECTICAL RELATION

The previous two sections allow us to conceptualize the notion of dialectical relation. There are two aspects to it: determination in the last instance and concrete realization. Or, *dialectical relation* is a process in which the determined instances, potentially existing within the determinant one, become its actual conditions of reproduction or of supersession and thus take on concrete features, through a process of mutual interrelation, and thus modification.

It follows that a dialectical relation is not a relation between dependent and independent variables. From the point of view of determination in the last instance, all variables are dependent on one another: the determinant depend on the determined because they need the determined in order to reproduce, or supersede, themselves; the determined depend on the determinant because they exist only as conditions of the latter's reproduction or supersession. From the point of view of concrete realization, all instances are equally dependent on one another, since they realize themselves in the process of mutual interrelation and thus modification. The same applies to the difference between a dialectical relation and a relation of mechanical causation in which some instances are cause and some are effect.[6]

Also, a dialectical relation is not one of simple mutual interrelation: Some instances are determinant and some are determined. It is not a relation between the essence, the necessary, and the contingent, that which has to be abstracted from in order to reach the essence. Both the determinant and the determined instances are essential. It is not a chronological relation, since some determined instances are born together with the determinant one. Even when other determined instances realize themselves after the determinant one has come to life (the determinant instance must constantly create new conditions of reproduction or of supersession), they modify the form taken by the determinant one so that there is contemporaneity in their concrete realization. It is not a relation between something pregiven (the determinant instance) and something to be determined: The determinant instance creates the determined ones in the process of realizing itself in its concrete, conjunctural form. It is not a process of allocation of elements (e.g., social agents) in an already preexisting structure: The process of allocation (e.g., of agents in a social structure) is at the same time a process of reproduction of the structure itself.

DIALECTICAL MOVEMENT

We have seen that instances are tied to one another by a dialectical relation—that they are tied by determination in the last instance and that they take on their specific and concrete features in the process of their mutual interrelation and simultaneous modification. But there is a logical link still missing between these two concepts. This is the notion of dialectical movement, the movement between one system of simultaneously realized instances tied by a dialectical relation to another system of simultaneously realized instances also tied by a dialectical relation.

Consider again the notion of determination in the last instance, or A => B, and suppose B is a condition of reproduction of A. In this case we say that there is *correspondence* between A and B. If B is a condition of supersession of A, there is *contradiction* between the two instances. In other words, correspondence means that the reproduction of B is a condition of reproduction of A; contradiction means that the reproduction of B is a condition of supersession of A (a change in the nature of A).

A relation of correspondence is not one of harmony. Actually, correspondence implies antagonism. More precisely, a relation of correspondence is *antagonistic* in the sense that in it each instance attempts to reproduce itself by reproducing the other instance, but must do so by attempting to change the other instance's *form* of realization, that is, the concrete features that instance takes when it is realized, and/or by attempting to change it from a realized *state* to a potential one, or vice versa. However, and this is the difference with a *contradictory* relation, the two instances do not attempt to change each other's *nature*, to supersede each other.

It is this antagonistic and contradictory nature of reality that explains the internal tension that manifests itself as movement. In the dialectical view, reality is seen not in static but in dynamic terms, as constantly changing. But movement and change do not come from outside; they are inherent in reality because they come from the antagonisms and contradictions inherent in it.

More specifically, *dialectical movement* has three dimensions. To begin with, since reality is the unity of potential and realized instances, movement means change (transformation) of potentially present instances into realized ones and change of realized instances back into a potential state. It is this aspect that allows us, for example, to understand the real nature of the so-called transformation problem, that is, the constant transformation of individual values into social ones and of these latter back into individual ones (see Carchedi 1991, chaps. 3 and 4). Second, since all instances realize themselves in the process of their mutual interrelations and thus modification, movement means change in the form of realization of all instances (e.g., variations in prices). Third, since reality is the unity of determinant and determined instances, and since these latter can be conditions either of reproduction or of supersession, movement means change of the conditions of reproduction into conditions of supersession and vice versa.

Thus, movement is inherent in the antagonistic and contradictory nature of the process of determination in the last instance. It is through this movement that what is potential realizes itself in its concrete form and either as a condition of reproduction or as a condition of supersession.

DIALECTICS

Dialectics is then the view of reality that explains both the simultaneous realization of all instances at one point in time and their change into a new system of simultaneously realized instances at another point in time in terms of the dialectical nature of the relation binding all instances and of the dialectical movement arising from it.

As applied to the analysis of social life, a *dialectical view of social reality* stresses the relation of existential interdependence and thus mutual interrelation between all social phenomena (both in their realized and in their potential state, i.e, as individual phenomena) in which (1) some realized social phenomena (determined ones) emerge from their potential state to become actual conditions of reproduction or of supersession of other realized social phenomena (the determinant ones); (2) all phenomena are subjected to a constant movement, which can imply a change from a potential to a realized state and vice versa, from a realized form to another realized form, and from being a condition of reproduction to being a condition of supersession and vice versa; and (3) there can be a change from a system ultimately characterized by a certain type of determinant instance to another system characterized by a radically different type of determinant instance.[7]

TENDENCIES

Particularly important for a method of research stressing the dynamic nature of reality are its laws of movement. These are those social phenomena that regulate the functioning and reproduction of the social system. Social laws can best be understood as natural laws, as laws independent of historical determination, which, however, can manifest themselves only in a historically determined and thus specific form. For example, "that the product of the serf must here suffice to reproduce his conditions of labor, in addition to his subsistence, is a circumstance which remains the same under all modes of production" (Marx 1967a, 3:790). More generally, "natural laws cannot be abolished at all. What can change in historically different circumstances is only the *form* in which these laws assert themselves" (Marx and Engels 1975b, 196).

It is because they are the specific expression of natural laws that social laws can regulate the functioning of the system, that they can become laws of motion of society.

Of particular importance for the present purpose is a specific feature of social laws: their being *tendential*. This means that in them the tendency can exist only in conjunction with its countertendencies. Thus, in order to understand the movement of reality, we must understand both the tendencies and the countertendencies. The tendencies are primary in the sense that they are the state toward which the countertendencies constantly gravitate; the countertendencies are secondary in the sense that they are deviations from the tendency.[8] This means, as we shall see shortly, that the tendency either cannot manifest itself at all or can manifest itself only partly or only cyclically. But, be this as it may, the tendency can exist only in conjunction with its countertendencies. The reason for this is that the same determinant instance that determines the tendency also determines the countertendencies.

Consider now Marx's hypothesis of the (tendential) equalization of all rates of profit into an average one. Marx is here interested in the *present tendency*, that is, in the hypothetical present situation that would result if only the tendential forces were operative. Or, to find the present tendency, one should ask: What would the situation be like *now* if, given the *present movement*, only the tendency were to realize itself? For example, given the present situation of a constantly changing hierarchy of rates of profit, the present tendential situation is the equalization of those rates of profit to the average of their presently realized level; thus, the present tendency is the hypothetical situation in which all branches (as represented by the modal capitalists) realize the same average rate of profit.

Suppose we want to inquire into the tendential course of technological development within a branch. Given that within a branch there is a modal production process (which produces the bulk of commodities) as well as more productive and less productive processes, the present tendency is the adoption by all capitals of the modal process. This is not the tendency at some future point in time, the *future tendency*, which is found by forecasting the future tendential reality on the basis of the present movement. To return to the example just mentioned, since all capitals within a branch would adopt the most profitable technique, the future tendency is the adoption by all capitals of this, the most advanced (because most profitable) technique; the present tendency is the adoption by all capitals of the presently modal technique.

Future tendencies should not be mistaken for present tendencies. Future tendencies are part of the forecast of the situation toward which the system presently moves. Present tendencies are part of the analysis of present reality.

THREE TYPES OF PRESENT TENDENCIES

Marxist literature has failed to distinguish not only between future and present tendencies but also between different types of present tendencies. This has hampered sharpness of analysis. Since a tendency manifests itself through the real movement of specific events, the different types of tendencies can be discerned by analyzing the real movement. More specifically, this work distinguishes among three types of present tendencies.

We have a *tendency of the first type* when the movement shows the tendency as the point or area in which the phenomena of a certain class are clustered; the countertendency is then revealed by the phenomena belonging to the same class that deviate from that point or area but gravitate toward it. As a rule of thumb, we can say that a tendency of the first type is indicated by what is usual or typical in a certain empirical situation.

This is the case, for example, of the tendential wage rate. The tendential wage rate is the modal one, the wage rate paid to the great bulk of the laborers, because this is the category of wage belonging to the modal level. But there always are, at any given moment, also countertendential forces (e.g., capital competition for scarce labor or capital's movement to low-wage areas), and thus wages above or below the modal rate. But all these (lower and higher) wage rates gravitate toward this modal rate.

We have a *tendency of the second type* when the movement shows the tendency only cyclically, that is, when the movement shows now the tendency (e.g., the fall in the average rate of profit) and then the countertendency (a rise in the average rate of profit). When the tendency realizes itself, the countertendency is present only in a potential state. Similarly, when the countertendency realizes itself, the tendency is present only in a potential state. Another way to put this is that the tendency reproduces itself within the countertendency once this latter has realized itself.

It should be stressed that the notion of *tendency* should not be confused with that of *trend*. In the movement of the average rate of profit, the trend is both downward and upward, according to which period is considered. However, the tendency is only downward and the countertendency is only upward. Or, the tendency is always present: in a realized state when the rate of profit falls and in a potential state when it either rises or stays at high levels. More generally, the tendency/countertendency hypothesis is a theoretical construction aiming at explaining reality, including the movement of the rate of profit in its upward and downward trends. The trend is a statistical construction that (like other statistics) can be used to verify the usefulness or correctness of a hypothesis (including the tendency/ countertendency hypothesis).

Finally, we have a *tendency of the third type* when only the countertendency, that is, the movement around the tendency (and not the tendency itself), is observable. This is the above-mentioned case of the empirically observable different rates of profit in the different branches, which, through their constantly overtaking each other, allows us to hypothesize a tendency toward an equalized average rate of profit. The countertendencies too have already been discussed.

In the first type of tendency, empirical reality contemporaneously shows both the tendency and the countertendency. The countertendency hampers the realization of the tendency in the sense that this latter can realize itself only partially (e.g., not all, but only the bulk of the workers belonging to a certain category are paid the same modal wage). In the second type of tendency, empirical reality alternatively shows either the tendency or the countertendency. The countertendency hampers the realization of the tendency (e.g., the fall in the rate of profit) in the sense that the latter can realize itself only cyclically. And, in the third type of tendency, empirical reality shows only the countertendency. This is the extreme case in which the countertendency completely hampers the realization of the tendency (e.g., the equalization of the rate of profit). In all three cases, it is the realized, empirically observable movement that indicates to us the existence of the tendency and the type to which it belongs. The tendency, in its turn, serves to explain that movement.

METHOD OF ANALYSIS AND METHOD OF PRESENTATION

In some of this work's contributions, the way to inquire into the logic of *Capital* is to reconstruct Marx's logical "moves," the sequence of "forms" or of categories, starting from some specific point and then unfolding one category from another. This logical unfolding is certainly an important aspect of Marx's work. But is *this* what characterizes his method? The answer to this question presupposes that a fundamental difference is made: that between the method of analysis and the method of presentation. Marx is very clear on this: "the method of presentation must differ in form from that of inquiry. The latter has to appropriate the material in detail, to analyze its different forms of development, to trace out its inner connections. Only after this work is done, can the actual movement be adequately described" (1967a, 1: 19). The reason for Marx's emphasis on this point is clear: If no difference is made between the two methods, the method of presentation is mistaken for the method of inquiry. This is a mistake, given that *the logical succession of categories, the organic-like unfolding of one category from another, characterizes the method of presentation but not that of inquiry.*

If this is so, any discussion of Marx's method should always state unequivocally which method is meant. Moreover, since one has to analyze something before it can be presented, one has to develop the method of analysis before the method of presentation can be developed. I should stress that the inquiry into the method of presentation is not only perfectly legitimate but also important. But the method of presentation can be developed only after the development of the method of inquiry. Disregard of this latter method collapses it in the method of presentation and leaves open the question as to the nature of the relation between the two methods.

It follows that, if we aim at discovering Marx's method of inquiry, we should *not* trace the sequence of categories in *Capital*, trying to discover the logic behind that sequence. This can reveal only the logic of the method of presentation. Rather, to discover the logic, that is, the dialectical logic, of his method of inquiry means (1) to distill the principles informing Marx's analysis of capitalist reality, (2) to study how Marx applies these principles in the course of this analysis, and (3) to develop, through this study, a dialectical view of reality. This is what I have tried to do in the preceding pages. Once this view has been developed, it can be applied to the analysis of new elements of reality and thus to the solution of new theoretical problems.

At the same time, since Marx is not simply a theorist but is a representative of the working class, to discover Marx's dialectical method of social inquiry means to discover how he reconstructs reality in thought (the concrete in thought) from the point of view of a certain class, the working class. In turn, this implies a critique of other, class-determined, theoretical systems. It is no accident that *Capital*'s subtitle is "A Critique of Political Economy." In short, the specificity of Marxian dialectics is the fusion of the dialectical view with the view of the working class into what can be called *dialectical class analysis.*

The method of presentation, on the other hand, must respond to a specific need: this is not simply that of finding an initial category whose analysis allows the development of other categories. This logical movement must also show (1) the validity of the Marxist analysis as an explanation, and ultimately as a tool of change, of reality; (2) the superiority of the Marxist analysis vis-à-vis other explanations; and thus (3) the superiority of the dialectical method of social inquiry. This is the logic guiding the choice of the initial category as well as the sequence of categories in the course of the presentation of the results of social inquiry. This logic of presentation stresses the logical development of a system of categories. However, there is no reason why this should be the only strategy followed in presenting the results of the analysis. For example, there is no reason why one should not anticipate some results in order to make some points clearer and prove those results only at a later stage of the presentation. The logical unfolding of categories is an aspect of Hegelian logic, where no distinction is made between the two methods. Any reconstruction of Marx's *Capital* on the basis of this logic fails to distinguish between the two methods, collapses the method of inquiry into the method of presentation, reduces the former to a one-dimensional preoccupation with the sequential logic of categories, and hampers the study and development of the dialectical nature of Marx's logic of inquiry.

FROM VALUES TO PRICES

THE CIRCULARITY CRITIQUE

The circularity critique is perhaps the best known. It was originated by Boehm-Bawerk in 1896 (1973), which, with the reply by Hilferding (1973) and the contribution by Bortkiewicz (1973), was brought to the attention of a wide readership in the Anglo-Saxon world by Sweezy's classical work (1968). Basically, the circularity critique argues that, in the computation of the prices of production, "the capitalists' outlays on constant and variable capital are left exactly as they were in the value scheme; in other words, the constant capital and the variable capital used in production are still used in value terms" (Sweezy 1968, 115). This has been formulated in modern terminology as follows: Inputs are expressed as values (individual values, in Marx's terminology), but outputs are expressed as prices of production (social values, in Marx's terminology).[9] This is a logical flaw, since the same commodity is bought as an input and sold as an output at the same price. Consider Table 1, where c, v, and s are constant capital, variable capital, and surplus value, respectively; V is the value produced by each unit of capital; PrPr(C) is the price of production per unit of capital, or value tendentially realized by each unit of capital; PrPr(C)−V is the transfer of value inherent in the transformation of values into production prices; OCC is the organic composition of capital; O is the output; and PrPr(O) is the price of production per unit of output, or value tendentially realized by one unit of output, in each branch.

As I submit in a later section, value is abstract labor expressed in money. Therefore, in Table 1, value quantities can be seen either as hours of labor or as quantities of money. Also, the hours of abstract labor are not the hours actually worked but are those hours after skilled labor has been reduced to unskilled labor and after more (or less) than average-intensity labor has been

TABLE 1. MARX'S TENDENTIAL EQUALIZATION OF THE RATES OF PROFIT

	c	v	s	V	PrPr(C)	PrPr(C)-V	OCC	O	PrPr(O)
BRANCH 1	80 +	20 +	20 =	120	120	0	4	100	1.2
BRANCH 2	90 +	10 +	10 =	110	120	+10	9	120	1.0
BRANCH 3	70 +	30 +	30 =	130	120	−10	2.3	130	0.92
	240	60	60	360	360	0			

reduced (or increased) to average-intensity labor. In other words, the quantities in Table 1 are hours of homogeneous abstract labor, which can be expressed in money terms. For example, in Branch 1 the 100 units of output have cost 100 hours of abstract labor. These would also be 120 hours actually worked only if they were all hours of average-intensity and of unskilled labor. If some hours were of more than average intensity or of skilled labor, less than 120 actual hours of abstract labor would be necessary to produce those 100 units of output, e.g., 80 actual hours. The money in circulation, which serves as a measure of value, expresses 120 hours of homogeneous labor, or 120 units of labor, and not 80 hours of (not homogeneous) actual work.

In terms of Table 1, Branch 1 sells its products at 120 (the price of production), but these products are bought at their not yet transformed value: 80 by Branch 1, 90 by Branch 2, and 70 by Branch 3. These products are sold at 120 but bought at 240. This discrepancy, it is argued, is due to a logical inconsistency in Marx's transformation procedure, since in that procedure the same commodities are bought as inputs at their (not yet transformed) values but sold as outputs at their price of production (i.e., transformed value). By far the most influential solution to this problem is that offered by Bortkiewicz (1973).

Bortkiewicz's solution, reduced to its essentials, assumes a situation of simple reproduction, given the three sectors of Table 1:

$$c_1 + v_1 + s_1 = V_1$$
$$c_2 + v_2 + s_2 = V_2$$
$$c_3 + v_3 + s_3 = V_3$$

where c, v, s, and V are the constant capital, variable capital, surplus value, and total value, respectively, of each branch, and where each of the subscript numerals refers to each branch. If demand equals supply:

$$c_1 + v_1 + s_1 = V_1 = c_1 + c_2 + c_3$$
$$c_2 + v_2 + s_2 = V_2 = v_1 + v_2 + v_3$$
$$c_3 + v_3 + s_3 = V_3 = s_1 + s_2 + s_3$$

The assumption is then made that with the transformation of values into prices of production, the price of the products of Branch 1 becomes x times greater than their value, that of the products of Branch 2 y times greater, and that of the products of Branch 3 z times greater. If we call the average rate of profit in price terms r, then the model of simple reproduction transformed in prices of production becomes:

$$c_1x + v_1y + r(c_1x + v_1y) = (c_1 + c_2 + c_3)x$$
$$c_2x + v_2y + r(c_2x + v_2y) = (v_1 + v_2 + v_3)y$$
$$c_3x + v_3y + r(c_3x + v_3y) = (s_1 + s_2 + s_3)z$$

Bortkiewicz thus obtains three equations with four unknowns (x, y, z, and r). In terms of mathematics, to solve this system we must supply a fourth equation. In terms of economics, this means that we must choose between two equally undesirable solutions. Either the fourth equation assumes that the total of prices equals the total of values, in which case the equality between surplus value and profits is not respected anymore; or our fourth equation assumes the equality of the total of profits and the total of surplus value, in which case the total of prices and of values does not coincide anymore. The two equalities do not hold, in general, at the same time. After Bortkiewicz, many other authors have worked out improved, or more complete, equally "consistent" solutions; however, they all share the same characteristic of severing either the equality between prices and values or that between surplus value and profits.

The consequences are far-reaching. If the former equality does not hold, it makes no sense to speak of "transformation" of values into prices. If the latter equality does not hold, profits no longer necessarily come from surplus value, and the theory of exploitation is dealt a fatal blow. Both conclusions are very grave for the Marxian theory of value. However, there is no reason to be concerned. What we have here is a pseudoproblem.

THE FALLACY OF THE CIRCULARITY CRITIQUE

Let us assume that the output of a certain process immediately enters a new production process as an input. Labor power is temporarily excluded from the present discussion because of its specific feature of not being the product of a capitalist production process. It will be dealt with later on. Here, only the inputs and outputs of capitalist production processes are considered. Therefore, outputs can be both means of production and means of subsistence, and inputs can only be means of production. Thus, a commodity that is both an input and an output must be a means of production. The discussion that follows focuses on means of production, unless differently stated.

Suppose that A is the output of a process P_1, which starts at time t_0 and ends at t_1, and also an input of a process P_2, which starts at t_1 and ends at t_2 and which results in the production of B. This is depicted in Figure 1.

FIGURE 1. THE CHRONOLOGICAL SEQUENCE OF TWO PRODUCTION PROCESSES

t_0 [———————————————] t_1

Inputs → P_1 → Output A

t_1 [———————————————] t_2

Input A → P_2 → Output B

The social value of A *as an output* is tendentially realized at t_1 and is thus expressed as its price of production at that moment. Therefore, A is sold as an output of P_1 and bought as an input of P_2 at that price. There has been a production of value and of surplus value during the t_0–t_1 period and a redistribution of that surplus value at the moment t_1. Now a new process starts and A enters P_2 as an input. The product of P_2, B, tendentially realizes its social value at t_2. The question now is: Does the value of A *as an input* of P_2 remain the same or will it not instantaneously change at the moment it enters the new production process P_2?

Suppose that the producer of B has used a greater quantity, or a more expensive quality, of A than is socially necessary, that is, than is needed by B's modal production process. As far as A is concerned, the value of B is given only by the socially necessary quantity and quality of A. The real process that ensures this is, of course, capitalist (price) competition. What the market tendentially gives the producer of B is not only a rate of profit proportional to his or her productivity,[10] but also the average value of A, the average value of the inputs. As Marx puts it:

> Though the capitalists have a hobby, and use a gold instead of a steel spindle, yet the only labor that counts for anything in the value of the yarn is that which would be required to produce a steel spindle, because no more is necessary under the given social conditions. (Marx 1967a, 1:188)

This case is similar to the one in which B's producer uses the socially necessary quantity and quality of A, but A's modal production process changes between t_1 and t_2. Here too, the value of A going into the value of B is not the value at which A has been bought at t_1 but the value A has at t_2. If, in this period, A has become either cheaper or more expensive, the value of B will accordingly be either reduced or increased. Again, this will be brought about by capitalist (price) competition.

Once the transformation process is seen as a real process, and thus as a sequence of real processes, it becomes clear that the social value of A as an output of P_1 enters the new production process P_2 as the individual value of A as an input. But the social value of A as an input of B will be determined only at the moment of exchange of B, at t_2. *At t_1, A has both a social value* (the value at which it is bought and sold—the price of production) *as the output of P_1 and an individual value* (the potential social value that will realize itself only at t_2) *as an input of P_2*. Thus, the moment at which A tendentially realizes its social value as an output (t_1) is not the moment at which it realizes its social value as an input (t_2).

In short, individual values are only potentially social values and tendentially realize themselves as social values only at the moment of exchange. This holds both for the social value of outputs, which tendentially realize themselves at the moment at which they are exchanged, and for the social value of inputs, which tendentially realize themselves at the moment the output of which they are inputs realizes itself.

The mistake inherent in the circularity critique is thus clear. This approach collapses two periods (t_0-t_1 and t_1-t_2) into just one, as Figure 2 makes clear.

Since two production processes and two moments of realization are collapsed into one, the illusion is created that, in Marx's transformation procedure, A is exchanged at both its social value and its individual value at t_1. But only the social value of A as an output tendentially realizes itself at t_1. The social value of A as an input tendentially realizes itself at t_2. The individual value of A does *not* realize itself as such; it realizes itself only as social value, and thus either at t_1 (as an output) or at t_2 (as an input). The

FIGURE 2. THE SUPERIMPOSITION OF TWO PRODUCTION PROCESSES

t_0 [———————————] t_1

Inputs → P_1 → Output A

t_1 [———————————] t_2

Inputs A → P_2 → Output B

individual values are the *potential*, not yet realized, social values, and the prices of production are the tendentially *realized* social values, the average form taken by the individual values at the moment of, and through, exchange. The *individual value* is thus the value a commodity has before being sold, including the value it has right after production.

The circularity critique thus makes a double mistake. On the one hand it considers as a chronological sequence what in fact is a chronologically contemporaneous process (the realization of individual values as social values). On the other hand, it considers as a chronologically contemporaneous process what is in fact a chronological sequence (the realization of the social value of A as an output and as an input). In reality, however, the value of A can appear only in its tendentially realized, social form, and the moment of its realization as an output is different from the moment of its realization as an input. Consequently, the value of the inputs in Table 1 cannot be their individual value. In short, constant and variable capital appear in Table 1 as already transformed values, as production prices of the previous production process, which are also the individual values of the inputs of the new production process.[11]

To sum up, the circularity critique shows a remarkable ignorance of Marxist methodology. It does not see the dialectical nature of the relation between individual and social values. It does not see that the value of a commodity does not realize itself first as an individual value (of the commodity as an input) and then as a social value (of the same commodity as an output). Rather, individual values realize themselves *as* social values so that a commodity, as an output, realizes its social value at the moment of its sale and, as an input, realizes its social value at the moment of the sale of the output of which that particular commodity is an input. The dialectic of the realization of value is, in the last analysis, the transformation of individual values into social values at the moment of exchange, that is, at the end of that production process; their transformation back into individual values when those products enter a new production process as inputs; and their transformation anew into social values when the output of which they are inputs is exchanged, sold.

The question that remains to be answered concerns the practical relevance of the change in the individual value of the inputs in the period during which they are transformed into the output. If all the social value of the means of production is transferred to the value of the product in just one production process, it is unlikely that the individual value of these inputs diverges from their social value, due to changes in the branch of production producing them. But if the means of production are used for more production processes, the individual value of these means of production can diverge from their social value during the period starting with the beginning of the first production period and ending with the termination of the last production period using those means of production. The longer this period, the more likely a change in the value of the means of production—that is, a difference between their individual value and their social value as inputs. One striking example is provided by IBM, which—under the pressure of competition—cut its computer workstation prices, on 8 May 1991, by up to 60% (Kehoe 1991). Those capitalists who had paid $130,000 for a machine that is now sold for $52,500 will be able to charge only this last amount for the remainder of that machine's life cycle.

But, more important, a productivity change in *any* capital causes a change in its OCC, in the surplus value produced by it, in the average rate of profit, in the price of production per unit of capital, and thus in the price of production per unit of output—that is, in the social value of all commodities. It follows that, quantitatively, the individual value of all inputs equals their social value *only in the case of a lack of technological change in the whole economy*, rather than only in the branches producing those inputs. This quantitative equality is then just a theoretical curiosity. Moreover, even if there were a quantitative equality, there would still be a qualitative difference between the individual and the social value of the inputs and thus a qualitative transformation of the former into the latter at the moment of the output's sale.[12]

THE INFINITE REGRESSION CRITIQUE

In the infinite regression critique, it is argued that if the inputs (A in the case of P_2 in Figure 2) are expressed as realized social value, and if they are prices of production, then to compute the price of production of A we must go back to the previous production process that produced A and from there to the previous one, thus falling into infinite regression. As Robinson put it:

> The constant capital was produced in the past by labour-time working with then pre-existing constant capital and so on, *ad infinitum* backwards. It therefore cannot be reduced simply to a number of labour hours that can be added to the net value of the current year. And there is no advantage in trying to do so. (Robinson 1977, 202)

It does not take much to see that, if this critique were sound, it would mean the bankruptcy not only of Marx's transformation procedure but also of social science in all its versions, including the neo-Ricardian one. This critique, in fact, would have to apply to any social phenomenon inasmuch as it is determined by other phenomena, both present and past. Social sciences, then, would become an endless quest of the origin. Fortunately, however, our predicament is not as gloomy as Marx's critics incautiously represent it. The reason is that the choice of the starting point depends on the scope and purpose of our research. If we want to determine the value of B, then it is perfectly warranted to take the value of A as given. If, for whatever reasons, we wanted to determine the value of A as well, we would have to take the value of its inputs as given. Infinite regression is a figment of neo-Ricardian imagination.

The neo-Ricardian theorists think that they can escape their own critique by computing the labor contents of physical inputs through the reduction to dated quantities of labour, that is, through "an operation by which in the equation of a commodity the different means of production used are replaced with a series of quantities of labour, each with its appropriate 'date'" (Sraffa 1960, 34). For example, the reduction equation of product A has the following form (Ibid., 35):

$$L_a w + L_{a1} w(1 + r) + \ldots + L_{an} w(1 + r)^n = A p_a$$

Here, the first term ($L_a w$) indicates the labor expended in the production of commodity A times the wage paid to it. The second term, $L_{a1} w(1 + r)$, indicates the inputs expressed in labor terms. Since these inputs have been the product of labor in the previous period, they are equal to the labor needed to produce those inputs in the previous period times the wage ($L_{a1} w$) plus the rate of profit on these inputs so computed (r times $L_{a1} w$). By so doing, we can compute the inputs needed to produce those inputs two production periods ago, and so on. The term $L_{an} w(1 + r)^n$ indicates the inputs expressed in labor terms in the nth period back in time plus the rate of profit on those inputs so computed.

But this procedure is far from being immune from the infinite regression critique. Sraffa seems to think that the further back we go, the smaller will be the commodity residue—that is, that part of the inputs expressed in physical terms--and thus the bigger will be that part of the inputs expressed in labor terms. In this case, the question becomes one of "how far the reduction need be pushed in order to obtain a given degree of approximation" (Ibid.). The point, however, is that it is simply not true that the commodity residue becomes smaller as we retrace the labor content of the physical inputs in the more and more distant production processes. Every time we make such a step back we compute the labor content not of a *decreasing physical residue of the inputs of this process but of the physical inputs of the previous production process.* And this means quite simply that this procedure too falls into the infinite regression trap. In any case, even if this method did find smaller and smaller physical residues—that is, greater and greater labor contents—of the means of production, this quantity would not be the social value of the means of production as inputs: This social value is given by their cost of reproduction at the time the output is sold.

A POINT OF CLARIFICATION

Occasionally, the objection is raised that in Table 1 the value of the outputs does not correspond to the value of the inputs needed for the production process to start anew on the same scale. For example, Branch 1 produces and realizes a value of 120. This is its output, which becomes the inputs of all three branches in the next production process. However, the inputs must have a social value of 240. Branch 1, then, produces less than what is needed by the economy for the next production process. This, of course, has nothing to do with the transformation problem. This quantitative inconsistency is due to the fact that each branch is represented by one unit of capital instead of displaying the actual, or absolute, amount of capital invested. It is clear then that, given that structure of the economy, Branch 1 would have to employ more units of capital per each unit of capital invested by the other two branches. For example, suppose the following two sectors:

$$\begin{array}{ll} \text{I} & 73.3c + 26.7v + 26.7s = 126.7 \\ \text{II} & \underline{60.0c} + \underline{40.0v} + \underline{40.0s} = \underline{140.0} \\ & 133.3c + 66.7v + 66.7s = 266.7 \end{array}$$

where Sector I produces means of production and Sector II produces means of consumption. After the equalization of the profit rates, each sector realizes 133.3. Sector I realizes a value of 133.3 for its means of production, which also is approximately the social value of the means of production needed by both sectors in the next production process (73.3 + 60). Similarly, Sector II realizes a value of 133.3 for its means of consumption, and this also is approximately the social value of the means of consumption needed by both sectors in the next production process (66.7 + 66.7).

INDIVIDUAL AND SOCIAL VALUES

It follows from what was said above that (1) given a certain output, the social value of the inputs is their cost of reproduction at the time the output is sold (time t_2 in Figure 2); and (2) this cost of reproduction is the price of production of similar inputs, also at the time the output is sold. We can now sum up Marx's notion of individual and social value of a commodity.

1. The individual value of a commodity is the value it has before being sold, but after production. Therefore, its computation must be carried out right before sale.
2. The social value of a commodity, or price of production per unit of output, is the value society assigns to it at the moment of sale. Therefore, its computation must be carried out at that moment.

   A commodity can be either an input or an output. In both cases, it has both an individual and a social value. Therefore:
3. The individual value of an input is equal to the price that has been paid for it. This, at this level of analysis, is its price of production per unit of output when it is bought.
4. The individual value of an output is equal to the individual value of its inputs plus the surplus value actually generated during its production.
5. The social value of an input is its cost of reproduction, that is, the price of production per unit of output of similar inputs, at the time the output is sold.
6. The social value of an output is the value of the modal commodity, that is, the price of production per unit of output. This is equal to the price of production per unit of capital divided by the modal output. In its turn, the price of production per unit of capital is equal to the social value of the inputs *used by the modal producer* plus the average rate of profit. If this commodity enters the next production process as an input, this social value becomes the individual value of the same commodity as an input (see point [3]).

A point of clarification can now be made. We know, from the analysis of the production process in Volume 1 of *Capital*, that labor is always both concrete and abstract. Concrete labor transfers the value of the means of production to the product. This is their individual value, their price of production at the time they are sold. For example, if a machine's price of production is equal to 100,000 and if each hour of concrete labor consumes one hundredth of that machine's use value (i.e., if that machine is completely used up in a thousand hours), each hour of concrete labor transfers a value of 100 to the product. However, at the time of the output's sale, this value counts as the cost of reproduction of the means of production. If there is a discrepancy between individual and social value, those capitalists whose means of production have lost (or gained) value lose (or gain) value to (from) other capitalists when the products are exchanged (sold). It is through this redistribution of value among capitalists that the individual value of the means of production is transformed into their social value.

Abstract labor creates new value, first the value of labor power and then surplus value. Since the value of labor power is the value of the means of subsistence, the individual value of labor power as an input is the price of production of the socially necessary means of subsistence at the time labor power is bought. The social value of labor power as an input is the cost of reproduction of the means of subsistence at the time the output is sold. It should be recalled that labor power differs from other commodities in that the quantity and quality of the means of subsistence change in accord to what society deems necessary for the laborers to reproduce themselves. Thus, the individual value of labor power as an input is modified not only by changes in the cost of reproduction of that basket of wage goods but also by changes in the composition of that basket at the time the product is sold. This is the value that must be created by abstract labor before it can create surplus value. If the individual value of labor power as an input differs from its social value, there is a redistribution of the newly created value between the value of labor power and surplus value. It is through this redistribution between capitalists and laborers that the individual value of labor power is transformed into its social value.

It follows that, contrary to what is commonly believed, the redistribution of value inherent in the sale of the product—that is, the transformation of individual into social values—encompasses not only the redistribution of surplus value among capitalists as a result of the tendential equalization of the rates of profit. It also encompasses (1) a change in the value of the means of production, if their individual value as inputs differs from their social value; and (2) a change in the value of labor power, if the individual value of a basket of wage goods at the time labor power is bought differs from the social value of a possibly modified basket of wage goods at the time the product is sold. The former is a redistribution of value among capitalists, and the latter is a redistribution between capitalists and laborers. *The transformation process, or the process of price formation, is a redistribution of value affecting all three components of a commodity's value*, not only the surplus value created during its production. It is not only a process of redistribution of surplus value among capitalists; it is also a process of redistribution of value both among the capitalists and between capitalists and laborers.

TWO COMMON MISUNDERSTANDINGS

It is commonly believed that for Marx the individual value is the value embodied in a commodity, meaning the labor that has been actually needed to produce it, and that the social value of that commodity should be equal to this individual value. In other words, the value realized by a commodity (a part of societal labor) should be equal to the value actually created during its production (the labor actually expended). Nothing could be farther from the truth.

First of all, *individual values are not values embodied.* It is impossible to compute the labor actually needed to produce the means of production and of subsistence without falling into the backward ad infinitum trap. The individual value of the inputs is already transformed: It is the price of production of the means of production and the social value of labor power (which depends on the price of production of the means of subsistence considered as necessary for the reproduction of labor power) at the time they enter the production process. Value embodied is not only a notion alien to Marxian price theory, it is also a quantity that cannot be known. However, if value embodied cannot be known, the individual and social value *can* be known and measured, once we start from a given social value of the means of production and of labor power. The other critique, that value is a metaphysical concept because "it cannot be observed" (Sawyer 1989, 226), can be easily disposed of once we realize that, for example, electricity is not observable either, yet it is anything but a metaphysical concept. Second, the individual value is equal to the social value only by way of exception. This is the case of those modal capitals that have an OCC equal to the average, if the change in the value of the means of production and of labor power as a consequence of the equalization of the profit rates is disregarded.

One reason for commonly identifying Marx's notion of individual value with that of labor embodied might be that traditionally the term *value embodied* has been used to translate two quite different concepts. On the one hand, Marx uses expressions such as *Wertding*, *verkörperter Wert*, *Wertkörper*, or simply *Körper* to indicate the physical body in which labor is materialized. These terms are translated as "value embodied." For example, in discussing the exchange of two commodities—20 yards of linen for one coat—Marx points out that they exchange in that proportion because the value of 20 yards of linen is equal to that of one coat. The linen is the relative form of value, the coat the equivalent form of value. The coat is "the mode of existence" of the value of the linen, its "value embodied" (Marx 1967a, 1:50). The coat "as equivalent of the linen . . . counts . . . as embodied value, as *body* that is value" (Ibid., 51; emphasis added). Or, "the value of the commodity linen is expressed by the *bodily form* of the commodity coat" (Ibid., 52; emphasis added); "the *use value* coat, as opposed to the linen, figures as an embodiment of value" (Ibid., 56; emphasis added); "*use value* becomes the form of manifestation, the phenomenal form, of its opposite, value" (Ibid.; emphasis added). It is the "incarnation of abstract human labor" (Ibid., 76), "the form of manifestation of the value of commodities" (Ibid., 89).

In short, in all these cases, the translation "value embodied" is used to refer to the *use value*, which serves as the embodiment of a certain quantity of exchange value, not to the *exchange value* contained in that use value. For this latter concept, Marx uses other terms such as objectified (*vergegenständlicht*) labor, or contained (*enthalten*) labor. But these terms too have been translated as embodied labor. It is the melting of these two opposite meanings in the term *value embodied* that is one of the likely sources of confusion.[13]

A second mistaken belief is that production prices are determined by the labor socially necessary to *produce* commodities, i.e., that they are determined only by the structure of production. Again, this is wrong. Production prices are determined both by the structure of production and by the distribution of (strong shifts in) social demand. The notion that production prices are solely determined by socially necessary labor time, understood as only technically determined, is a Ricardian, rather than a Marxian, one. In other words, *the socially necessary labor time is not found directly by computing how many hours are technically needed by the modal producers*. This would exclude the role played by social demand. Rather, it is given by the equalization of the rates of profit into an average rate that is tendentially realized only by the modal producers. This presupposes the active role of social demand, inherent in the D = S assumption. Once this computation has been carried out, it is possible to compute how many hours of labor are expended for the production of, and are appropriated by, each commodity. This computation is carried out below. Here it suffices to stress that it is this socially necessary labor time (or price of production in labor terms) per unit of output that explains why a certain use value, which incorporates a certain socially necessary labor time, is exchanged for a multiple (or a fraction) of a different use value that incorporates the same socially necessary labor time.

WHAT IS VALUE?

Often one runs into expressions such as surplus value being "produced by labor" (Castells 1980, 45), as labor being "the substance of value," and so on. Used in a figurative sense, these expressions are acceptable. However, taken acritically, they can be used to support an idea of value as being something endowed with a reality of its own, possibly even a physical reality. This interpretation is mistaken and rests on a confusion between concrete and abstract labor, between use value and (exchange) value.

Let us recall, from *Capital*, Volume 1, that labor is both concrete and abstract. As concrete labor, it creates new use values. In this sense, the use of the term *creates* is justified. But labor is also abstract in the sense of expenditure of human energy, irrespective of the specific tasks performed. In this sense we cannot say that (abstract) labor creates (exchange) value. Value is *not* created by (abstract) labor. Value *is* labor, that is, abstract labor performed under capitalist production relations that must express itself as money. Moreover, if the distinction between productive and unproductive labor is introduced, we must add the further specification that value is abstract labor transforming, as concrete labor, use values. Value is the product of labor *power*, that is, the expenditure of labor power as abstract labor.

Put in different words, value is a category developed to understand the production of wealth *for* the capitalist class *by* the laborers.[14] Value is a historically specific and thus a *socially specific* concept. This holds for both individual value and social value, for value both before and after it is redistributed through the price mechanism, since value expresses a relationship between classes typical of a specific historical period. Ultimately, value expresses the fact that capitalism is first and foremost the appropriation of labor and that the production of use values is only a means for such an appropriation.

Notice that abstract labor is a category of thought that corresponds to something real, to the expenditure of human energy irrespective of the specific forms of activity carried out (concrete labors). The abstraction from these specific forms of activity is made in order to focus on what all these forms have in common—for example, consumption of proteins, calories—in order to focus on a real process. The concept of abstract labor, thus, is different from the concept of, say, fruit. This latter merely serves to subsume under one category different objects, such as peaches and melons. The concept of fruit has no reality of its own (there is no such thing as a fruit). The concept of abstract labor, on the contrary, does have a reality of its own, that part of reality we focus on when we analyze the exertion of human energy without taking into consideration its specific forms. Abstract labor must manifest itself as social value, as value quantitatively transformed, at the moment of exchange, but it already exists at the level of production. Actually, it can manifest itself at the level of exchange only because it exists before being exchanged.

An alternative interpretation (generally referred to as the "value-form" interpretation) stresses that it is the act of exchange that reduces the different use values to a common ground, that of also being (having) exchange value (see, e.g., Reuten 1988, 52 and Chapter 4 in this volume). In this view, abstract labor "constitutes itself at the moment of," or "is grounded in," exchange. This view denies reality to abstract labor before exchange and reduces Marx's notion of abstract labor, a concept Marx grounds in production, to an abstraction with no reality of its own (just like the notion of fruit). It follows that individual values are denied reality and only social values are said to exist. Then the transformation "problem" vanishes, but with it also vanishes the possibility of developing a Marxist price theory, which is based on that transformation.

One more point must be made in this connection. The abstract labor that goes into the value of a product is not only the labor carried out in the present production period but is also the abstract labor carried out in the previous period. This latter is incorporated in this period's means of production. As we have seen above, the value transferred to the value of this period's product counts as the abstract labor that would be socially necessary to produce the means of production at the moment the product is sold. And, as we know from the first volume of *Capital*, this value is transferred through *concrete* labor. Or, the labor that is value (abstract labor) is not the same as the labor that transfers value (concrete labor). This is another reason why the value of a product cannot be said to be created by abstract labor. Even if value were created by abstract labor, it would be the new value that is so created: The other part of the product's value is transferred by concrete labor.

If all these qualifications are kept in mind, the expressions "value is created by abstract labor" or "labor is the substance of value" can be used as convenient, but imprecise, short-cuts.

PRODUCTION PRICE AND SOCIALLY NECESSARY LABOR TIME

It has been submitted above that the socially necessary labor time (SNLT) can be found only after the rates of profit have been equalized. Let us now engage in this computation. First of all, to hold that value is abstract labor (with the above-mentioned qualifications) does not imply that the total *new* value is equal to the total number of hours actually worked. In fact, hours of higher than average intensity or of skilled labor create more value than hours of average-intensity or of unskilled labor. Yet value can be measured in terms of labor hours once above- or below-average-intensity labor is reduced to average-intensity labor and skilled labor is reduced to unskilled labor. For example, given a certain average intensity of labor, one hour of labor of double intensity is equal to two hours of labor of average intensity. Or, given the value of an unskilled laborers's labor power, one hour of skilled labor expended by a labor power whose value is twice the value of unskilled labor's labor power is equal to two hours of unskilled labor and counts as (because it is) twice as much value. Both the value produced by different levels of intensity and the value produced by different levels of skills can be quantified: the former by measuring, for example, the rapidity of certain movements; the latter by measuring the value of labor power. In the previous pages as well as in what follows, therefore, the computation assumes homogeneous hours—hours of unskilled labor of average intensity.

Let us begin by computing the *individual* value of a commodity in terms of labor hours, starting from money quantities. We know the total value produced in the previous period expressed in money (M_0) and the price of production of the means of production also expressed in money (PP_0). Then the percentage of the latter relative to the former is $z = PP_0/M_0$. If we know the total of homogeneous labor hours expended in the previous period (TL_0), the SNLT incorporated in these inputs is z times TL_0. This computation applies also to labor power. Its value is given by the price of production of those goods (of a certain quantity and quality) deemed necessary for the reproduction of the laborers at the time labor power is bought. Let us call the price of production of these goods in money terms PL_0. Then for labor power $y = PL_0/M_0$. By multiplying y by TL_0, we obtain the SNLT incorporated in the wage goods. This is also the number of homogeneous labor hours the laborers have to work in order to reproduce the value of their labor power. Given the length of the working day, the remaining labor hours are surplus labor expended to produce that commodity. By adding these three components, we obtain the individual value of the commodity in terms of labor.

Let us now compute the *social* value of that commodity also in terms of labor, under the simplifying assumption that the SNLT incorporated in the inputs does not change. Since we know the average rate of profit in terms of money, we know the surplus value realized (s^*) by that commodity, also in terms of money. This is a percentage of total value (M_1), again in terms of money, or $j = s^*/M_1$. Since we also know the total labor expended in this period (TL_1), the surplus labor corresponding to s^* is j times TL_1. By adding this number to the SNLT incorporated in the inputs, we get the labor time socially necessary to produce that commodity. The difference between the labor time incorporated in the commodity before and after the equalization of the rates of profit gives the gain or loss of labor inherent in the price mechanism, or unequal exchange of labor. Under the assumption of capital mobility, the labor time socially necessary to produce a commodity is its price of production.

VALUE AND FULL AUTOMATION

What was said above allows us to understand why machines do not produce value. If value is abstract labor performed by laborers under capitalist relations of production, the less labor is expended the less value is created, by definition. This becomes clear in the hypothetical case of a fully automated economy. In this case, machines could not create value or surplus value, they could only transform use values. In fact, the nonowners of the means of production would cease to exist as laborers, and capitalists could sell their different products (use values) only to one another. But then value, the expenditure of labor by a class for another class, would cease to exist. Capitalists would cease to exist too and would become producers of use values both for their own consumption and for exchange. Since value is a socially specific concept, based on the existence of two categories of agents of production, if one category, the laborers, disappears, the other category, the capitalists and their agents, disappears too: The owners of the means of production cease to be capitalists and become independent producers. The advent of a fully automated economy would mean the end of capitalism. However, this would not necessarily mark the birth of socialism.[15]

Notes

1. This part draws heavily upon Carchedi 1987, ch. 2. For a more detailed presentation of the following concepts, the reader is referred to that work.
2. Of course, I do not refer here to the "actually realized socialism" whose economic and moral bankruptcy has been there for all to see at least since the 1960s.
3. Postulates are concepts that (a) are not immediately evident, (b) are conditions of existence of other concepts, and (c) can somehow be shown to be true. This last point requires a theory of verification, something that the reader can find in Carchedi 1987, ch. 3, appendix. Axioms, in comparison, are commonly accepted, self-evident notions the truth of which cannot be verified. Each and every theory (social or not) is based on some postulates, and to argue the contrary is pure nonsense. Whether the chosen postulates are useful (to understand reality) or not is a question that can be answered only on the basis of a theory (process) of verification. This is the *ex-post* reason for accepting a postulate, and not its *ex-ante* "reasonableness." If we were to reject those postulates that are not immediately evident, the application of the same method

(i.e., that postulates must be immediately evident) to science would greatly hamper scientific discovery. For example, Einstein would never have discovered his special theory of relativity if he had not turned the "absurd" notion of the constancy of the velocity of light into a postulate.

4. What is potential is something that either has not realized itself at all or has realized itself at a certain level of analysis but must change before appearing at another level of analysis, the one we are dealing with. In this latter case, what is potential and what is realized depends on the part of reality we want to consider. Thus, when we analyze social values (prices), the values commodities have before sale (realization) is their individual value.
5. In Carchedi 1987, ch. 1, I have used a simpler, but less precise, terminology. There, the determined instance *is* a condition of reproduction or of supersession of the determinant instance. Here, the determined instance *is called into existence* as a condition of reproduction or of supersession of the determinant instance. The expression "called into existence" is intuitively acceptable in cases in which human agency is obviously involved, for example, when a legislative system needs a certain police force to implement laws. But this expression would seem to be less suitable in cases in which institutions or, more generally, structures are involved (as, for example, the structure of production determines the structure of individual values). But it is precisely in these cases that "called into existence" is a useful expression. In fact, it indicates that determination always needs human agency. For example, individual values can be determined by the structure of production only because people engage in production and create value.
6. This, of course, does not imply that all variables should be taken into account in order to carry out a certain inquiry. This is obviously an impossible task. What it does mean is that, having chosen our field of inquiry (thus including only some selected variables), we should consider the interrelation among them as one of dialectical relation.
7. This approach aims at making sense of reality without claiming to be a "reflection" of reality in our thought. By "reflection" I mean here a view that is not affected by social reality and especially by the social position of the subject of knowledge. Traditionally, in the reflection approach (typical Second International Marxism), it is the individual, not class, who is the subject of knowledge.

   The view implicit here, on the contrary, holds that knowledge is class determined (it is indeed produced by individuals, but they are carriers of ideological class relations) and that a "correct" view of reality is both subjective (it is imbued with the subjectivity of a class) and objective (reality is known in its objectivity). Or, what is known is objective in the sense that it exists independently of our perception of it but is subjective because it can be known only through a class-determined system of knowledge. A "correct" knowledge of reality is then one that finds a correspondence between facts and theory. But it should immediately be added that both the facts (not only the part of reality chosen for inquiry but also our perception of it) and the principles establishing when there is such correspondence (the principles of verification) are themselves part of that theory and thus class determined.
8. The choice of the elements of reality that we define as tendencies reflects our conception of the nature of reality. This conception is in fact a hypothesis that must be subjected to verification. There is no room here to discuss verification within a dialectical approach. Here it is sufficient to stress that verification is a

more complex procedure than the simple empiricist comparison of theories with "neutral" facts would have us believe. I deal with this in Carchedi 1987, ch. 3.

9. "The real value of a commodity is, however, not its individual value, but its social value: that is to say, the real value is not measured by the labor-time that the article in each individual case costs the producer, but by the labor-time socially required for its production" (Marx 1967a, 1: 317).

10. I have shown in Carchedi 1991, ch. 3, that the average rate of profit is tendentially realized only by modal capitals and that nonmodal capitals tendentially realize a rate of profit proportional to their level of productivity relative to the modal level.

11. A slightly different version of the circularity critique stresses that if in Volume 3 of *Capital* constant and variable capital are bought as inputs at their individual value and sold as outputs at their price of production, the same logical inconsistency must apply to Volume 1 of *Capital*. But, and this agrees completely with the interpretation submitted here, in Volume 1 too Marx considers the value of the inputs as already transformed. I will cite only one of the many quotations that support my argument. In considering the value of the cotton needed to spin yarn, Marx says: "We have no need at present to investigate the value of this cotton for our capitalist has, we will assume, bought it *at its full value*. . . . In this price, the labor required for the production of the cotton is always expressed *in terms of the average labor or society*" (1967a, 1: 186–87; emphasis added).

12. There have been many reactions to the circularity critique. Baumol 1974, Rubin 1972, Shaikh 1977, Gerstein 1976, and Fine and Harris 1979 are discussed in Carchedi 1987, ch. 5. Foley (1986, 104) submits that there are in Marx's work two definitions, rather than only one, of the value of labor power: "as concrete labour embodied in the commodities workers consume" and "as the amount of abstract social labour workers receive in wages for 1 hour of labour power." The transformation procedure would then hold if we chose the latter definition. But the circularity critique should not be countered by creating an artificial separation in Marx's notion of labor power. Itoh (1976, 338) seems to move in the same direction as the approach submitted here by stressing that the transformed values show "the result, not the starting condition of exchanges" and that *c* and *v* reappear again "in the following period," as inputs of the following production process. However, Itoh does not develop these points. Recently, a very good collection of articles has been edited by Mandel and Freeman (1984). Aside from specific differences, these contributions and the approach submitted here are broadly complementary. Kliman and McGlone (1988) agree on the validity of the method submitted here but argue that my distinction between realized social values (tendentially, prices of production) and potential social values (individual values) "denies the actuality of values as distinct from prices" (78). Unfortunately, this is a misreading of my position. In the dialectical view submitted here, potential social phenomena are just as "actual," i.e., real, as realized social phenomena. Finally, for an important but relatively undiscussed paper broadly consistent with these submitted here, see Mattick, Jr. 1981.

13. I would like to thank Werner de Haan for bringing this point to my attention. Smith (1990c, 71) argues that "only concrete labour can be 'embodied.' Abstract labour, labour specific to one type of social production, is labour which has proven to be socially necessary. Measuring the magnitude of embodied labour is

a relatively straightforward procedure of simply summing up the direct and indirect labour inputs." There are at least four objections that can be made to this passage. First, by labor embodied Marx means labor that has found a concrete body, a use value. It is thus both concrete and abstract. Second, abstract labor is not labor that has proved to be socially necessary. Abstract labor is the expenditure of human labor power irrespective of the specific features associated with concrete labor. Labor that has proved to be socially necessary is quantitatively transformed (redistributed) abstract labor, the production price. Labor that has not (yet) proved to be socially necessary is the individual value, abstract labor before transformation (redistribution). Third, not only abstract labor, but also concrete labor, is specific to one type, i.e., the capitalist type, of social production. This is the issue, which cannot be dealt with here, of the capitalist nature of the labor process, of the transformation of use values. Fourth, measuring embodied labor is impossible. These critical notes are not meant to detract from Smith's remarkable achievement in his discussion of the Hegelian criticisms of Marx.

14. This, and related points, are skillfully developed in Arthur 1986.
15. Smith 1990c submits that, "In a world where *all* production was completely robotized we obviously would no longer be dealing with a form of *social* production at all" (70). This would indeed be the case if the robots were privately owned, which is the case considered by Smith (and under the implicit assumption, to be relaxed shortly, that production is only material). The reason is that, since the physical act of producing is carried out by robots, the owners of the robots do not interact at the level of production. But it might be interesting to add that, if the robots were collectively owned, production *would* be social. In fact, the cause of the social nature of production should not be sought in whether the physical act of producing is carried out by people or by machines. Production is social or not according to whether the agents of production are tied by production relations. If the decisions about what to produce, how to produce it, and for whom to produce it are made collectively by the associated producers, production is a social process, whether the actual transformation of material use values is carried out by people or by machines. In contrast, in a capitalist economy production is social because, for the production of value and thus of surplus value, two categories of agents of production are needed, the owners and the nonowners of the means of production.

But production is also production of knowledge. In the case hypothesized by Smith, robots might take over material production, but if they were also to take over mental production, humans would become redundant. Therefore, the owners of robots would have to engage in the production of knowledge, and this production would have to be collective, i.e., social (since information would have to be exchanged, new generations would have to be schooled, and so on).

Contributors

CHRISTOPHER J. ARTHUR is Honorary Lecturer of Philosophy at the University of Sussex. He is the author of *The Dialectics of Labor: Marx and His Relation to Hegel* (Basil Blackwell 1986). He is also a member of the Editorial Board of *Radical Philosophy* and *Capital & Class*.

MARTHA CAMPBELL teaches economics at the University of Denver. Her research specialty is Marxian monetary theory.

GUGLIELMO CARCHEDI teaches economics and sociology at the University of Amsterdam. He is the author of *On the Economic Identification of Social Classes* (Routledge & Kegan Paul 1977), *Class Analysis and Social Research* (Basil Blackwell 1987), and *Frontiers of Political Economy* (Verso 1991).

PAUL MATTICK, JR., teaches philosophy at Adelphi University in New York. He is the author of *Social Knowledge: An Essay on the Limits of Social Science* (M. E. Sharpe 1986). He is also the Editor of the *International Journal of Political Economy*.

FRED MOSELEY teaches economics at Mount Holyoke College. He is the author of *The Falling Rate of Profit in the Postwar United States Economy* (St. Martin's Press 1992). He is also the Book Review Editor of the *Review of Radical Political Economics*.

PATRICK MURRAY teaches philosophy at Creighton University in Omaha, Nebraska. He is the author of *Marx's Theory of Scientific Knowledge* (Humanities Press 1988).

GEERT REUTEN teaches political economy and the philosophy of economics at the University of Amsterdam. He is the author of *Value-Form and the State: The Tendencies of Accumulation and the Determination of Economic Policy in Capitalist Society* (with Michael Williams) (Routledge 1989).

TONY SMITH teaches philosophy and political science at Iowa State University. He is the author of *The Logic of Marx's Capital* (SUNY Press 1990), *The Role of Ethics in Social Theory* (SUNY Press 1991), and *Dialectical Social Theory and Its Critics* (SUNY Press 1992).

Bibliography

Arthur, C. J. 1979a. "Dialectic of the Value-Form." In *Value: The Representation of Labor in Capitalism*. Edited by Diane Elson. Atlantic Highlands, NJ: Humanities Press.

———. 1979b. "Dialectics and Labour." In *Issues in Marxist Philosophy*. Vol. 1, *Dialectics and Method*. Edited by J. Mepham and D. H. Ruben. Brighton: Harvester Press.

———. 1986. *The Dialectics of Labor: Marx and His Relation to Hegel*. Oxford: Basil Blackwell.

———. 1988. "Hegel's Theory of Value." In *Value, Social Form and the State*. Edited by M. Williams. London: Macmillan.

Backhaus, Hans-Georg. 1980. "On the Dialectics of the Value-Form." *Thesis Eleven*. Vol. 1, no. 1, 99–120.

Bacon, Francis. 1960. "The New Organon." In *The New Organon and Related Writings*. Edited by Fulton H. Anderson. Indianapolis: Bobbs-Merrill.

Bailey, S. 1967. *A Critical Dissertation on the Nature, Measure, and Causes of Value*. London: Frank Cass. (Originally published in 1825)

Banaji, Jarius. 1979. "From the Commodity to Capital: Hegel's Dialectic in Marx's *Capital*." In *Value: The Representation of Labor in Capitalism*. Edited by Diane Elson. London: CSE Books.

Baumol, William. 1974. "What Marx Really Meant." *Journal of Economic Literature* 12 (March): 51–62.

Bellofiore, Riccardo. 1989. "A Monetary Labor Theory of Value." *Review of Radical Political Economics* 21 (Spring-Summer): 1–25.

Boehm-Bawerk, E. von. 1973. "Karl Marx and the Close of His System." In *Karl Marx and the Close of His System*. Edited by P. Sweezy. Clifton, NJ: Kelley.

———. 1975. *Karl Marx and the Close of His System*. London: Merlin Press.

Bortkiewicz, L. von. 1952. "Value and Price in the Marxian System." *International Economic Papers* 2: 5–60.

———. 1973. "On the Correction of Marx's Fundamental Theoretical Construction in the Third Volume of *Capital*." In *Karl Marx and the Close of His System*. Edited by P. Sweezy. Clifton, NJ: Kelley.

Campbell, Martha. Forthcoming. "The Commodity as Necessary Form of Product." In *Economics as Worldly Philosophy: Essays on Political and Historical Economics in Honor of Robert L. Heilbroner*. London: Macmillan.

Carchedi, Guglielmo. 1984. "The Logic of Prices as Values." *Economy and Society* 13(4): 431–55.

———. 1986. "The Logic of Prices as Values." In *The Value Dimension*. Edited by Ben Fine. London: Routledge & Kegan Paul.
———. 1987. *Class Analysis and Social Research*. Oxford: Basil Blackwell.
———. 1988. "Marxian Price Theory and Modern Capitalism." *International Journal of Political Economy* 18(3): 6–112.
———. 1991. *Frontiers of Political Economy*. London: Verso.
Carver, Terrell. 1980. "Marx's 1857 Introduction." *Economy and Society* 9 (May): 197–203.
Castells, Manuel. 1980. *The Economic Crisis and American Society*. Princeton, NJ: Princeton University Press.
Cohen, G. A. 1978. *Karl Marx's Theory of History. A Defence*. Oxford: Clarendon Press.
Cutler, A., A. Hussain, B. Hindess, and P. Q. Hirst. 1977. *Marx's "Capital" and Capitalism Today*. Vol. 1. London: Routledge.
Descartes, René. 1960. *Discourse on Method and Meditations*. Translated by Laurence J. Lafleur. Indianapolis: Bobbs-Merrill.
De Vroey, Michel. 1982. "On the Obsolescence of the Marxian Theory of Value: A Critical Review." *Capital & Class* 17: 34–59.
Dumenil, Gerard. 1980. *De la valeur aux prix de production*. Paris: Economica.
———. 1983. "Beyond the Transformation Riddle: A Labor Theory of Value." *Science and Society* 47 (Winter): 427–50.
Echeverria, Rafael. 1978. "Critique of Marx's 1857 Introduction." *Economy and Society* 7(4) (November): 333–65.
———. 1980. "The Later Marx and Hegel: A Study on the Development of the Marxian Concept of Science." *Research in Political Economy* 3: 155–208.
Eldred, Michael. 1984a. *Critique of Competitive Freedom and the Bourgeois-Democratic State*. Copenhagen: Kurasje.
———. 1984b. "A Reply to Gleicher; History: Universal Concept Dissolves Any Concept!" *Capital & Class* 13: 135–40.
Eldred, Michael, and M. Hanlon. 1981. "Restructuring Value-Form Analysis." *Capital & Class* 13: 24–60.
Eldred, Michael, and M. Roth. 1978. *A Guide to Marx's "Capital."* London: CSE Books.
Elson, Diane. 1979. "The Value Theory of Labor." In *Value: The Representation of Labor in Capitalism*. Edited by Diane Elson. London: CSE Books.
———. 1988. "Market Socialism or Socialization of the Market?" *New Left Review* 172: 1–44.
Elster, Jon. 1985. *Making Sense of Marx*. New York: Cambridge University Press.
Engels, Frederich. 1906. *Ludwig Feuerbach*. English ed. London: Lawrence & Wishart.
———. 1970. "Review of Karl Marx." In *A Contribution to the Critique of Political Economy*. New York: International Publishers.
Fine, Ben. 1982. *Theories of the Capitalist Economy*. London: Edwin Arnold.
Fine, Ben, and Laurence Harris. 1979. *Rereading "Capital."* London: Macmillan.
Foley, Duncan. 1982. "The Value of Money, the Value of Labor-Power, and the Marxian Transformation Problem." *Review of Radical Political Economics* 14 (Summer): 37–49.
———. 1986. *Understanding Capital: Marx's Economic Theory*. Cambridge, MA: Harvard University Press.

Gerstein, Ira. 1976. "Production, Circulation and Value." *Economy and Society* 5(3): 243–91.

Gleicher, David. 1983. "A Historical Approach to the Question of Abstract Labor." *Capital & Class* 21: 97–122.

———. 1985. "A Rejoinder to Eldred, Abstract Labor, the Rubin School and the Marxist Theory of Value." *Capital & Class* 24: 147–55.

Grossman, Henryk. 1929. *Das Akkumulations- und Zusammenbruchs-gesetz des kapitalistischen Systems*. Leipzig: C. H. Hirschfeld.

Hayek, F. A. 1961. "The Non Sequitur of the 'Dependence Effect.'" *Southern Economic Journal* 28 (April): 346–48.

Hegel, G. W. F. 1892. *The Logic of Hegel*. Translated by W. Wallace. Oxford: Oxford University Press.

———. 1942. *The Philosophy of Right*. Oxford: Oxford University Press.

———. 1955. *Lectures on the History of Philosophy III*. Atlantic Highlands, NJ: Humanities Press.

———. 1962. *Lectures on the Philosophy of Religion*. Vol. 1. Translated by E. B. Speirs and J. Burdon Sanderson and edited by E. B. Speirs. Atlantic Highlands, NJ: Humanities Press.

———. 1967. *The Philosophy of Right*. Translated by T. M. Knox. London: Oxford University Press.

———. 1969a. *The Science of Logic*. New York: Allen & Unwin.

———. 1969b. *The Science of Logic*. Translated by A. V. Miller. Atlantic Highlands, NJ: Humanities Press.

———. 1971. *Philosophy of Mind*. Translated by W. Wallace. Oxford: Oxford University Press.

———. 1975a. *Hegel's Logic*. Translated by William Wallace. Oxford: Clarendon Press.

———. 1975b. *Logic*. Translated by W. Wallace. Oxford: Oxford University Press.

———. 1985a. *Hegel's Logic*. Translated by W. Wallace. Oxford: Oxford University Press.

———. 1985b. *Introduction to the Lectures on the History of Philosophy*. Translated by T. M. Knox and A. V. Miller. Oxford: Clarendon Press.

———. 1989. *Hegel's Science of Logic*. Translated by A. V. Miller. Atlantic Highlands, NJ: Humanities Press.

Hilferding, Rudolph. 1973. "Boehm-Bawerk's Criticism of Marx." In *Karl Marx and the Close of His System*. Edited by P. Sweezy. Clifton, NJ: Kelley.

Himmelweit, Susan, and Simon Mohun. 1978. "The Anomalies of Capital." *Capital & Class* 6: 67–105.

Hodgson, Geoffrey M. 1988. *Economics and Institutions*. Cambridge: Polity Press.

Itoh, Makato. 1976. "A Study of Marx's Theory of Value." *Science and Society* 40(3): 307–40.

Kehoe, L. 1991. "IBM Cuts Its Workstations by Up to 60%." *Financial Times*, May 8.

Keynes, John M. 1936. *The General Theory of Employment, Interest and Money*. London: Macmillan.

Kliman, A., and T. McGlone. 1988. "The Transformation Non-Problem and the Non-Transformation Problem." *Capital & Class* 35: 56–83.

Krahl, Hans-Jurgen. 1970. "Bemerkungen zum Verhältnis von Kapital und hegelscher Wesenslogik." In *Aktualität und Folgen der Philosophie Hegels*. Edited by O. Negt. Frankfurt: Suhrkamp.

Lakatos, Imre. 1974. "Falsification and the Methodology of Scientific Research Programmes." In *Criticism and the Growth of Knowledge.* Edited by I. Lakatos and A. Musgrave. Cambridge: Cambridge University Press.

Lipietz, Alain. 1982. "The 'So-Called Transformation Problem' Revisited." *Journal of Economic Theory* 26 (February): 59–88.

Mage, Shane. 1963. *The Law of the Falling Tendency of the Rate of Profit.* Ph.D. dissertation, Columbia University, New York.

Mandel, Ernest. 1988. "The Myth of Market Socialism." *New Left Review* 169: 108–20.

———. 1990. "Karl Marx." In *Marxian Economics.* Edited by J. Eatwell, M. Milgate, and P. Newman. London: Macmillan.

Mandel, Ernest, and Alan Freeman, eds. 1984. *Ricardo, Marx, and Sraffa.* London: Verso.

Marshall, Alfred. 1979. *Principles of Economics.* 8th ed. London: Macmillan.

Marx, Karl. 1939. "Urtext." In *Grundrisse der Kritik der politischen Oekonomie.* Frankfurt am Main: Europaische Verlagsanstalt.

———. 1963. *Theories of Surplus-Value.* Vol. 1. Moscow: Progress Publishers.

———. 1964. *Economic and Philosophic Manuscripts of 1844.* Translated by Martin Milligan and edited by Dirk J. Struik. New York: International Publishers.

———. 1967a. *Capital.* 3 vols. New York: International Publishers.

———. 1967b. "Excerpt Notes." In *Writings of the Young Marx on Philosophy and Society.* Translated and edited by Lloyd D. Easton and Kurt H. Guddat. Garden City, NY: Doubleday.

———. 1967c. "Theses on Feuerbach." In *Writings of the Young Marx on Philosophy and Society.* Translated and edited by Lloyd D. Easton and Kurt H. Guddat. Garden City, NY: Doubleday.

———. 1968a. *Oeuvres.* Vol. 2. Edited by M. Rubel. Paris: Gallimard.

———. 1968b. *Theories of Surplus-Value.* Vol. 2. Translated by Renate Simpson and edited by S. Ryazanskaya. Moscow: Progress Publishers.

———. 1970a. *A Contribution to the Critique of Political Economy.* Translated by S. W. Ryazanskaya and edited by Maurice Dobb. New York: International Publishers.

———. 1970b. *Critique of Hegel's "Philosophy of Right."* Translated by Annette Jolin and Joseph O'Malley and edited by Joseph O'Malley. Cambridge: Cambridge University Press.

———. 1971a. *A Contribution to the Critique of Political Economy.* Translated by S. W. Ryazanskaya and edited by Maurice Dobb. London: Lawrence & Wishart.

———. 1971b. *Theories of Surplus-Value.* Vol. 3. Moscow: Progress Publishers.

———. 1972. *Theories of Surplus-Value.* London: Lawrence & Wishart.

———. 1973. *Grundrisse.* Translated by Martin Nicolaus. New York: Vintage Books; Harmondsworth: Penguin.

———. 1975a. "Notes on Wagner." In *Texts on Method.* Translated and edited by T. Carver. Oxford: Basil Blackwell.

———. 1975b. *Texts on Method.* Edited by T. Carver. Oxford: Basil Blackwell.

———. 1976a. *Capital.* Vol. 1. New York: Random House.

———. 1976b. *Capital.* Vol. 1. Translated by B. Fowkes. Harmondsworth: Penguin.

———. 1977a. *Capital.* Vol. 1. New York: Random House.

———. 1977b. *Capital.* Vol. 1. Translated by Ben Fowkes. New York: Vintage Books.

———. 1978. *Capital*. Vol. 1. Moscow: Progress Publishers.
———. 1981. *Capital*. Vol. 2. New York: Random House.
———. 1982. *Capital*. Vol. 3. New York: Random House.
Marx, Karl, and Frederich Engels. 1962. *Werke*. Vol. 3. Berlin: Dietz.
———. 1966. *Karl Marx, Friedrich Engels: Studienausgabe in 4 Banden*. Vol. 2, *Politische Oekonomie*. Edited by Irving Fetscher. Frankfurt am Main: Fischer Taschenbuch Verlag.
———. 1975a. *Collected Works*. Vol. 3. London: Lawrence & Wishart.
———. 1975b. *Selected Correspondence*. Moscow: Progress Publishers.
———. 1976. "The German Ideology." In *Collected Works*. Vol. 5. New York: International Publishers.
———. 1983. *Letters on "Capital."* Translated by A. Drummond. London: New Park Publications.
———. 1987. *Collected Works*. Vol. 29. New York: International Publishers.
———. 1988. *Collected Works*. Vol. 30. New York: International Publishers.
———. n.d. *Selected Correspondence*. Moscow: Foreign Language Publishing House.
Mattick, Paul, Jr. 1981. "Some Aspects of the Value-Price Problem." *Economies et Societes* (Cahiers de l'ISMEA Series) 15(6–7): 275–81.
———. 1986a. *Social Knowledge: An Essay on the Nature and Limits of Social Science*. London: Hutchinson.
———. 1986b. *Social Knowledge: An Essay on the Nature and Limits of Social Science*. Armonk, NY: M. E. Sharpe.
Mattick, Paul, Sr. 1959. "Value Theory and Capital Accumulation." *Science and Society* 23 (Winter): 27–51.
———. 1969. *Marx and Keynes: The Limits of the Mixed Economy*. Boston: Porter Sargent.
Medio, Alfredo. 1972. "Profits and Surplus-Value: Appearance and Reality in Capitalist Production." In *A Critique of Economic Theory*. Edited by E. K. Hunt and J. Schwartz. Baltimore: Penguin.
Meek, Ronald L. 1976. *Studies in the Labor Theory of Value*. 2d ed. New York: Monthly Review Press.
Mepham, J. 1979. "From the *Grundrisse* to *Capital*: The Making of Marx's Method." In *Issues in Marxist Philosophy*. Vol. 1. Edited by D. Ruben and J. Mepham. Atlantic Highlands, NJ: Humanities Press.
Mill, John Stuart. 1965. *Principles of Political Economy*. Toronto: University of Toronto Press; London: Routledge & Kegan Paul.
Mirowski, Philip. 1990. "Learning the Meaning of a Dollar: Conservation Principles and the Social Theory of Value in Economic Theory." *Social Research* 57(3): 689–717.
———. 1991. "Postmodernism and the Social Theory of Value." *Journal of Post Keynesian Economics* 13(4): 565–82.
Moore, S. 1963. "The Metaphysical Argument in Marx's Labour Theory of Value." *Cahiers de l'institut de Science Économique appliquée* 140: 73–97.
Moore, Stanley. 1980. "Marx and Lenin as Historical Materialists." In *Marx, Justice, and History*. Edited by Marshall Cohen, Thomas Nagel, and Thomas Scanlon. Princeton, NJ: Princeton University Press.
Morishima, Michio. 1973. *Marx's Economics*. New York: Cambridge University Press.
Moseley, Fred. 1982. *The Rate of Surplus Value in the United States Economy, 1947–1977*. Ph.D. dissertation, University of Massachusetts.

———. 1992. *The Falling Rate of Profit in the Postwar United States Economy*. New York: St. Martin's Press.

Murray, Patrick. 1988a. "Karl Marx as a Historical Materialist Historian of Political Economy." *History of Political Economy* 20(1): 95–105.

———. 1988b. *Marx's Theory of Scientific Knowledge*. Atlantic Highlands, NJ: Humanities Press.

Musgrave, Alan. 1981. "'Unreal Assumptions' in Economic Theory: The F-Twist Untwisted." *Kyklos* 34(3): 377–87.

Negt, O., ed. 1970. *Aktualität und Folgen der Philosophoie Hegels*. Frankfurt: Suhrkamp.

Nove, Alex. 1987. "Markets and Socialism." *New Left Review* 161: 98–104.

Okishio, Nobuo. 1961. "Technical Change and the Rate of Profit." *Kobe University Economic Review* 7: 86–99.

O'Malley, J., and F. E. Schrader, eds. 1977. "Marx's Précis of Hegel's Doctrine of Being in the Minor Logic." *International Review of Social History* 22: 423–43.

Paolucci, Henri. 1974. "Truth in the Philosophical Sciences of Society, Politics and History." In *Beyond Epistemology: New Studies in the Philosophy of Hegel*. Edited by F. G. Weiss. The Hague: Martin Nijhoff.

Pejovich, S. 1982. "Karl Marx, Property Rights School and the Process of Social Change." *Kyklos* 35: 383–97.

Petry, Michael. 1970. "Introduction." In *Hegel's Philosophy of Nature*. Vol. 1. London: Allen & Unwin.

———. 1978. "Introduction." In *Hegel's Philosophy of Subjective Spirit*. Dordrecht, Netherlands: D. Reidel.

Pilling, Geoffrey. 1980. *Marx's "Capital": Philosophy and Political Economy*. London: Routledge & Kegan Paul.

Reuten, Geert. 1988. "Value as Social Form." In *Value, Social Form and the State*. Edited by Michael Williams. London: Macmillan.

Reuten, Geert, and Michael Williams. 1989. *Value-Form and the State: The Tendencies of Accumulation and the Determination of Economic Policy in Capitalist Society*. London: Routledge.

Robinson, J. 1977. "Ideology and Analysis." In *The Subtle Anatomy of Capitalism*. Edited by J. Schwartz. Santa Monica, CA: Goodyear Publishing.

Roemer, John E. 1982. *A General Theory of Exploitation and Class*. Cambridge, MA: Harvard University Press.

Rosdolsky, Roman. 1977. *The Making of Marx's "Capital."* London: Pluto Press.

Rubin, I. I. 1972. *Essays on Marx's Theory of Value*. Detroit: Black and Red Press.

Sawyer, M. C. 1989. *The Challenge of Radical Political Economy*. Hemel Hempstead: Wheatsheaf.

Sayer, Derek. 1987. *The Violence of Abstraction. The Analytic Foundations of Historical Materialism*. Oxford; Cambridge, MA: Basil Blackwell.

Schmidt, Alfred, ed. 1969. *Beiträge zur Marxistischen Erkenntnistheorie*. Frankfurt am Main: Suhrkamp.

Schnädelbach, Herbert. 1970. "Zum Verhältnis von Logik und Gesellschaftstheorie bei Hegel." In *Aktualität und Folgen der Philosophie Hegels*. Edited by O. Negt. Frankfurt: Suhrkamp.

Schrader, F. E. 1980. *Restauration und Revolution*. Hildesheim: Gerstenberg.

Sekine, T. 1984. *The Dialectic of Capital*. Vol. 1. Tokyo: Yushindo Press.

———. 1986. *The Dialectic of Capital*. Vol. 2. Tokyo: Toshindo Publications.

Seton, F. 1957. "The 'Transformation Problem.'" *Review of Economic Studies* 24: 149–60.
Shaikh, Anwar. 1977. "Marx's Transformation of Value and the 'Transformation Problem.'" In *The Subtle Anatomy of Capitalism*. Edited by J. Schwartz. Santa Monica, CA: Goodyear Publishing.
Skinner, Andrew. 1985. "Introduction." In Adam Smith, *The Wealth of Nations*. Harmondsworth: Penguin.
Smith, Adam. 1933. *An Inquiry into the Nature and Causes of the Wealth of Nations*. Vols. 1 and 2. London: Dent & Sons.
Smith, Tony. 1990a. "Analytical Marxism and Marx's Systematic Dialectic Theory." *Man and World* 23: 321–43.
———. 1990b. "The Debate Regarding Dialectical Logic in Marx's Economic Writings." *International Philosophical Quarterly* 30(3) (September): 289–98.
———. 1990c. *The Logic of Marx's "Capital": Replies to Hegelian Criticisms*. Albany, NY: State University of New York Press.
———. 1991. *The Role of Ethics in Social Theory*. Albany, NY: State University of New York Press.
Sohn-Rethel, A. 1978. *Intellectual and Manual Labour*. London: Macmillan.
Sraffa, P. 1960. *The Production of Commodities by Means of Commodities*. New York: Cambridge University Press.
Steedman, Ian. 1977. *Marx After Sraffa*. London: New Left Books.
Suchting, William. 1986. *Marxism and Philosophy*. New York: New York University Press.
Sweezy, Paul. 1968. *The Theory of Capitalist Development*. New York: Monthly Review Press.
Taylor, Charles. 1975. *Hegel*. Cambridge: Cambridge University Press.
Wagner, Adolph. 1879. *Allgemeine oder Theoretische Volkswirthschaftslehre Lehrbuch der Politischen Oekonomie*. Leipzig, Heidelberg: CF Winter'sche Verlagshandlung.
Williams, Michael, ed. 1988. *Value, Social Form and the State*. New York: St. Martin's Press.
Witt-Hansen, J. 1960. *Historical Materialism. The Method. The Theories*. Vol. 1. Copenhagen: Munksgaard.
Wolff, Richard, Antonio Callari, and Bruce Roberts. 1983. "A Marxian Alternative to the 'Transformation Problem.'" *Review of Radical Political Economics* 15: 115–35.
Yaffe, David. 1973. "The Marxian Theory of Crisis, Capital, and the State." *Economy and Society* 2(2): 186–232.
Zeleny, Jindrich. 1980. *The Logic of Marx*. New York: Rowman & Littlefield.

Name Index

Subject Index